H O N

SOMEWHERE BETWEEN HEAVEN AND EARTH

HONG KONG:
Somewhere Between Heaven and Earth

AN ANTHOLOGY
SELECTED AND EDITED BY

Barbara-Sue White

HONG KONG
OXFORD UNIVERSITY PRESS
OXFORD   NEW YORK
1996

Oxford University Press

Oxford New York
Athens Auckland Bangkok Bombay
Calcutta Cape Town Dar es Salaam Delhi
Florence Hong Kong Istanbul Karachi
Kuala Lumpur Madras Madrid Melbourne
Mexico City Nairobi Paris Singapore
Taipei Tokyo Toronto

and associated companies in
Berlin Ibadan

Oxford is a trade mark of Oxford University Press

First published 1996
This impression (lowest digit)
1 3 5 7 9 10 8 6 4 2

Published in the United States
by Oxford University Press, New York

© Oxford University Press 1996

British Library Cataloguing in Publication Data
available

Library of Congress Cataloging-in-Publication Data

Hong Kong: somewhere between heaven and earth/selected and edited
by Barbara-Sue White.
p.   cm.
ISBN 0-19-587696-2
1. Hong Kong—History—Sources. I. White, Barbara-Sue, date.
DS796.H757H64   1996
951.25—dc20   96-5160
                                                              CIP

Printed in Hong Kong
Published by Oxford University Press (China) Ltd
18/F Warwick House, Taikoo Place, 979 King's Road,
Quarry Bay, Hong Kong

Once again, to my family—with love

ACKNOWLEDGEMENTS

I would like to extend special thanks to Coonoor Kripalani-Thadani, Edward Chen, and Carol Chan of the Centre of Asian Studies at the University of Hong Kong for office space and amenities, and to Y. C. Wen and the staff of the Hong Kong Collection at the University of Hong Kong Library.

I would like to thank Kenneth Andrew, Amina el Arculli, Robert Bagley, Gillian Bickley, Helen Braverman, Nigel Cameron, John Chan, Mimi Chan, Mary Child, Austin Coates, Peter Cunich, Robert Elegant, Jane Gardam, Jean Gittins, Piers Gray, Emily Hahn, Anthony Hedley, Susan Henders, Susanna Hoe, Anthony Lawrence, Perry Link, P. K. Leung, Rebecca Lloyd, Richard Mason, Christopher Mitchell, Jane Mont, Doris Edith Mount, Michael Montgomery, Drummond Mulberry, Christopher New, Norman and Roberta Owen, Loren Pfister, Priscilla Roberts, Alastair Scott, Ian Scott, Elizabeth Sinn, Carl Smith, Joyce Stevens Smith, the late Walter Sulke, Elsie Tu, Peter and Nancy Thompson, Jeremy T. White, Kevin M. White, Lynn T. White III, Maude McArthur White, Janice Wickeri, Kate Owens Wright, and the late Joseph Wong.

I would also like to thank people at the following institutions: The Duchess of Kent Children's Hospital at Sandy Bay, The Gest Library at Princeton University, The Hong Kong Museum of History, The Hong Kong Branch of the Royal Asiatic Society, The Hong Kong Public Records Office, Jardines Ltd., the Syndics of Cambridge University Library, the Library of the School of Oriental and African Studies, the Media Resources Centre at the University of Hong Kong, and Princeton University Library.

The publishers would like to thank the following for permission to reproduce copyright material: 'The Pig Boy' from *Pangs of Love* by Jane Gardam, published by Abacus Books, reprinted by permission of David Higham Associates; 'Hongkong' from *Journey to a War* by W. H. Auden and Christopher Isherwood, copyright© 1939 and renewed 1967 by W. H. Auden and Christopher Isherwood. Reprinted by permission of Curtis Brown Ltd, Random House Inc, and Faber and Faber Ltd on behalf of the Estate of W. H. Auden; *The World of Suzie Wong* by Richard Mason, published by J. M. Dent, reprinted by permission of A. M. Heath & Co. Ltd; *The Chinese Box* by Christopher New, published by W. H. Allen, reprinted by permission of the Peters Fraser & Dunlop Group Ltd; from *Renditions* Nos. 29 & 30 (Spring & Autumn 1988) Hong Kong: Research Centre for Translation of the Chinese University of Hong Kong: 'My Sojourn in Hong Kong' by Wang Tao, p. 37, 'One Night in Hong Kong' by Ai Wu, p. 59, 'Hong Kong Nights' by Ba Jin, p. 54, 'A Ge-Ware Incense Burner with "Flying" Handles and Six Legs in Crackled *Fenqing* Glaze' by Ni Kuang, p. 150.

CONTENTS

CONTENTS

INTRODUCTION

I am so entranced with Hong Kong as a city and a setting, that I will read almost anything set in the territory. Sometimes it is a thriller found in an airport book store, or a novel with a strong Hong Kong section. The compilation of this anthology has allowed me to explore a wide range of writing about Hong Kong, and to share some of its written treasures.

Why this fascination with Hong Kong? Compared to other great cities of the world, Hong Kong's history as a metropolis is strikingly brief. Its specific dates as a colony began with the British flag-raising in 1841 and the handover to China in 1997—years of tremendous development into a dynamic international centre. Its intensity and uniqueness draw many visitors back to the Territory, while writers seem compelled to try and capture its excitement, scenery, and *mélange* of cultures.

This book reveals this fascination through impressions of Hong Kong written in letters home, journals and memoirs penned on long sea voyages, poems, reports, descriptions, and fiction. Writers offer reasons for their entrancement with the colony, as well as reservations about Hong Kong. There are pre-colonial writers as early as the Tang and Song Dynasties, and the reactions of later writers, from Queen Victoria to a Chinese prison inmate.

Fiction in this collection by both Chinese and Westerners covers the Victorian age to the 1990s. 'Dolly's' 1890s spoof of Hong Kong society was written for local newspaper entertainment while Bella Woolf's short stories satirize 1930s colonial foibles. In modern Hong Kong, Ni Kuang explores the eagerness of many people to match wits and grab a bargain.

The descriptive passages written by visitors can be as lively as the fiction. Albert Smith, an English entertainer, writes about the performance he gave at the Hong Kong Club in the 1850s, while Rudyard Kipling offers his reactions to a tour of the Colony's red light district. Around the same time, Matilda Sharp and her sister set up housekeeping on the Peak, remembering to pack pistols on their sojourns to the cathedral. Each writer, whether dashing off letters home or writing for publication tried to capture the vivacity and rapid pace of the Colony. Austin Coates' retelling of a court case as a young District Officer in the New Territories in the 1950s reads like a short story—except that it actually happened.

Hong Kong has never been free from tensions, and strains increased as World War II approached. Its effect on the Colony is expressed in Emily Hahn's autobiography and then in the memoirs, letters, and poem from a Hong Kong under Japanese rule. Christopher New experienced the effects of China's Cultural Revolution on Hong Kong and combined his description with colonial backbiting in 'Lunch at the Hong Kong Club' from his novel *The Chinese Box*. The collection closes with an ironic piece by Louise Ho about modern Hong Kong—complete with modern problems.

If you have lived in Hong Kong or visited, may these descriptions awaken memories of your own experience: after dark, the illuminated vessels in the Harbour are framed by twinkling lights from skyscrapers, vehicles, and roads; on a misty morning you feel the eerie sensation of the Kowloon hills rising from the clouds 'somewhere between heaven and earth'. And if you have never been to Hong Kong, your imagination can travel as it pleases, arriving with Captain Belcher in 1841 or more recently with Jane Gardam.

My own initial arrival in Hong Kong by passenger ship from Taiwan remains one of my most vibrant memories. It was in April 1968, and my husband and I had been living as students in Taipei where four storeys made a building tall, and the dusty streets were miles from the sea. The ship still had massive metal gates which could be slammed shut against pirate attacks, last needed little more than a decade before. We anchored off Hong Kong Island, and I remember climbing up on the deck about 7 a.m. to find our ship surrounded by lighters being loaded with the ship's cargo while tiny sampans rocked with life and enterprise. Chinese men and women worked equally hard unloading, but many women had babies strapped to their backs in red cotton carriers, exuberantly embroidered. The scene was lit with the early morning sun, bathing to an unreal intensity pristine new skyscrapers, decaying arcaded buildings, and myriad vessels.

The green hillsides above North Point then featured clusters of ramshackle squatters' huts, while below hundreds of small wooden houseboats and sampans bobbed along the water's edge. On the Star Ferry concourses lining both sides of the Harbour, emaciated rickshaw-pullers squatted before long rows of Chinese-red wooden vehicles calling out to tourists and local residents alike. Rickshaws were then a real mode of short distance transport rather than a tourist photo opportunity.

By the early 1970s, the China Products outlets, affectionately known as the 'Commie Stores', were filled with scrolls and exquisite antique silver stolen by Red Guards during the Cultural Revolution. Cheap shiny metal Mao badges and rubber Red Guard squeaky dolls adorned the desks of Western scholars, and our Kowloon flat, overlooking a rooftop Communist school, was inundated each morning with a blaring rendition of 'The East is Red'. Busloads of tourists motored up to Lo Wu to gape over the border at China, forbidden to most Westerners and absolutely to Americans.

Readers may see this anthology as a window into Hong Kong's past: as a collection of visions by a variety of outsiders, of what they found beautiful, exciting or exotic, and what they yearned to give to or to get from the Territory. Many of these excerpts show Hong Kong as earlier Westerners saw it, with the attitudes, hopes and prejudices of previous decades. They share the reality of Hong Kong's past, and suggest the strength with which she will face her future.

I hope that readers will find all the selections enjoyable, but not every piece included is or even aspires to be great writing. Some have been chosen because they capture the spirit of an age as it unfolded in Hong Kong, seen, for example, in the romantic Victorianism of 'The Steamer with the Buff-coloured Funnel'. Unique impressions have sometimes been preserved in privately printed works such as the poems of Governor Clementi or the memoirs of Judge Goodman—and a host of others waiting to be discovered. Some works have been chosen for the time and place at which they were written, including the amateur poem rhymed in a Kowloon prisoner-of-war camp or the postcards sent at various times from Hong Kong to those back home.

The collection opens with a contemporary short story, 'The Pig Boy', in which we feel the reactions of a modern visitor, initially overwhelmed by Hong Kong. The excerpts are then presented chronologically beginning with Chinese glimpses of Hong Kong long before the British first landed. Wherever possible, spelling, grammar, and punctuation have been left as originally written. This means that the word 'Hong Kong' itself is hyphenated, written as one word or two; while the word 'harbour' switches to 'harbor' with the nationality of the writer. In addition, nineteenth-century paragraphs can meander on for pages: sometimes I have divided them and made cuts, but I hope the flow has been maintained.

In much of the earlier colonial writing, the British see themselves as benevolent colonists, racially superior to the Chinese, and other Westerners write with similar arrogance. Even the title of 'John Chinaman at Home' shocks today, as do the assumptions of Sir Charles Dilke in 'English Arrogance'. Some of the liveliest writing is by intrepid Victorian lady travellers, but many people in Hong Kong view white women as creatures to be protected and carted around in sedan chairs by coolies, whenever possible. Some Westerners see Chinese men, when not pulling rickshaws or other primitive forms of conveyance, as lying stupefied in exotic opium dens, running Lyndhurst Terrace brothels, or as wily compradors. Chinese writers, on the other hand, did not flinch from describing Western barbarians as 'round-eyed, large-nosed foreign devils'. A very anti-British view is expressed in the passage by Ai Wu, incarcerated for a night in Hong Kong *en route* from Burma to China. All of these sentiments, rarely expressed today, formed part of the ethnocentric slant of our predecessors in Hong Kong.

Many themes recur in the writing of the early settlers, including mail day with letters hurriedly finished to catch the boat, typhoons, and the threat of disease. Then there is the constant importance of money, its getting and spending, and, of course, opium, legal in the colony until after World War II.

The Hong Kong writing of some well-known contemporary writers such as John Le Carre, Timothy Mo, James Clavell, Jan Morris, and Han Su Yin are readily available and have not been included, although some are quoted below.

Relations between races and ever-important social distinctions are constant themes of many authors, and Hong Kong's Peak is of continued significance, both for its rugged beauty and as the exclusive pinnacle of social heights for Westerners until the wealthy

Eurasian, Robert Hotung, was granted permission to build there. The result was 'Idlewild', his mansion which included a Chinese temple, visited by George Bernard Shaw during a brief visit to Hong Kong in 1933. Shaw described his visit as follows:

When I was in Hong Kong, I was entertained very agreeably indeed by Sir Robert Ho Tung. We were both of an age at which one likes a rest after lunch. He took me upstairs into what in England would have been a drawing room. It was a radiant miniature temple with an altar of Chinese vermillion and gold, and cushioned divan seats round the walls for the worshippers. Everything was in such perfect Chinese taste that to sit there and look was a quiet delight. A robed priest and his acolyte stole in and went through a service. When it was over I told Sir Robert that I had found it extraordinarily soothing and happy though I had not understood a word of it. 'Neither have I,' he said, 'but it soothes me too.' It was part of the art of life for Chinaman and Irishman alike, and was purely aesthetic.

Shaw adapted the temple for the third act of a play, *Bouyant Billions*, and he and Robert Hotung corresponded after the visit.

In addition to being an exclusive residential area, the Peak has entranced many authors. Although Jan Morris has written an entire travel book on Hong Kong, she captures its elusive magic in a short chapter in *Pleasures of a Tangled Life* (1989) called 'The Walk of Walks'.

But of all the promenades I know, one more than any other seems to me the walk of walks. It is the path that runs around Victoria Peak—'The Peak' for short—on the island of Hong Kong. When I am in that demanding colony I do the Peak walk every morning before breakfast, and I come down to my cornflakes in the city feeling not just the fitter for it, but the more serene too—as if, striding rhythmically as I do around the half-hour circuit of the hill, I have started the day with a commitment to the organic order of things.

Through these writings, a kaleidoscope of Hong Kong emerges with its colonial and modern architecture, dramatic scenery, history, and colourful population. A surprising view of the relations between the British and the Chinese in Hong Kong was expressed by Anton Chekhov after a visit:

They have excellent roads, horse-drawn streetcars, a funicular railway, museums, botanical gardens; whenever you turn you see how solicitous the English are for their employees; there is even a sailors' club. I rode in a jinrickshaw, that is, on people, bought all sorts of baubles from the Chinese, and became outraged when I heard my fellow travellers, Russians, vilifying the English for exploiting the natives. Yes, the English exploit the Chinese, the Sepoys, and the Hindus, I thought, but in return he gives them roads, water mains, museums, Christianity. You do your own exploiting, but what do you give in return?

Writings about Hong Kong are scattered in libraries and collections throughout the world. As a British colony, much writing associated with Hong Kong is in Great Britain, of course, and part of the interest of putting together this anthology were the hours spent rummaging through very dusty boxes of reports and correspondence in the Cambridge University Library.

I had applied specifically for permission to examine some of the papers of the firm of Jardine Matheson, and I flipped through boxes of letter books copied by professional scribes for company records. I chose the letter to Jamsetjee Jejeebhoy to underscore the early involvement of Indians in Hong Kong's business life. That connection is continued in the schoolboy essay about the 1906 typhoon by Abbas el Arculli.

After presenting me with more boxes of Jardine Matheson records than I could wade through in a year, the Cambridge University librarian asked unprompted if I would like to see the original papers of Stella Benson, a reformer partially responsible for having prostitution in Hong Kong declared illegal in the early 1930s. Her tour of the Hong Kong brothels is related in this collection, and I lingered in the library until closing time reading her letters and reports.

One unexpected aspect of compiling the anthology has been the letters from now elderly authors, expressing delight that excerpts from their books, some long out of print, could be shared once again. And so Kenneth Andrew, author of 'Gangsters & Hatsnachers' from his memoir, *Chop Suey*, wrote at the age of 101, that his years with the Hong Kong police were the most exciting of his life. Emily Hahn and Jean Gittins, both in their late eighties, wrote respectively from England and Australia, and Richard Mason, in Italy, offered to send a photocopy from *The World of Suzie*

Wong if I couldn't find a copy. Happily, the book has been reprinted in Hong Kong.

Months spent in the Hong Kong Collection at the University of Hong Kong were among the pleasures of gathering pieces for the anthology. Library material is non-circulating, and so even popular paperbacks, designed to be read in bed with a box of chocolates, had to be consumed in the library. No chocolates were allowed in the reading room, but narrow slices of Hong Kong Harbour could be glimpsed between the skyscrapers, underscoring the physical reality of often absurd fictional harbour chases and smuggling. The Hong Kong Collection also holds numerous rare documents and books related to the Territory. Some are deadly dull—shipping or business reports aren't the most thrilling reading—but then I would stumble across an absolute gem such as the illustrated letters, included here, sent home by Herbert James to his 'Dear People' back in Ireland.

The cover painting by Constance F. Gordon-Cumming belongs to Nancy Ma Thompson and her husband Peter Thompson who possess an admirable collection of original Hong Kong art. Once I knew about Gordon-Cumming's watercolours, I tracked down her writing at the Princeton University Library in the United States. Although I focused on Hong Kong, I inevitably read more of the travel adventures of the author. In the case of Lady Brassey's *Voyage of the Sunbeam*, wildly popular in the Victorian era, I, too, fell under her spell as she described fires and shipwrecks at sea. For Lady Brassey, Hong Kong was an intriguing port on a world voyage, but with the entire book in hand, I could hardly stop with her 'Visit to the Hongkong Races'. Libraries abound with the works of Victorian travellers, and I recommend them for more than the Hong Kong sections.

A plea for original letters in a newsletter of the Hong Kong Branch of the Royal Asiatic Society resulted in a meeting with Kate Owens Wright, born in the territory just before World War II. Several of her relatives spent the war years interned at Stanley on Hong Kong Island and at the Shamshuipo Camp in Kowloon. She was happy to share the fascinating and moving cards and letters they wrote home during and after the hostilities.

Some parts of this collection were unearthed in attic trunks, some in library books not withdrawn for decades, while others were former bestsellers. This book contains part of the written record of those who came to Hong Kong before most of us, and I hope these excerpts will lead you to read some of the works in their entirety. These are all echoes of Hong Kong's past, worthy of being perused by those interested in her present and future. I hope these writings will link you to Hong Kong's heritage, and if you are in Hong Kong, encourage you to write your own impressions of the territory, whether in journal form, the great Hong Kong novel, or exuberant postcards back home.

Barbara-Sue White
Hong Kong
January 1996

A TOURIST'S IMPRESSION
1990s

'Oh, I think I'd hate Hong Kong.'

'I think you're beginning to like it.'

JANE GARDAM, 1991

1
THE PIG BOY

JANE GARDAM

To open the collection, let us arrive in Hong Kong with Veronica, a modern, first-time visitor. At first repelled by Hong Kong, events cause her to reconsider the multi-faceted Territory. Jane Gardam, a prize-winning British author, published this story in The Pangs of Love *in 1991.*

Veronica smelled the pig boy before she saw him and the smell was the essence of her loathing and hatred of Hong Kong.

A wet, grey, bad-tempered, blowy day and cold. She was wearing a new warm jersey under her white summer suit. Back at the hotel were all the thin summer clothes she had brought with her, still unworn. She had felt the room-boy's disdain as he unpacked them. Here was a first-time-out wife. She didn't know a thing. Didn't know that as late as March it could be cold and wet and bleak. Colder than England.

Colder than Barnes, she thought. She had left London with the grass on Barnes Common brightening and long and all the candles shining on the avenue of chestnuts that crosses the pretty railway line. London had had the smell of summer—airy and fresh. Here there was grit in the air and rubbish blew about the streets like rags.

Her husband was at work. He would be at work tonight until eight o'clock. Then there would be the usual drinks party. Perhaps two parties. Then the usual meal in a restaurant with friends. Then the usual wander in the streets among the stalls. Then bed. At the weekend—her last weekend—the firm had offered them a hired car.

But it wasn't being much of a holiday, alone all day. Well, of

2

course it was not meant to be a holiday. She was just there. There
as a wife. A brought-out wife, paid for by Geoffrey's firm. She was
to be brought-out (tourist class) every six months for a few weeks
until he finished the job. Like most other wives with husbands
working abroad she was safety-valve procedure against executive
breakdown.

The air must be full of flying wives, thought Veronica—airlines
to Singapore, Hong Kong, the Philippines, Colombo—heavy with
wives flying husbandwards: oil wives, lawyers' wives, army wives—
complacent on the journey out, glum or tense or relieved on the
flight home again, leaving their husbands not necessarily to any
great amusement. Geoffrey had said, 'Look round. Look at all the
men sitting eating alone. Not exactly the glossy life, is it?' 'Yes—
my wife's at home,' said the husbands. 'No—well she can't really.
Children's education.' Or, 'No. She can't. She has her job. No, it's
not much fun, but it's not forever. You learn to manage.'

And the world was full of people pitying the wives, thought
Veronica. In Barnes the drinks parties glittered with sharp eyes—
if you were lucky enough to be invited to any without a man. 'Yes,
I'm married,' you said, 'my husband's working in Hong Kong. Oh
yes—but I do get out there you know. Several weeks twice a year.'

'That sounds terrible.'

'It's very usual. Very usual nowadays. After all, it's not new.
Look at army wives and sailors' wives—they've always done it.
One's independent after all.'

'Not much fun though.'

'Oh, I don't know.'

The guarded look behind the eyes which said, 'Is she faithful?
I'll bet she's not. I'll bet he's not either. Asking too much—alone
six months of the year.'

Then would come the invitation—or no invitation. Whichever
happened, it was insulting.

And for Veronica, even in the liberated streets of Barnes, staying at home was harder to explain than for many because she had
no children. Being a painter she could have worked anywhere.

'No—we have no children.'

'Don't you think of being with him then?'

'Oh—I think I'd hate Hong Kong. And there are things here I
can't really leave.'

'What is it she can't leave?' they thought. 'She's probably just

3

found that she could never really stand him. There's probably trouble. I wonder what her lover's like?'

But there was no lover and there had never been trouble, and it was a surprise to find that when she arrived in Hong Kong this first time she found herself thinking, 'What if he's changed? What if I don't like him?' Dazed still by the idiot film she had watched on the flight and a couple of magazines the woman sitting next to her had loaned her, she thought, 'I wonder what his woman's like? Chinese? They're very pretty. Doting too. Everyone will know about her except me. They'll think nothing of it. It's the custom of the job, the times. Probably always was. Insane to be chaste. I wonder why I am?'

'I don't want to see him,' she thought, waiting for her luggage to lumber up on the roundabout. 'I'm frightened.' The roundabout went hypnotically, smoothly round, black and quiet like a roulette wheel. The Englishwoman with the magazines came up to her looking fuzzy and excited—little suits and brooches. 'Forget—did you say you were army? Are you an army wife? Are you going to the married quarters?'

'No, I'm not.' Suddenly angry, Veronica said, 'I work. I do a job.'

'Oh,' said the woman eyeing her, unbelieving. 'I thought if he wasn't here to meet you we could share a taxi.'

'I'm staying at the Peninsula.'

'Oh my! I'm sorry.' She looked hard at Veronica, not believing that a woman she had seen looking so uncertain could be staying at the Peninsula, though—Geoffrey had let his flat and was spendthrifting weeks of pay—this was true. They went through Customs together. An aggressive Chinese man-woman in police-type uniform shouted at them and glared. It was cold and the wind whined.

'I hadn't expected this,' said Veronica.

'First time out then?' The woman perked up.

'Yes.'

'Oh—you'll love it. I've been out five times. Lovely shopping.'

And there was Geoffrey, a tireder looking Geoffrey, rather redder in the face and flabbier, his shirt bloused out a bit over his trousers, but his eyes bright. Looking for her.

At once all thoughts of mistresses and lovers became ridiculous, their recognition of each other complete. Hurtling in the taxi through up-and-down rivers of lights, they held tight to each other's hand, and all the old pleasures flowed back.

It was the day time without him that had become so deadly boring. She felt so ashamed—the first time in the East—to be bored.

Geoffrey got up at seven-thirty and they had breakfast in their room—a great trolley wheeled in by two waiters, like an old film. The trolley had huge silver dish-covers, a pyramid of butter (which Geoffrey, because of the blousing out of the shirt, did not eat. 'Chinese call it cow's grease. Puts you off. Convenient.') And there were shiny cloth napkins the same colour as the cloth and fresh flowers in a glass.

When he had gone to work she would dress slowly and wander about. Then she would go down in the lift with its bowing attendant and leave the room-key in the lobby. Then she would walk purposefully out of the great white and gold hall into the street and let the crowd sweep her along.

For the first days, just to be in the marching streets was something, being swept up with the rest into a whirlpool at traffic lights, then like water, surging across. She crossed to Hong Kong side and the crowds at the ferries nearly trampled her under. She loved this at first. It was like going out further from the shore where the bigger waves might knock you down and bear you away and nobody know.

But after a week or so she grew used to it—used to the pace and the impersonality. It was just a richer, madder Oxford Street on a Saturday afternoon. She began to notice a pair of shoes in a display window in the side of the Peninsula Hotel. Two hundred pounds. The first day the price of the shoes had seemed ludicrous. After a week or so of Hong Kong it seemed just the price of shoes.

She grew used to the legless woman who shuffled her way about the pavement under the shoes, and around the corner, among the little clutch of street stalls that appeared by magic every morning. People stepped over the woman as if she were a moving stack. Food from the stalls dropped on her as she held up her tin cup for money. 'She has to pay for that pitch,' said a lawyer friend of Geoffrey's, 'like the door-man at Claridges.'

Veronica got used to the Hakka gypsy woman with the two-year-old squatting beside her and the sharp professional gypsy wag of the head as she sent the child running after her down Nathan Road to pull at her skirt. 'Money, money, money,' the child said—angrily, like the Customs official. Its mouth was covered in sores. She grew used to this.

One day she took the harbour cruise and sat in a cold green-house of a boat to see the city from the sea. The lunatic, concrete growths stuck up amid a forest of sharp-edged temples. They looked pushed into holes in the hills, and at their feet, among the dark little tents of the squatters was the noise of more cranes, more drills, more bulldozers, tearing away, knocking down, building yet more. It seemed like no country.

Another day she took a taxi and watched the boat families at Aberdeen from another glass greenhouse. She watched the chickens and babies and birds in cages on the decks and the screaming women in huge shields of hats all tipping and tossing over the choppy cold waves. All looked an exhibition, put on for the brought-out wives. It was not real. She was bored.

Lunch somewhere, if she remembered, and then back to the hotel for a rest (a rest from what? She was twenty-five, healthy and a full-time painter), then maybe an invitation from one of the resident wives to go shopping. They might be Chinese or French or American or English, but the conversation was always the same. Then the noisy, boozy, sociable evening in the glaring streets with Geoffrey and friends. All in the streets at night was self-consciously wicked—the transvestite street, the blue-film and massage-shop street, the nude-photograph street. Thousands of tourists.

And she was bored.

It might have been Soho except for the crazy zig-zag glitter of the lights—soft yellow and pink and gold and white and green. 'It's the pale green ones that make it Chinese,' said Geoffrey. 'The rest could be anywhere—though nowhere so many. I love the pale green.'

It was the first time he had said that he loved something here.

'D'you not long for proper green?' she said. 'You said you did. In letters.'

'Proper green?'

'You said you'd start watching television just for the scenery. Watching Westerns to see the grass.'

'Oh—there's grass here if you look. Up in the New Territories grass all the way to China. You can walk for miles. We'll go at the weekend in the car. And there's green on the islands. It's wonderfully beautiful. You can sunbathe on Cheung Chau. Next time you come out it will be really hot.'

'I think you're beginning to like it.'

'Oh—yes. What?' He was watching five little boys spooning what looked like baby snakes into their mouths from blue and white egg-cups. The naked lightbulbs over the stalls swung in the wind. They looked like Christmas tree fruits. They made shadows come and go across the five pale faces. Hair shone like tar.

'You aren't beginning to want to stay? I mean *stay*? Not go home—stay here permanently?'

'God no,' he said, 'I'm here for quick money like everyone else. You know that. We can earn more here in six months than in ten years at home. It's why we did it. Hell!'

They walked back through the packed midnight. The tenement walls hung above the narrow streets like the flanks of galleons, dressed over-all, night and day, with long poles of washing. From the lamp-lit rooms behind came the soft shuffling knock of the mah-jong games, floating out over the night until it was part of the night, like cicadas in Italy.

So now, towards the end, Geoffrey had an all-day meeting and would not be in until after eight o'clock and Veronica was to have lunch with the wife of his boss—an English woman from Kent who had come out to live in Hong Kong permanently. She and the wife would then go shopping for silk and perhaps some jewellery which the wife would advise about and get a good discount. Veronica took a taxi from the Hong Kong-side ferry and it wound up the Peak, round flower beds and gardens. But cement piles were going up even among these. A shining building that looked scarcely finished was being pulled down again to make way for something more modern. A speeded-up film of the building of Hong Kong, thought Veronica, would be like the waves of the sea, rising and breaking to rise again. The gardens were certainly doomed, she thought. However much must this land be worth? The Cathedral must be sitting on a fortune. A thousand pounds a centimetre. Ten thousand pounds a geranium.

The taxi swung off the road into a tunnel of expensive white tiles and cork-screwed up it to a double-meshed door. A servant in a long black dress answered it—hair screwed back, waxed yellow face, tight cheek bones, greying hair and a sweet smile. She seemed uncertain though about letting Veronica in and disappeared for quite some time. Veronica stood in the windy tunnel.

Then down in a flurry came the lady from Kent, by no means so flawlessly dressed as at the party where Veronica had met her. Her hair flopped about. The finger nails of one hand were painted and held a brush for the fingers of the other hand were still plain. She embraced Veronica wildly with both arms. Veronica hoped the lacquer wasn't spilling down her back.

'My dear! But it's terrible! I'd forgotten.'

'It doesn't matter at all.'

'Sit down. A drink. Oh but this is awful. I've never done it before. That party—so noisy. I do this. I *throw* invitations about. But I've never, never forgotten. Ever. I could die.'

'It's quite all right.' Veronica wondered why she couldn't just stay. 'There's heaps I can do instead.'

'Are you here for a nice long time?'

'Another week.'

'Look, I'll get the diary. We'll fix something now. Wednesday—no, I can't do Wednesday. Say Friday and I'll cancel my hair. Or Sunday—what about this Sunday and Geoffrey can come too?'

'We were—hoping for a car this weekend. To go to the New Territories.'

'Oh dear, well, Monday then?'

'I'll be gone by Monday. Look—don't worry. It's nice to be here now. Nice to come for a drink.'

'You see I have a Bridge.'

Veronica thought for a moment of teeth. Perhaps new teeth making lunch difficult.

'A Bridge—the wife of—well, it's a Royal Command sort of thing. There are two tables—a French table and an Anglo-Chinese table. And tea. Look—do you play Bridge?'

'No I'm afraid—'

'Of course not. You work, don't you?'

'I'm a painter.'

'Oh, a *painter*. Oh wonderful. I'm sure there are a lot of painters in Hong Kong. Well, I believe there's a wife at Jardines—does Chinese heads. Makes quite a little business of—Look why don't I take you to the Bridge? It'd be quite an experience for you. It's quite serious stuff you know. It might amuse—it's *real* Bridge.'

'No, no—'

But the woman had decided. She was stretching for the jade green telephone and talking ten to the dozen. They ate some biscuits and drank some more gin.

'You don't want to bother with lunch, do you? The food here is the big danger. We get as greedy as the Chinese. Aren't you loving the restaurants?'

'Yes, loving them.'

'I hope Geoffrey's doing you proud? We hardly see him. I hear he's moved to the Pen. with you?'

'Yes.'

'Oh, *rather* fun.'

A taxi took them to a house even higher up the Peak—servants, glass, marble floors, rare pieces of curly black ebony and small figurines of jade. The French table was already under way—tight mouths, severe hair-cuts, fast conversation. The sharp faces on the cards looked back. The Chinese/English table was more relaxed except at moments when a deep silence fell and eyes became a silk screen and watched the rings shining on the confident international fingers. Outside the window birds tipped and soared on the cold wind.

An older, Chinese woman came across to Veronica when tea was brought and sat by her. She said, in a Knightsbridge voice, 'How are you liking Hong Kong? I believe it is your first time?'

'Oh very much. Yes, it is.'

'You are from London?'

'Yes. From Barnes.'

'Ah—from Barnes.'

A louder Chinese lady came across. She had round red spots painted on her cheeks and corkscrew curls. She spoke in a high, rather cockney sing-song.

'You will be going to London soon? Then you must stay in my flat. In Ken Sing Tong.'

'But I live in—'

'You like Hong Kong?'

'Oh, yes, very—'

Little cakes made of chestnut purée wrapped in pale green marzipan were handed with the tea. The purée was piped in little worms like the things the boys were eating at the street stalls. The pale green marzipan was like the green neon. 'The pale green that is Chinese.'

9

'But it isn't,' thought Veronica. 'It is just pale green. I've seen those cakes in Fortnums, just as, come to think of it, I've seen that queer stuff on the street stalls. It was noodles. This place isn't any more foreign than London. None of it.'

The lady who had offered her a flat in Kensington took three little cakes, ate them greedily and licked her painted fingers, heavy with diamonds.

'Nothing Chinese here,' thought Veronica, looking at all the ebony and jade and silk and the Chinese carpet on the floor. 'It is the Finchley Road.'

'I am hating it,' she thought, and got up.

'I must go,' she said. The women were going back to the tables. 'Oh dear,' said the Boss's wife. 'Oh hell—I did bish it up, didn't I? Must you go?'

'I must, I'm afraid. I'm meeting someone Kowloon side.'

It was the most inconvenient moment to leave and she knew it. The hostess was trying to get the tables back together again against a lot of fast talking by the French in corners. Servants were gliding about trying to gather unobtrusively the remains of the tea. 'So glad you could come,' said the hostess with a far-away calm that did not disguise her alertness to developments in more significant parts of the room. 'We'll meet again—won't we?' said the Boss's wife. 'We've all so wondered what dear Geoffrey's wife would be like.'

Two of the French women stopped talking then and looked at Veronica quickly.

Looking round, Veronica thought, 'They are all devious. Every one of them. What are they really thinking about behind all the witty talk and the picking up of the cards and the laying down of them?' Laughter followed her out of the room and she thought that it did not sound very kind. I liked the noise of the mah-jong players better than that, she thought. Getting off the ferry Kowloon side, it was still not five o'clock. Over three hours to go. She had not a thing to do.

When she reached the Peninsula she found that she could not go in. She walked instead along the side of it, past the little inset shop windows and the two hundred pound shoes. She thought of the rings and the earrings and the even more beautiful shoes of the women playing cards on the Peak. As she stood, a woman passed her, bouncing and busty. She was coming from a hairdresser, the hair raised up in a cushion, stiff with lacquer. She was the woman from the aeroplane, the army wife. She walked jauntily past Veronica, not recognizing her. It might be Barnes, thought Veronica, or Ken Sing Tong.

Then she found that she was walking away and away from the hotel and away down Nathan Road. At first she walked quite slowly, but then she began to walk fast, watching for the traffic, but beginning to walk in and out of it. She began to march at the same quick, steady pace as everyone else in the crowded street.

And soon she found that she was caught up with the people on the pavement. She was in a marching army. Nobody looked at her, touched her, jostled her. Nobody in the street ever seemed to touch anybody else. And they made way for you without noticing you. You began to melt through the crowd like a spirit. There were no collisions. It was like radar, like bats. Up on their toes they all walked, their faces looking straight ahead, their arms to their sides. Perhaps, thought Veronica, if you live so closely, so densely together, you have to develop this isolation. Nobody noticed her, walking, walking, walking, marching, marching. And, as she turned off into a side street for no real reason and marched on she realised that she had stopped being unhappy.

On a corner a minute old woman sold purple chrysanthemums and Veronica bought six. They seemed very cheap. The old woman with little yellow hands wrapped the stalks in yellows paper. Her hands were like fans. Ivory fans. They had no pictures on them. No faces.

'I think I'm a bit mad,' said Veronica. 'What shall I do with these flowers?'

The wind blew and it began to rain. The rain was cold on her face and the paper round the flowers grew sopped and useless. She let it float away and into the gutter with other rubbish, and walked on.

'I think I must be hungry,' she said. 'I ought to have eaten some of those Mr Kipling chestnut things. I'll find a street stall.' Geoffrey said, 'Never a street stall. Never in Hong Kong. Singapore yes. Hong Kong never. Look at the pots they cook in. Slopped round with a greasy cloth. Never washed up.'

'I'll eat at a street stall,' she said.

But there seemed now to be no stalls. She had walked since leaving Nathan Road down a dozen small streets and got back to a main road again—dirtier and greyer with only a faint glitter from the tram lines and overhead wires tossing with rain and wind. Traffic screamed by. The people thinned. The trams and buses were packed with those going home from work and other thousands arriving for the evening shift. She didn't know whether to try and cross this road or not, and realized she was quite lost. Also, it seemed—but this must surely be because there was a storm coming—to be getting quite dark.

Then she was out of the street and on a great motorway, a huge clover-leaf junction. The crowd had disappeared and there was no one about. Only traffic—mostly big square lorries—steamed by. It was an enormously wide road, two triple carriageways and a scruffy central reservation. At the far side there seemed to be grass and a large, low, sad-looking building, a sort of club house. Maybe she could get a taxi back from there?

All alone in the ridiculous white suit she ran from the edge of the motorway to the central reservation and stood there between the whizzing lorries, waiting for the second dash to the far shore. And there she smelled the pig boy.

He was in a lorry—a lorry still far away up the road, but the smell was so huge and terrible that she looked about her, up and down the road, to see if some great sewer were leaking near her feet. The wind then carried the smell in a blast into her mouth so that she retched and dropped the flowers and pressed her hands over her face. Her eyes streamed with water. She struggled to get her handkerchief—anything—out of her bag, and with a clashing, cranking roar the lorry came up beside her.

The back of it was filled to the brim with screaming pigs—dark with dirt, tossed in a writing mass, suffering, fighting with pathetic, inadequate feet to get somehow steady and in control of their great bodies. The pigs at the bottom of the heap—their gaping faces pressed into the slats—seemed already dead.

But it was the smell. It made her nearly faint.

'You want help?'

It was the driver. The pig boy. High above her head he looked down. She turned away sick. 'No, no.'

'You lost? English? You want help?'

He was not Chinese like the flower-seller, or the servants on the Peak, or the ivory-carved room-boys at the hotel, or even the red faced Hakka professional beggar. He had a broad face, laughing cheek-bone, long, bright Mongolian eyes and curly hair.

'Thanks,' she gasped. 'No. It's fine, thanks. I'm just going—over there. To get a taxi.'

'That place shut there now over there. That place shut. For new building. Re-settlement. Old English tennis club. Nobody now. Where you stay?'

'The Peninsula.'

'Four-five mile, soon dark.'

'It's all right. Please go.' She—still nearly fainting—tried to cross the road behind the lorry.

But he had jumped down and came towards her. He took her wrist and pulled her to the front of the lorry and tumbled her up and in. She retched again and her forehead fell down against the dashboard.

'You ill?' He had started the engine though it could hardly be heard against the screaming of the pigs. He turned on the radio. Chinese music wailed through the cab, too.

'The smell, the smell!'

'Oh, *smell*,' he said and began to laugh. 'Terrible, terrible smell.' He laughed with his eyes and his shoulders and his mouth and with every bit of him. Clusters of good luck charms hung across the windscreen of the cab—tokens, ribbons, silly animals dangling from strings, and several photographs of girls. Veronica turned from all of them and leaned her head against the rattling, vibrating door. 'Terrible smell!' He laughed with pride. She remembered how the room-boys had laughed and laughed, Geoffrey had told her, when he had hurt his back soon after he arrived and had had to lie down on a hard board. 'Terrible pain,' they had laughed. And someone else, telling her of a visit to a Chinese dentist—and on the Peak at that—had asked 'Is this going to hurt?' 'Oh yes—it going to hurt all right,' and had roared with laughter. Something at last was different here.

The lorry had turned off the motorway and down a drab road, seeming to turn away from the Centre again. It rattled past warehouses and long grey sheds. By one of them it stopped. Some people came out, wearing cloths across their faces. The driver jumped out and went over to them and they all went into the shed. Veronica, still holding the handkerchief to her mouth, sweating with sickness, struggled with the door but it wouldn't open from the inside. She felt utter terror now through the sickness, and began to cry.

Then the door was opened and she fell out into the pig boy's arms. He jumped back at once. He looked shocked and only when he was sure she was safe on her feet did he shout above the pigs, 'Please—come with me now.'

She could think only of getting away from the hell of the lorry and as he turned she followed, out of the filthy yard, along a wire fenced road, then down an alley that led to another alley that led to another that led to a busy road again. They walked, one behind the other along this road until they came to an iron bridge. Under the bridge were some stalls selling kites—sharp yellow and red and blue. Around them people were eating and talking and shouting and under the bridge a man was squatting in vest and underpants playing an instrument balanced with a spike like a miniature cello on the pavement. It looked like something between a guitar, a cello and a lute and the noise that came from it was like chalk drawn across a blackboard and in its way hurt like the smell of the pigs.

As Veronica watched, the musician looked up and smiled at her and the sun came out. All the coloured kites blazed for a moment in the sunset.

'Quick, quick,' said the pig boy and walked lithe and fast under the bridge and into a dark street. As they reached it, out came the sun again and Veronica saw the street crumbling before her. A lumpish, medieval machine, very different from the mechanics on the Peak, slowly swung a huge iron ball at a tall, papery old building. The whole front of the building slipped quietly to the ground and the sun went in again.

'I am being shown things,' said Veronica, 'like Faust.' They went on down the dark and filthy street. 'Or maybe I am being kidnapped. Perhaps I am about to be raped. Or knifed. Geoffrey—all of them—said, "Never go Kowloon side alone."' 'I am mad.' But she walked quietly on behind the pig boy.

He stopped and said, 'Tea?'

'No—no. Please—I want to go home. Can you find me a—bus or a taxi or something? I must get back.'

'You are ill. Tea first and then home.'

They were standing outside a dirty, blackened house with a very narrow, dark doorway. It was the oldest house she had seen in

Hong Kong. Outside it, on two ancient basket chairs there sat an old woman and a very, very old man dressed in black tunics and black trousers. They sat very straight, like royal people. The woman looked at Veronica and bowed. The man looked gravely at her for rather longer, and then bowed. Nobody spoke, and in the quiet Veronica could still hear the piercing music of the lute player that now sounded the only right music for the scene.

Then, from across the road, next to the house that was being pulled down, people came running and gathering round a queer, high car, piled high with paper flowers—pink and red and yellow and white. They chattered and laughed and fussed and took no notice of Veronica or the ancient royal personages or the demolition.

The pig boy had disappeared, but he now came out of the dark doorway between the two basket chairs with a painted Chinese girl who looked at Veronica and smiled. From the thickness and symmetry of the paint Veronica saw that the girl was a prostitute. Several other girls came out who looked like her sisters. They seemed dolls from a box. Then someone else came and laid a cleanish sheet of white paper on the pavement and bowed to Veronica to sit on it. Then an older woman in a thick woollen suit and a gold bangle round her ankle brought a tiny bowl of tea.

Veronica drank it, and caught the eye of the old people. The old woman smiled, showing a mouth full of gold teeth. The old gentleman touched first one side of his long moustaches and then the other before smiling, too. Across the road the wild party surged about the car, filling and covering it with more and more paper flowers. The pig boy, who had been talking to the painted girls, came over and said, 'You happy and well?'

She drank the tea.

'It is a funeral,' said the boy. 'You have come to a funeral.' He repeated this to the others in some sort of language and everyone laughed tremendously. He said, 'You are dressed in white for the funeral.' Their laughter mixed with the laughter and shouts of the funeral party across the road, as it moved off.

The sun had gone in now. The dust from the demolished building hung heavy. The pig boy stank. Rubbish was piled in the gutter. The woman brought more tea. The queer music went faintly on.

'You happy and well?'

15

Veronica said, 'Oh I am happy. I am well.' This was translated, and the old aristocrats bowed. There was silence.

Veronica realised sadly that they were expecting her to go. She stood up and said to the pig boy, 'I wish I had kept my flowers, my flowers to give them. I let them drop.'

This was translated and there was more bowing. Veronica shook hands with everyone. They took her hand with a very slight hesitation. Following the pig boy, she turned at the end of the road to wave to them, but there was no one on the street at all except the two old people and they seemed to be sitting thoughtfully looking in another direction.

The pig boy walked ahead and then after a while beside her, saying nothing. She could hardly keep up. He had fallen quite silent and she said, 'Please—can I get a bus or taxi now? I thought I saw a taxi just then.'

'No taxi.' he said. 'You are back hotel.'

'Where?'

'One minute now. Two minute.'

'It can't be.'

Yet the streets were different, noisier, busier. There were tourists about. Then all at once, there was the Hakka beggar with her child, but now, the pig boy beside her, the child did not come after her crying 'Money'.

'I should tell you,' said the pig boy, 'that you must not take hands. You must not take hands here or embrace.'

'I'm sorry. I just wanted to say thank you to them.'

He walked on, filthy and beautiful and rough in the rich street. The crowd was changing every moment, growing smarter, faster, better dressed. He wove expertly among them.

'What are you? Who are you?' she said.

'A pig boy. I bring pigs everyday out of Red China into Hong Kong. Chinese pigs. Big trading.'

'Yes, I see.'

'Good job,' he said. 'Sweet and sour'—he laughed. 'Only for strong men.'

'Oh goodness,' she said—here were the shoes. 'Oh goodness, we're back at the Peninsula. Oh thank you, thank you.' She turned to the pig boy and not able to help it held out to him both her hands. He looked at them unsmiling.

'You took my wrist,' she said, 'to pull me into the cab.'

Briefly he touched her hands with his own and was gone.

'My God!' It was Geoffrey beside her getting out of a taxi. He carried a brief case and a pile of papers. 'You just back? You've had a long day. It's past nine. God, this bloody place. I hate it. Let's get a bath and—heavens, you smell dreadful. Wherever's the memsahib been taking you?'

'Do you hate it?' She could not move one step until Geoffrey had answered. If she moved she knew that something would break. 'Do you hate it here?'

'Well—no. But you do.'

'Do I?'

'You know you do. I know you do. I've known all the time.'

They stood on the pavement and the crowds washed effortlessly by. 'You couldn't live here, Veronica.'

'I might,' she said, 'I might.' ▧

PART II

OUTPOST OF THE CELESTIAL EMPIRE AD 700-1729

'They live by fishing and salt-making'

SONG DYNASTY GAZETTE

2
NEW PEACE COUNTY
FROM A CHINESE GAZETTER OF THE HONG KONG REGION

Jane Gardam offers a view of contemporary Hong Kong, but let us now go back to early days, long before the British, and read some of the reports and documents of Hong Kong through its history.

Judging from Western reports written in the mid-nineteenth century, it might be assumed that before the British commenced their rule of Hong Kong, the place sported only a handful of local fishermen, the odd pirate, and little culture or history. Instead, archaeologists have unearthed artefacts which suggest many centuries of civilization. Written records include governmental reports, gazettes for Southern China and a Tang poem.

During China's Tang Dynasty (AD 618–906), a military garrison was established at Tunmen in what is now known as Hong Kong's New Territories to protect the entrance to China's Pearl River. Han Yu, a famous eighth-century Tang poet, composed a couplet describing Tunmen engulfed in storm. It is inscribed on a stone tablet standing above a sixth-century Buddhist monastery.

Though Tunmen is considered high, The waves have swallowed it up.

*

Civil unrest followed the end of the Tang Dynasty, and Hong Kong and Guangdong were under the jurisdiction of the Southern Han Dynasty rulers until they fell to the Song in AD 971. Hong Kong emerged as a centre of pearl fishing at Tolo Harbour, then known as Meichuan. This description has survived.

Liu Chang [the last Southern Han ruler] occupied Ling Nan and recruited eight thousand men for the specific purpose of gathering pearls at Meichuan Dou [Hong Kong]. Each man had a stone tied to his foot and had to dive to a depth of five to seven hundred feet [sic]. Drownings were commonplace. In due course the emperor's treasuries became so well stored with pearls that the pillars and curtains of his palace were all decorated with them and were extremely magnificent.

*

During the subsequent Song Dynasty, Chinese writers described Hong Kong in government gazettes. A local gazette depicted the people of Hong Kong's Lantau Island.

The inhabitants neither farm nor make silk, nor do they pay taxes or do labour service. They live by fishing and salt-making.

*

The last Song emperors came to Hong Kong, setting up court near Kowloon City, and a large percentage of their army settled in Hong Kong. Hong Kong continued to be the subject of reports, and in 1729, during the Qing Dynasty, a provincial report urged an end to an activity still popular in Hong Kong: gambling.

From earliest days loafers and idlers have been anathema to those who rule. But gamblers are worse than mere idlers. They neglect their proper occupations and waste away their family fortunes, day by day their natures become more corrupt and their schemes more crooked. When fathers become addicted they are unable to give moral teachings to their sons, and when the master is addicted he cannot control the slave as he ought. Gambling is a cause of fights, a source of lawsuits, a reason for the rise in banditry, and a centre of attraction for the disaffected, damaging in countless ways the good morals and customs of the people.

For years now edicts repeatedly have been sent down strictly forbidding gambling, but the practice has not stopped, nor have makers of gambling equipment ceased to exist, or those who are responsible for the prohibition employed their full energies in the task.

We consider that the reason why gambling proliferates is that when fathers and elder brothers indulge in it, their sons and younger brothers take notice and emulate them; when masters indulge, their slaves and servants observe and copy them; and even women and young girls fall into the slough and do not think it blameworthy: and because so many are addicted many more become corrupted. If the prohibition were strictly enforced, no one would dare to go on infringing the law, and in course of time young men would not take up the habit; and if no one were acquiring the habit, then it would of course die out and there would be no necessity for further orders of this kind.

From now on when gamblers are apprehended there must be a careful examination of their equipment to see where it was made, and when there is clear evidence of the country of origin of the equipment the county magistrate of that place shall be dismissed for dereliction of duty, the prefectural magistrate shall be deprived of title but allowed to remain in office, and all their superior officers in the province shall be demoted one grade but allowed to remain in office.

If a county magistrate manages to discover and bring to justice someone manufacturing gambling equipment in his own territory he shall be promoted two grades, his prefectural magistrate shall be promoted one grade, and their provincial superiors shall each receive a double record of merit entry. This scheme of reward and punishment shall be permanent and shall commence in AD 1730. The provincial authorities shall ensure that even in the remote corners of town and country everyone shall be aware of it. ▨

PART III

THE BRITISH RAISE THE UNION JACK
1840-1860

'Albert is so much amused at my having got the Island of Hong Kong.'

QUEEN VICTORIA, 1841

'I was agreeably disappointed in Hong Kong; it was not the dog's hole I had heard of.'

OSMOND TIFFANY JR., 1849

VOYAGE OF HMS *SULPHUR*

SIR EDMUND BELCHER

Everyone seemed to keep diaries and journals in the nineteenth century, often prompted by long sea voyages. Sometimes the entries included descriptions of historically important events. Sir Edmund Belcher was captain of the HMS Sulphur, *one of the first ships to land at Hong Kong after the cession of the island to the British.*

We landed on Monday the 25th January, 1841, at fifteen minutes past eight a.m., and being the *bona fide* possessors, Her Majesty's health was drunk with three cheers on Possession Mount. On the 26th the squadron arrived; the marines were landed, the Union Jack hoisted on our post, and formal possession taken of the Island by Commodore Sir. J. G. Bremer, accompanied by the other officers of the squadron, under a *feu de joie* from the marines and the Royal Salute from the ships of war. On the Kowloon peninsula were situated two batteries, which might have commanded the anchorage, but which appeared to be but thinly manned; these received due notice to withdraw their men and guns, as agreed by the late treaty. ▓

4
LETTER TO QUEEN VICTORIA
FROM VISCOUNT PALMERSTON

British government officials felt that Captain Elliot did not drive as hard a bargain as possible in the Opium Wars with China, accepting the rather dubious island of Hong Kong, plus an indemnity of six million dollars and rights for customs collections. Palmerston was embarrassed by Elliot's behaviour, and no monument exists in Hong Kong for the recalled envoy, who was then sent as Consul to Texas.

Foreign Office, 10th April 1841

Viscount Palmerston presents his humble duty to your Majesty, and has the honour to submit the accompanying letters, which he received yesterday, about the operations in China. Viscount Palmerston has felt greatly mortified and disappointed at this result of the expedition to China, and he much fears that the sequel of the negotiation, which was to follow the conclusion of these preliminary conditions, will not tend to render the arrangement less objectionable. Captain Elliot seems to have wholly disregarded the instructions which had been sent to him, and even when, by the entire success of the operations of the Fleet, he was in a condition to dictate his own terms he seems to have agreed to very inadequate conditions. Even the cession of Hong Kong has been coupled with a condition about the payment of duties, which would render that island not a possession of the British Crown, but, like Macao, a settlement held by sufferance in the territory of the Crown of China.

Viscount Palmerston has sent a small map of the Canton River, which your Majesty may like to keep for future reference. ◉

25

5

LETTER TO THE KING OF THE BELGIANS

FROM QUEEN VICTORIA

Many of Queen Victoria's thousands of letters are stiff, formal epistles to officials. However, her real feelings come out in her informal and more relaxed letters to her uncle. This suggests, perhaps, her real reaction to the acquisition of Hong Kong.

13th April 1841

MY DEAREST UNCLE,—I thank you very much for your kind letter of the 9th, received yesterday. I think, dear Uncle, that you would find the East not only as 'absurd' as the West, but very barbarous, cruel and dangerous into the bargain.

The Chinese business vexes us much, and Palmerston is deeply mortified at it. *All* we wanted might have been got, if it had not been for the unaccountably strange conduct of Charles Elliot who completely disobeyed his instructions and *tried* to get the *lowest* terms he could. . . . The accounts of the cruelty of the Chinese to one another are horrible. Albert is so much amused at my having got the Island of Hong Kong, and we think Victoria ought to be called Princess of Hong Kong in addition to Princess Royal. 🏵

6

NOTE ON THE ISLAND OF HONG KONG

A. R. JOHNSTON

As the British Empire expanded, educated people delighted in describing exotic lands far from fog-bound Britain. In contrast to the Hong Kong of today, this earlier version of the island with its red deer and mango trees seems remote indeed.

The Island of Hongkong, seen from a distance at sea, is, like all the islands on this Coast of China, precipitous and uninviting. Its high hills often terminate in sharp peaks, and are thickly strewed with masses of black rock of primitive formation, frequently piled upon one another in a most remarkable and sometimes fantastic nature with here and there two or three lower hills covered with gravel and sand. From the summit to the water's edge there are few or no trees; and, except in the months May, June, July and August, when these islands look green, they might be supposed to be quite barren.

On landing and examining the island of Hongkong, the N. and N.E. side is found to be separated from the S. and S.W. by one continued range of hills, in no place less than 500 feet, in most parts upwards of 1000, and on more than one pinnacle 1741 feet above the level of the sea, by barometrical observation. When to this is added that the utmost breadth of the island does not exceed four or five miles, it may easily be imagined that the descent to the sea on either side is very abrupt.

A course kind of grass is found on all the hills, but on those with a northerly and north-easterly exposure it is generally choked by ferns and stunted brush-wood: while on the face of the hills fronting the south it grows in clumps unchecked, except when burnt by natives.

There are no towns on the island, excepting the flourishing

one of Victoria, which was founded by the English in 1841, and formally ceded to the British Crown under the Nanking Treaty. This town is fast springing into importance, and a fifty-foot road runs through it for more than three miles to the valley of Wong-nei-chung, where it becomes narrower, and, diverging, crosses over a range of hills by the ravines already described, to Tai-tam Bay, and from thence to Chek-choo [Stanley] on the south side of the island.

No public buildings were found on any part of the Island of Hongkong when it was first occupied by the English, except a small tumble-down Chinese house at Chek-choo, and another at Shek-pie-wan [near Aberdeen], where the petty mandarins stopped occasionally, and three Chinese temples, one at Chek-choo, one near Soo-kun-poo [near Causeway Bay], and the third and finest at Shek-pai-wan, situated on a little island not exceeding an acre in extent, and covered with trees. The existence of this last temple, with the ruins of many houses in the same vicinity, gives rise to the impression that Shek-pai-wan has seen better days; and it is known to have been one of the principal resorts of the pirates when they infested this coast of China many years ago; and that it would again lately have been so, had the island of Hongkong not been occupied by the English, is more than probable. . . .

The only animals found on the island are a few small deer, a sort of armadillo, and a land-tortoise. There are several sorts of snakes, but no one has yet been found to suffer from their bite.

Among the fruits and vegetables produced on the island, are the mango, lichee, longan, orange, pear, rice, sweet potatoes, and yams; a small quantity of flax is grown, and prepared for household uses by the villagers. Since the occupation of the island by the English, the potato of Europe and fruits of Canton and Macau have been introduced; and lately a great many European seeds have been brought out by the agent of the Horticultural Society of London, and distributed.

The agriculturists of Hongkong use the common Chinese wooden plough, drawn by bullocks or buffalos; and their other agricultural implements are like those used on the mainland. Their threshing flour is made on the first convenient spot outside their farmhouse; the ground being smoothed, is afterwards covered with lime and beaten flat. The grass is sometimes trodden on by cattle, and at other threshed with a flail, quite like our own, except that one piece revolves on a pin with a head, which is fastened into the side of the other. Some of the labouring women wear a hat like the usual Chinese one, but it has a blue nankin curtain of five or six inches deep, sewn around the edge of the rim to keep off the glare from the face. ▩

7

THE COLONY OF HONG KONG

THE REVEREND JAMES LEGGE

The Reverend James Legge founded Hong Kong's Union Church, a coalition of Protestants. The congregation first assembled at the Reverend's home on Hollywood Road, before building Union Chapel, and finally at the current church on Kennedy Road. As an early missionary and admired citizen in Hong Kong, Legge delivered a lecture of reminiscences of his many years in the Colony at the City Hall on 5 November 1872. His last years were spent in England as an eminent professor of Chinese literature at Oxford.

In the month of May, 1843, I reached Macao, and, a few days after, came over with my family to this place [Hong Kong]. Our passage was made in a small cutter, chartered for the occasion, and I have not forgotten the sensations of delight with which, when we had passed Green Island, I contemplated the range of hills on the north and south embossment, between them the tranquil waters of the bay. I seemed to feel that I had found at last the home for which I had left Scotland; and here has been my abode, with intervals occupied by visits to the fatherland, for nearly thirty years. . . .

In the early days there was next to no police guardianship; and the consequences were frequent disorders on the streets during the day, and many burglaries on a grand scale during the night. I once witnessed from my house in D'Aguilar Street an engagement between nearly a hundred Chinese coolies on each side, on the ground now occupied by the Club-house. Bamboo on bamboo, and bamboo on skull, resounding pretty equally, until parties were obliged to give up from exhaustion. I thought that nothing wilder or better-sustained had ever been seen at Donnybrook Fair. . . .

There was a rumour of a scheme to re-enact the gunpowder plot by means of a tunnel under the cathedral, when the governor, the bishop, and the congregation were to be blown up. The facts of this case, however, if there were any, I could never satisfactorily ascertain.

The most successful exploit of this kind was perpetrated as late as January, 1865, by a gang who tunnelled by the hard labour of several weeks right under the treasury of the Central Bank of India, and carried off upwards of $100,000 in gold and bullion and notes. In 1863 twenty-two prisoners made their escape from the gaol by tunnelling under it into a drain. Not long after, I did the service to the Government of disconnecting a scheme on a larger scale, by which within a few hours, eighty-nine men would have got away. . . . The secrecy, skill, and perseverance with which the mining operations had been conducted were astonishing, and made me think it was a pity the ability of the scoundrels could not have been utilized in Cornwall or other parts of Great Britain.

At the terrible subject of piracy I can only glance. That it was for many years a terrible evil I need not say. There is no doubt, I think, that the bands who attempted the violent burglaries of which I have spoken were mainly composed of pirates, and that when the land was no longer safe for them, they confined their operations to the sea.

It is thought, I know by many, that my views on this subject [the Hong Kong Police] are visionary and Utopian—derived from my acquaintance with Chinese literature more than from acquaintance with the Chinese people. I will only say that during my many years of residence here, my intercourse was quite as much with the people as with their books. Several hours of every day were spent in visiting them from house to house, and shop to shop; conversing with them on all subjects, and trying to get them to converse with me on one subject [Christianity]. When I went home in 1867, I could say that, excepting the brothels, there was hardly a house in Victoria and the villages in which I had not repeatedly been, and where I was not known as a friend. . . .

Well;—what is to be the future of Hongkong? When I try to pierce into the future, I see a railway from Kowloon to Canton, and branch lines connecting with it. I see this island the natural outlet to all Europe, and by the Pacific lines to the United States. I see itself the home of a happy population, three times more numerous than the present, and foreigner and Chinese dwelling together in mutual appreciation. I see its harbour a forest of smoking funnels with hardly a white-winged sailing vessel among them; opium is a phantom of the past. The emigration of the poor goes on from it on principles approved and guarded by the Chinese and other governments, while the enterprise and integrity of its merchants, the kindness, forbearance, and purity of all its inhabitants are spoken of with delight from Peking to Hainan, from the farthest west of Szechuan to the borders of the Eastern sea. 🔲

8

LETTER FROM HONG-KONG, DESCRIPTIVE OF THAT COLONY

FROM 'A RESIDENT'

Since the identity of the author remains a mystery, the accuracy of the contents were presumably not questioned. Complaints about the cost of accommodation will strike a familiar note with anyone recently paying Hong Kong rents.

Victoria, 16th November, 1844

Sir,
I was duly favoured with your letter of the 2nd June. As a vessel sails to-day for Bombay, I shall give you my opinion on the points you wish for, only stipulating that in the event of your publishing the information, you will not give my name, unless the statement is disputed, when you are at liberty to use it.

I have resided at Hong-Kong since August, 1843. The climate, as might be expected from the latitude, is warm, but not so much so as many places further north. . . .

It is very difficult to describe the state of society in the island. The distance at which we live from each other,—the town extending over a long, narrow stripe along the shore, between the sea and the hills; the short time most of us have been here; the nature of the climate—un-favourable for going out, except during the evenings which are exceedingly short; darkness following very close upon sunset, and probably also the nature of the pursuits of most, have a tendency to encourage seclusion. Our military gentlemen are the same all over the world. Perhaps I might say the same of the upper classes of British merchants, who here, as elsewhere, are most respectable. As might be expected, a low class of adventurers, though not yet very numerous, are finding their way here, not calculated to raise the character of our nation.

Much cannot be said to the credit of the Chinese population who have resorted hither. None of the native merchants have yet formed establishments here, deterred, it is believed, by the fear of being 'squeezed,' as they term it, by their own mandarins. The shopkeepers, nevertheless, are numerous, though few even of these have their families here. The coolies are, probably, as thorough a set of scoundrels as are to be found; at present, however, from the number of works going on they are all employed, and since the police system was put on a proper footing, the place has been quiet and passably honest as far as acts go. When we are a little further advanced, there is some reason to hope for much improvement. Some Hongs are building at present, which are expected to be occupied by Foh-Kien [Fujian] merchants. The presence of wealthy natives, holding a large quantity of goods in their possession, will ensure a more respectable class of workmen, and a good police, backed by an efficient court of justice, will infallibly drive away many of the bad.

If you have not already heard of the prices of land, you will be surprised at the sums drawn by Government. A lease for seventy-five years only is granted, and for that £400 sterling per annum is a common rent for an imperial acre, many even higher. This too is given for lots that require an expenditure of from one to three thousand dollars to prepare a site for building on. Houses are scarce and let high, which is probably the cause of this high price; from twenty to thirty per cent is often got upon money so expended; but as a very great number are now building, rents may be expected to fall, and then the Government rent will be felt more burdensome.

Living is expensive, and the butcher market not very well supplied. Mutton and beef are sometimes not to be had. Fowls are plentiful and cheap, always bought by weight (alive). Fish also is plentiful and good, and there is no want of vegetables or fruits. . . .

A medical friend has just called. Among the causes of sickness he thinks intemperance holds a prominent place, and, unfortunately, his opinion is but too well-founded. The number of low tippling houses is large, and spirits are very cheap. Every day people may be seen reeling about under a burning sun, scarce able to stand, and the result is all attributed to the climate. Parties of from 50 to 100 are occasionally allowed to land from the ships in the harbour, with leave of absence for two days, during which they are not an hour sober; and in all probability the great mortality in the army has some connection with the same cause.

I believe this is the best information I can give you on the matters you inquire about. I have lately seen several plates illustrative of Hong-Kong and China. Of the latter I cannot judge, but I have seen none from which a proper idea can be had of the former. . . .

I am, Sir, yours faithfully,

J——C——

9

AN AMERICAN IN HONG KONG

OSMOND TIFFANY, JR.

Over a hundred and fifty years after Osmond Tiffany's book was written, the fax machine has replaced the rush to finish a letter before the next ship sails for Bombay.

In most ways, this description by an American depicts a very different Hong Kong from that of today. But although the style of architecture has changed radically, those stacks of bamboo construction poles remain—as does the continued clatter of perpetual building. This excerpt comes from Osmond Tiffany Jr.'s 1849 memoirs, The Canton Chinese or The American's Sojourn in the Celestial Empire.

After a dinner more extraordinary, if possible, than the morning meal, we read until nightfall, and then anchored again not far from Hong Kong. Before the first hint of dawn our crew were up, and it being still calm, resumed their oars, and after an hour's paddling, emerging from a narrow passage, we suddenly beheld the crags on either side stretch into deeper gloom, and disappear in total darkness.

We were on the lip of Hong Kong harbor, but could behold nothing. Under us was the tossing surge, above us the starry heavens, and we floated on, as it seemed, into a universe of blackness.

The veil of night gradually lifted from the waters, and so, without accident, we were in sight of the goal.

The apprehensions of pirates were not altogether unfounded; there are a savage set of villains cruising about the mouth of the river, who will plunder, if not murder, anyone at the first opportunity. They often go in fast boats with their crews concealed, run alongside of unwary craft, and board them in a moment.

We saw no pirates, though during the second anchoring we were prepared for them, and slept with one eye open.

Our nervous Hindoo who had waked us up the night before, when there was not the slightest danger, took occasion to snore comfortably when we might reasonably expect visitors. The crew went to sleep as usual, and the next morning assured us with significant shakes of the head, that they were perfectly prepared for any intruders, and had been on the lookout, and that they would have stood by us most unflinchingly, in case of need. We, of course, believed them, as every man is supposed to speak truth until he is detected in a lie.

As we had moved about half way across the harbor we saw a long dark object looming up, and which presently assumed the shape of an English steamer. It was a government vessel, drawing only a few feet of water, and very serviceable for river navigation.

The buildings are almost all of substantial stone or brick, and considerable taste has been displayed in the architecture and internal arrangement of the dwellings. But we are getting on much too fast, and must not describe Hong Kong before we arrive there. As we neared the town it became light, and we skirted along the hill, looking out for a convenient place to land. The crew became remarkably industrious, and all took hold of the oars, and were so very much occupied, that they did not look out for breakers ahead, and bumped us high and dry on a rock with stunning force, just as we were coming in shore. The fast boat's bottom grazed the rock, and her bow went high in the air, and so disturbed the equilibrium of the pirate-haunted Hindoo, that he vanished head foremost into the water tank in the bow, and received a washing that he never would have volunteered to undergo.

We could not get ashore, and, as it was very early, let the crew employ themselves in running out a kedge and tugging at it, until we went souse into deep water. This operation occupied near an hour, and we philosophically ordered breakfast. To our dismay we learned that every thing was gone, nothing could be shown but some crockery, and a corkscrew. The boy who had catered for us was as hungry as we were, and when we finally pushed up to the stone steps of a pier, he immediately volunteered to lead us to the hotel. One of the Austrian gentlemen, armed with his letters of introduction, stepped ashore, found out the 'Astor House' of Hong Kong, reported that its boarders in large proportion were cock-roaches, drew one of his letters, brought down his man, and then sent to us to quarter on the same individual.

The boy who professed absolute knowledge of Hong Kong, undertook to guide us remaining two, while the damp Hindoo brought up the rear. The boy did admirably, only he led us to the wrong end of town first, and the tramp without breakfast, and with the thermometer at 90°, was thoroughly invigorating. As we went along we saw pasted on the fences genuine English hand-bills, and delighted ourselves, while the boy was looking around for the right house, with reading them. Among others were plac-ards of the Haymarket, Drury Lane, and Her Majesty's theatre.

After five hundred inquiries, the meandering youth found the house, and we were glad to take shelter from the burning sun in the hospitable mansion of Capt.—. We were soon enjoying a cap-ital meal, attended by several Malay servants, who are more docile and plastic than Chinese.

The furniture was European; there were several English prints on the wall, and, what was still more like home, we found a Yan-kee clerk in the office, one of the sharpest of the sharp, with a nasal twang like a violin string near the bridge, and who had 'come to Chiny all the way from Barnstable.'

We soon found the cause of what had arrested our attention in the street, viz., the number of idlers who were congregated there, and the general dullness of the town. We learned that a rebellion had taken place among the Chinese. One of the Chinese had struck or stuck an officer, and a party of five or six had prevented the bakers from delivering bread at the doors of the Europeans. The rebellion was quelled in a day or two, the tax was reconsid-ered but not withdrawn, and all the trouble ended when the one Chinaman was hung and the half dozen flogged.

The Chinese suffered many indignities at Hong Kong; no doubt the rascally natives deserved punishment often, and were kept in check by the strong arm of power; but the worthless adventurers of the town took every occasion to disgust the Chinese, and did not even spare any portion of the better inhabitants.

Scapegoats and scoundrels from the purlieus of London, crea-tures that only missed Botany Bay by good fortune, were to be found in the town of Victoria, lording it over the natives, many of whom were more respectable and respected than they had ever been or ever could be. Low Wapping dock loafers, who had never at home put their heads into decent houses, would swagger along three or four abreast, elbowing quiet men out of the way, and replying to a word by a blow.

The season of the year was late in the autumn; it was in November when Americans button up their coats, and build large fires, and yet we were roasting in garments of the thinnest linen. But in Hong Kong we were cautioned by good friends to beware of the sun, and were followed, every time we went near the front door, by a servant with an oriental umbrella. We soon found, however, that walking on the hot sand was too uncomfortable, and until the setting sun threw its long shadows over the bay, we lay still beneath the broad verandahs.

I was agreeably disappointed in Hong Kong; it was not the dog's hole I had heard of. . . .

As the town was rapidly increasing when I was there, go where you would your ears were met with the clink of hammer and chisels, and your eyes were in danger of sparks of stone at every corner. The buildings were run up and finished with magic ease; one day the cellar would be dug, and the next the roof was being finished.

It was not that the houses were hurried and slighted, but that such numbers of the Chinese were at work, that, like bees, the hive was soon ready for honey. The intense power of the sun drives all the workmen to shelter, and before a house is commenced a staging of bamboo is erected and covered with matting. As the building rises the bamboo poles are run up story by story, the matting elevated, and the whole house completely protected from the glare of day until the last nail is driven.

Many of the buildings are of a kind of sandstone easily worked when first quarried, but becoming harder the longer it is exposed to the weather.

The English have made, as usual with them, most excellent roads around the island, and have also introduced a strong police force. At night one always walks attended by a cooley carrying a lantern, and at the distance of every ten paces a policeman is stationed, and the light of the lantern shows him armed to the teeth.

The shops in Hong Kong are of the most wretched order, there being no rich natives on the island, and the Europeans being supplied from several shops kept by English, and in which the wares of London are retailed at enormous profits. But the ravening wolves

---

THE

HONGKONG & SHANGHAI HOTELS, LTD.

HONGKONG:

Telegraphic Address:—**KREMLIN, HONGKONG.**

HONGKONG HOTEL   -   -   REPULSE BAY HOTEL.

PENINSULA HOTEL (Under construction)   PEAK HOTEL.

CANTON:

CANTON HOTEL (Under construction)

SHANGHAI:

Telegraphic Address:—**CENTRAL, SHANGHAI.**

ASTOR HOUSE HOTEL   -   PALACE HOTEL.

MAJESTIC HOTEL   -   -   GRAND HOTEL KALEE.

PEKIN:

Telegraphic Address:—**WAGONLITS PEKIN.**

GRAND HOTEL des WAGONS LITS.

THE HONGKONG & SHANGHAI HOTELS, LTD.

IN CONJUNCTION WITH

THE GRAND HOTEL des WAGONS LITS, LTD.

---

most successful in Hong Kong are the hotel keepers. Their houses are of the first order, overrun with rats and mosquitoes, and they manage to charge more and give less than any other 'publicans and sinners.' They go upon the Grahamite principle of buttering bread, they put as little as they can on, and scrape as much as they can off.

Hong Kong for some years to come is likely to be the center of British trade; it is eligibly situated, and easily defended. Ships can get into the harbor, or out again, with almost any wind, and the passages are so narrow that a vessel could be riddled with balls and sunk in the water at a moment's warning. The British have also been wise enough to adopt the liberal policy and make Hong Kong a free port. ▓

10
EARLY DAYS IN THE COLONY

STEEN ANDERSON BILLE

Steen Anderson Bille visited Hong Kong in 1846 as commander of the Danish ship, Galathea. He published his memoirs of his voyage around the world in 1853, and went on the become Denmark's Minister of the Navy. He offers a European but non-British view of the new Colony.

At Macao Capt. Flensborg brought me on board a couple of Chinese pilots who the next morning, June 22, 1846, were to bring us to Hongkong. . . . However, I must admit that had I known these men beforehand, I should have thought twice before taking them on board. . . . I went through the channel in the *Galathea*. Hongkong is to remain under English rule and its harbour to be a free port for world trade. Ten thousand Chinese were taken in the service of the Government, rocks blasted, stones hewn, streets traced, macadamized, lighted, mighty aqueducts hewn out of the granite and houses were built.

And what houses: the English vanity showed itself again in the fullest measure. Those who came from England and sacrificed home and family for the hoped-for profit would at least bring English comfort to the Chinese soil, those who came here from Calcutta did not wish their new city to take second place to the one they had left. The result was that already one palace raises its head by the side of the next and many more are being built, everyone one of them threatening to eclipse the magnificence of the other and older neighbours. Rich shops, great hotels, splendid dining rooms, balconies turned toward the sea and pillars to support them form airy vestibules, short all the luxury and magnificence produced by architecture.

Hongkong consisted, when I was there, of only one long street, Queen's Road, which is close to and parallel to the beach. When

it is considered that every foot's width of earth has to be blasted out of the rock, it is quite consistent that the start has been made from below. Extension up the hill was already proceeding. The Government House, the house of the general in command, the club, the half-finished Exchange and several other buildings were lying higher up and many private houses were being built, while roads and streets were already laid out between them.

I have very little to say about the social life of Hongkong. The inhabitants are too busy with their trade and acquisition of wealth to spend any time on social enjoyment. I have in the actual sense of the word not spoken to one lady during the whole of my stay here. Very few families are found here; most of the men have left their families in England or they are unmarried. But even many of those who have their families out there have them living in Macao, which is considered much healthier, and they take the steamer over there on Saturdays and return to Hongkong on Monday.

Even though social life was restricted to the often and elsewhere mentioned colonial dinners, I found something in Hongkong which I have not met in any other colonies, a small private theatre, the premises of which was the Chinese 'Sing-song' or playhouse. The exhibition to which we had been invited consisted of two comedies, 'Mr. Thompson' or 'Which is He?' and 'The Rival Valets.' These pieces were quite funny, almost irreproachable when one did not make too great demands, the character of a lady played by a Dane even exceptionally good. The machinery on the other hand was so imperfect that the curtain had to go down every time the setting of the stage had to be changed, and the building was so airy and leaking that we might as well have been standing under the sky. People were sitting with umbrellas open over their heads, but as the gutters under the roof soon were filled we got a shower bath from them also over us and we had to give up the game. Besides the noise from the rain on the roof was so strong that nothing whatever could be heard from the stage and the play was stopped for about ten minutes.

After the play, some of the gentlemen from the *Galathea* as well as several English naval officers accepted an invitation to a small club, where they spent the rest of the evening, but from which they carried no high opinion of the social life of Hongkong. The chairman of the party was the captain of an opium clipper, and, for his age, a very corpulent, jovial and vivacious man with a round and rubicund face. He did everything in his power to put life and humour into the party, but all his labour was in vain; one glass was emptied after another, but the whole row down exhibited only the most indifferent faces. Toasts were brought, compliments exchanged, the one more tedious and tiresome than the former. Songs were sung, 'Rule Britannia', 'Yankee doodle', German and Danish drinking songs. But the same heavy and depressed mood continued: the company was incorrigible. The only one, though he did not look elated himself, who tried to make as much noise as possible, was a Yankee, who came from the play in full theatrical costume and who put one foot on the table every time he made one of his many over-excited speeches. He also saw that no toast was honoured with less cheers than 'three times three' usually followed by 'once more hep, hep, hep'. 🔲

11
LETTER TO SIR JAMSETJEE JEJEEBHOY
FROM JARDINE, MATHESON & CO.

In the nineteenth century, business firms hired professional scribes with perfect 'copper-plate' handwriting to copy all letters sent out by the company. These letters were found in over-sized leather-bound Letter Books in the Cambridge University Library. Here is a business letter sent to the Indian Parsee business associate of Jardine Matheson, Sir Jamsetjee Jejeebhoy, the first Indian knighted by the British. The subject, not surprisingly, is opium, central to Hong Kong business. Malwa and Patna are types of this drug.

Jardine, Matheson & Co., Hong Kong,
7 December, 1846

Sir Jamsetjee Jejeebhoy
Bombay, India

My dear Sir Jamsetjee,
There has been no change in markets here since the departure of the Steamer with the exception perhaps of Malwa which continued to assume a more unfavourable aspect from day to day. The stock of that description cannot be less than 10.000 chests chiefly of *passable* quality.

The *Anonyma* arrived here on the afternoon of the 4th Instant after a splendid passage full equal to the *Lanrick*'s. She brings a Small Cargo. This, however, will give some firmness to our Patna Market, and we think rates will be supported till the new drug comes in. The present quotation for Patna is $640. We shall not decide on the future movement of the *Anonyma* till the next mail arrives.

2 copies 1st—*Lanrick* 2nd—HM *Brig Espegle* ▓

12
DIARY OF A HONG KONG DOCTOR

BENJAMIN LINCOLN BALL

Benjamin Ball was an American ship's doctor whose work took him throughout the Far East, including Hong Kong in its early days. Like many other writers, he describes a walk on Queen's Road and mentions the lack of vegetation on Hong Kong Island. Extensive forestation was a project of the latter nineteenth century. Dr Ball's diary, published as Rambles in Eastern Asia, including China and Manilla, during Several Years Residence, *creates a vivid picture of 1840s Hong Kong.*

*H*ong-Kong, August 31st [1848].—It has been raining hard all day. At one of the Chinese shops, where I was making some inquiries, I saw a Chinaman who spoke good English, and appeared so polite that I stopped a while, and entered into conversation with him. He told me his name was Ayou; that he had lived two years in Boston; that formerly he was comprador to Mr. Cushing at Canton, and afterwards lived with him in America. Preferring his own country, he returned, and now has a large alum [a crystalline substance used for medicine] establishment, in which, he says, he is doing a good business; he added, that a Chinaman who speaks both English and Chinese can make 'plenty money' in China.

This evening I was present at a dinner party given by Mr. W. at the hotel. He called it a christening party for his little child. There were twenty or thirty present, of whom a few were ladies. Dinner was served at six, and supper at eleven p.m. Toasts were freely given and drank, and our company so composed of different nations that there was much mirth and humour. I was the only American, and, the stars and stripes being toasted by an Englishman, I of course responded to the everlasting friendship of the

45

two countries. Songs were sung, and at twelve the party broke up. But a storm was raging without, and had increased to a typhoon. We hardly stepped out the door before we retreated within again. It was raining and blowing in great gusts, and the air was of Egyptian darkness. Glass was breaking, blinds slamming, boards rattling, tiles falling from the roofs, and bricks from the chimneys, and broken shutters were falling into the street. It sounded as if everything was unloosed and in motion. The blinds and windows seemed ready to break in with a crash; missiles were clattering over the house in different directions, and within was occasionally heard the falling of glass or earthenware. Several times we essayed to go home, but our eyes could not penetrate the blackness, and it was considered unsafe to make any further attempt. Mr. W. very kindly provided us all with sleeping apartments, and made us welcome for the night.

Friday, September 1st.—The night has been fearful, and one that I shall not soon forget. I could not sleep in the noise of so much clatter and crash till past three o'clock. The house itself shook so that several times I was on the point of springing up, thinking that the roof was actually being wrenched off. Everything was made as secure as possible, and yet there was a constant din of cracking and falling glass. The wind gathered and groaned as if with herculean efforts to level all with the ground. Again and again it came with increased power. Sometimes it seemed as if an immense serpent had encircled the building in its folds, and that the timbers, one after another, were giving way, and the sides of the house being crushed in its fearful embrace. Amid the raging of the storm I at length fell asleep, and dreamed that I was in a terrible tempest at sea. I thought the vessel was driven with such force that it skimmed over the surface of the water, and then, leaving the sea, flew through the air over the land, coming in contact with the hills, and bounding along like a balloon across the valleys.

I arose this morning at eight, and, in returning home, was wet by a driving rain. It was so dark at Mr. Drinker's that we had lights on the table at breakfast, although at nine o'clock in the forenoon. All here had been terrified, and many fears entertained for the safety of the house. The doors and windows were barricaded, and required at times the united strength of all. The garden was in ruins. Plantain-trees were broken down, other trees nearly destroyed, and flower-pots were strewed about and broken up. The water in the harbor had torn and washed up into the garden large stones from the sea-wall; the walks had caved away, &c.

I walked out with a friend to see what havoc had been made elsewhere. We found the shore lined with wrecks of Chinese junks. Vessels were dismasted, and some were on shore. The bodies of drowned Chinamen were being carried away on boards. Sides of buildings were blown out, and the water near the shore was full of spars and drift-wood of various kinds. The slight bamboo houses were in ruins, while those more strongly built exhibited, more or less, evidences of the storm. Capts. Watson and McLacklan walked down the shore, looking for their vessels, but could not anywhere identify them. Last night at the hotel they were quite anxious to get off to them, but no boat could be hired to hazard the attempt, and the Chinese boats were all on the opposite shore. Captain Clarkson of the *Chicora*, is here this eve. He saved eighteen Chinamen from a boat containing eighty, which drifted upon him in the night. To save one of them he descended by a rope into the water, and, by a rope fastened to the body of the drowning man, drew him up. They had specie and opium on board, all of which was lost.

Tuesday, September 5th.—We have more news of the effects of the typhoon. Mr. W. says that to-day he passed, in his boat, numbers of dead bodies floating in the water. Most of them were Chinese, but there were some Malays, blacks and Europeans. The US ship *Plymouth* saved a vessel and cargo boat that had gone ashore at a Chinese port. Several hundred natives were assembling off to capture her in the night, when the *Plymouth* put men aboard and saved her. She had on board six hundred chests of opium, with many thousands of dollars in silver, of which the *Plymouth* has two thirds as salvage.

Wednesday, September 6th.—In making a professional visit to-day, my boy expressed much reluctance at taking a case of instruments. He wished to get a cooly to carry them: but I objected, as one servant was enough, and I gave him in addition my umbrella and gloves to carry. Servants do not like to do anything that strictly belongs to those of a lower order. My boy does not like to take a bundle or package, because it is the business of a cooly to bear burthens. I gave him a letter to take to a gentleman, and observed that he handed it to a cooly, who carried it.

A lady seems very dependent when she is obliged to send a servant to call two others for the purpose of moving a rocking-chair, or to put another in its place. I should not have felt myself disgraced had she asked me; and I could have done it while she was giving directions to the servant, although I might have lost caste with her by so *menial* a service.

Some think it strange that I do not take a sedan-chair in preference to walking; and they advise me not to expose myself in the sun in the middle of the day. It is customary for Europeans to ride in a chair when they go any distance. Two coolies are generally sufficient, but a heavy person requires four. Doctors in visiting their patients ride in chairs; though Dr. M. usually appears in a low carriage, drawn by a pair of handsome Chusan ponies. His boy rides with him, holding an umbrella over his head, and takes care of the horses in his absence, being obliged continually, with a cloth, to drive off the flies which torment them.

Sunday, September 10th.—I went this morning to the hotel, and breakfasted with Mr. R. At dinner, at Mr. D.'s there were nine masters of vessels, making in all about twenty persons. There were Americans, and seemed to enjoy a meeting with so many of their countrymen. Capt. Nickels, of the *John Q. Adams*, from Boston, came in this morning. His arrival with letters and papers from America made the day an eventful one. I was much disappointed in receiving nothing myself, but accepted, with much pleasure, an invitation to take part in looking over Mr. and Mrs. B.'s large package.

Wednesday, September 16th.—In looking over my clothing to-day, I found my coats, pants, colored and white gloves, &c., covered with mould and mildew. I set my boy to cleaning them, and he went about it as though he had engaged in a endless job. The air is so damp here that trunks, hats, &c., will mould, or articles exposed merely in the room. My instruments begin to look as if the smallpox would soon exhibit itself upon them. Dr. M. informs me that they will rust and spot in spite of every precaution, and that it is impossible here to keep any instrument in order.

13

SAILING INTO HONG KONG

WILLIAM MAXWELL WOOD

Dr Wood served as navy surgeon to the fleet of the United States East India Squadron, but one suspects his real joy was retiring to his room and indulging in his endless and endlessly vivid travel writing. He is the author of Victorian tomes such as A Shoulder to the Wheel of Progress *and* Wandering Sketches in South American Polynesia, *as well as* Fankwei, or the San Jacinto in the Seas of India, China, and Japan *from which this extract comes. Despite the density of his description, in this account he presents one of the liveliest portraits of early Hong Kong.*

Owing to the defect in our engine, and some delay in repairing it, we did not arrive in Hong Kong until the 11th of June, 1856—within a few days of eight months since leaving New York.

From the lonely waters and level flats of the Gulf of Siam, to the green islands, rugged mountains, and thronging vessels of the harbor of Hong Kong, is a transition of marked contrast.

Our first contact with Chinese qualities introduced us to their indomitable energy, perseverance, and industry. An enterprising Chinese pilot had picked us up far out at sea, and another had been for a month steadily on the look-out for us; and, as we ran up to our anchorage, we encountered a Chinese invasion. A fleet of boats, propelled by mat sails, by sculls and oars, borne down upon us. The principal object of competition was to get the office of comprador—the privilege of supplying the various messes, and of being the ship's bum-boat; that is, trading with the men at certain fixed hours. This is a very profitable position, and those who engage in it get rich. Then, there were tailors, painters, shoe-makers, peddlers, washermen, and washerwomen, besides aspirants for the honourable appointment of 'fast-boat'—the boat which, being the home and dwelling-place of the proprietor and his family, wives, and children, is employed, instead of the ship's boats, to take us to and from the shore.

On came the competing fleet, regardless, apparently, of being run down by our heavy steamer. We were not then familiar with the great skill with which these boats are managed—being suddenly turned and changing their course just as they appear to be rushing upon an object. Stimulated by the prize before them, and confident of their skill, they paid no attention to the orders to warn them off, if, indeed, these could be heard above the clamor and the screeching of their own tin-toned throats. Some of the greater tacticians had small American ensigns flying, and one bold diplomatist, determined to command success by assuming it, flew home his mast-head a white flag, painted in large characters— BUM-BOAT, US STEAMER, *SAN JACINTO.*

Up alongside the ship they dashed, and, despite their skill, not without some damage to them, crashing bamboo spars. Men and women clambered up to ship's sides, and thrust forth bundles of certificates from their former patrons in our service, at the same time assuring us that he or she was No. 1 in their respective vocations.

A great and absorbing interest drew us for the time from these novel sights. Owing to the courtesy of the house of De Silver & Co., the accumulated letters of an interval of eight months' absence from home were sent on board to us by the time we had anchored, and the hopes, the fears, and the anxieties of all this time were to be confirmed or dispelled.

The hurry and bustle of a fresh arrival, the reception of visitors, and the firing of salutes having subsided, in a day or two we are in a state to make a more detailed examination of this fruit of English civilization which had sprung up in what, twelve years ago, was a den of Chinese pirates and a collection of miserable fishing huts. . . .

Standing out to catch the breezes of the hill-top, with the Union Jack flying in its front, is the yellow-washed castle of the Governor, the residence of the Bishop of Victoria, and the cathedral, with fortifications and military quarters capping off nature's granite summits with the same material molded by the lines of architecture and masonry. Over all, from an elevation of eighteen hundred feet, looks down Victoria's Peak, over city and bay, sampan, lorcha, and junk, the merchantmen of many nations soon to be lying in the stagnation of war and blockade.

Under English fortresses and men-of-war we are tolerably safe. But the opposite or Kowloon side of the bay, inviting as it looks, only two miles away, is at all times pretty certain death to any wandering Fankwei [foreign devil: Westerner]. Hostility to the barbarian is increased by his proximity, as some unfortunate Englishmen have recently experienced. . . .

By the time we are ready to return the sun is gilding the hilltops, and the labouring life of Hong Kong is astir. As we re-enter the suburbs of the city, the mechanics are busily at work in their open shops. The bamboo chair-maker and the rattan shaving mattress-maker are topographical trades, but the blacksmiths, tinmen and braziers are numerous, and the barbers are everywhere, in shops and in the streets, shaving heads, plaiting queues, shampooing backs, cleaning out ears and eyes. Then we have a range of marketshops; the pork-butcher is dealing out his slender cutlets, the fruiterer his pines, bananas, oranges, and huge pomellons. Next to this golden-coloured merchandise, are masses of green salad, cabbages, peas, beans, with radishes and tomatoes. There are dried fish and fresh, with bunches of dried ducks, split open, pressed flat, as if rolled between heavy rollers, and dried with transparent thinness.

The labouring coolies, with their burden-sticks across their shoulders, fill the streets, all dressed with much uniformity in broad-brimmed, sharp-peaked hats, made of palm-leaves, blue cotton shirts, or frocks, coming to their hips, trowsers of the same reaching half way down the leg, and either bare or straw sandal-shod feet. The women wear precisely the same costume,

51

except that the outer frock hangs lower, and the trowsers reach the ankle. Even among the lower classes, a few small-footed women are seen tottering along like a child on short stilts, but most of them are either barefoot or wear a shoe with a sole two inches thick, shaped like a rocker skate; mothers are tottering along with children lashed to their backs by a square cloth, of which the prevailing fashion is crimson.

At a later hour, when we would meet the better classes of Chinese, another style of costume varies the streets. Black satin or embossed velvet shoes with thick white soles, white leggings reaching to the knees, and meeting blue silk breeches which are fastened by silk garters, or the silk breeches, may descend the leg, fitting it tightly and being fastened at the ankles with ribbons. The outside garment is either a figured silk or a woollen cape, or a long robe either light and flowing, or quilted and trimmed with rich furs, according to the season. In fact, although there is a general style of costume, it admits as much variety almost in fashion as is seen on Broadway. The cap of these gentry is a close-fitting skull cap made of eight sections, with a crimson knot on the top. Rain or shine, cold or warm, in the day time, cloudy or clear, every Chinaman has an umbrella, and at night a lantern.

By the time we have passed through the Chinese suburbs, and reached the large and capacious buildings of the European settlement we find we are bounded on all sides by the British government. First we come to a guard-house, and then a long range of granite buildings, called the war department; a little further, on the opposite side, the military hospital, a large central building with a fountain amid the shrubbery of the front yard, and two wings. Then on and on, other public buildings—a navy yard. Then again, on both sides of the street, long ranges of military quarters with shady walks under rows of tress in their front, and sentries posted at the gate. Here we fall in with specimens of the military guardians of the empire. European soldiers in the tight-fitting crimson jackets, or dark coloured, curly-haired Sepoys [Indians], with loose white robes, flowing trowsers and crimson turbans; or the same fellows dressed in tight-fitting European military dress, looking like flexible black snakes stiffened in tin jackets.

Having passed these military establishments, we come upon another small prairie expanse, the parade ground, opening to the bay on one side, and overlooked at the other by the Episcopal cathedral perched upon an eminence.

A row of trees on each side of the road shades our walk across this space, and at later hour of the day there would be much to keep us loitering along this thoroughfare. In the shade of these trees is the place of business of respectably dressed and sage look- ing old Chinamen—conjurors, physicians, and magicians. . . .

Such is a glance at the capital of the island over which is ruler and governor Dr. Sir John Bowring, the philologist and philan- thropist—poet and philosopher—the statesman and chartist—an apparently worthy gentleman, whose literary reputation is far greater than that of his position of Governor of Hong Kong. According to the colonial press, he does not possess one good quality or a solitary virtue. Sir John, it has been said, has some- what humorously said he was the great supporter of the colonial press, as but for abuse of him, the writers would have no material for their pens to work upon.

It seems so essential a condition of a Hong Kong governor's position to be abused, that, as a thing of course it resolves itself into a mere form of speech, and is diluted into a Pickwickian sense. After all, the governor, who has earned a world-wide repu- tation as a man of letters, may be as able as those of whom the world has never heard, and morally may be no worse than the commercial community of which the leading business is opium smuggling, and the daily excitement, gambling upon its price. ▣

14

COMEDIAN IN THE COLONY

ALBERT SMITH

Albert Smith was celebrated in Victorian England as a novelist, playwright, humourist, and popular entertainer. After a number of years in medical practice, he switched to a more bohemian literary life, becoming a friend of Dickens and of the showman, P. T. Barnum.

This extract comes from To China and Back, *his diary written with publication decidedly in mind. It is the tale of his trip to the Orient to gather material and props for what was to be his last theatrical extravaganza, for he died suddenly in 1859 of bronchitis. Staged in London's Piccadilly, the ornate Egyptian Hall was aglow with Chinese lanterns illuminating scrolls and curios. Especially popular were two wooden crosses acquired from the Canton execution grounds.*

*S*aturday, *21st August 1858.*—At 2 p.m., passing Green Island, we entered Hong Kong Harbour. In a few minutes, Lieutenant Douglas Walker came on board from the flag-ship, the *Calcutta*, for letters, and was kind enough to offer me a berth until I could determine where I should go; for there are no hotels, properly so called, at Hong Kong. A well-conducted house would make a fortune. Then all the boats of the different merchants swarmed alongside for newspapers, intelligence, &c., and the *Home News*, the *Overland Mail*, and the *Straits Times* were at a high premium. Mr. J. Darby Gibb, to whom I was introduced, was good enough to go off to the Hong Kong Club, and propose me there. Mr. Maclean, of Jardine's house, seconded me, and I was elected at once. Then Mr. Howe took me and my luggage in his own boat to the landing-place at Pedder's Wharf, and I walked up to the Club, where Mr. Chisholm Anstey was waiting to offer me a room in his house; but now it was not necessary, as there are bed-rooms in the Club. I got a charming bed-room, No. 7, at the north-east corner of the building—large and airy, with a pleasant look-out, commanding the harbour in front, and the church, the Bishop's palace, Sir John Bowring's, Colonel Caine's and the principal street at the side.

Dined by myself in the Club. Had an odd fish, whose name sounded like 'groper' [garoupa], and a little fowl, with good pale ale. There was very bad attendance, as the native servants had all been recalled by an imperial edict, but the ice, and the room, and the steadiness were agreeable, after so much steamboat living.

After dinner went out for a stroll—my first walk in China! The shops were very alike, but a little superior to those at Singapore; and some were closed by bars of wood, like wild beast cages. . . .

Monday, 23rd August.—. . . I walked with Mr. Anstey along the parade ground, and the latter told me an odd anecdote connected with the doubtful results of the missions here. A Chinaman had been hung at Hong Kong a short time ago, and the missionaries of different creeds had all fluttered down on him to claim the lost sheep as their own. The man had a notion, that by the English law, a condemned criminal may have whatever he wishes to eat and drink. He said to the missionary who appeared highest in favour, 'My wanchey (*I want*) facey washey,' meaning baptism. This was done, and then when asked to explain his reasons for this, he replied, 'My wanchey roast duck.' This not being complied with, he died a Buddhist. The story requires no comment.

In the night rain fell with a violence I had never before witnessed.

Wednesday, 25th August.—While at breakfast heard a monotonous chant going on in the street, so went to the balcony. A Lascar [Indian seaman] funeral was passing. Just as they got opposite the club one of the mourners suddenly punched another's head, upon which a general row began at once, and they broke one another's umbrellas into splinters. The remainder of the procession still went on singing their hymn, but looking back at the fight, until, at last, they all started once more together.

Paid a visit to Messrs. Negretti and Zambra's photographer, M. Rossier, who lived at the Commercial Hotel, belonging, I believe, to Messrs. Lane and Crawford. He complained much of the effect of the climate on his chemicals. . . .

The young men in the different large houses have a sad mind-moundering time of it. Tea-tasting, considered as an occupation, does not call for any great employment of the intellect: and I never saw one of the young clerks with a book in his hand. They loaf about the balconies of their houses, or lie in long bamboo chairs; smoke a great deal; play billiards at the club, where the click of the ball never ceases, from earliest morning: and glance vacantly over their local papers. . . .

Thursday, 26th August.—At two, Mr. Rozario, the police interpreter, called on me: and I arranged with him to be my companion, during my stay in China. He bought me two long matchlocks from Mr. Mitchell, taken in the junk-hunt last week. Started off with Rozario to shop, and bought many 'properties' for the Egyptian Hall.

We then went to a Chinese Restaurant. The lower room was the second-class one, but the upper one was very nicely fitted up, with panels carved *au jour*, and painted and gilded recesses, for private parties and opium smokers. We sat down at a little table, and presently they brought us tea. There were already on the table five or six little saucers, some holding soy, and others little condiments and mixtures of mustard, spice &c. The tea was put into the cups, and water poured on it. Then they covered the cup with the saucer, which fitted into it; and thus you strained the leaves back from the tea, when you drank. I thought our London tea much better—but everything in London is the best. . . .

Monday, 30th August.—To the Police-office, where Mr. May was conducting an inquest, and the body was lying in the street on a stretcher, for the people to look at. . . . Then, next day, to lunch with Captain and Mrs. Twiss. He took me to see a man very clever

VICTORIA, HONGKONG.

Programme

OF

Mr. Albert Smith's

ENTERTAINMENT,

CHIEFLY RELATING TO

THE TRAVELLING ENGLISH,

AND

THEIR AUTUMNAL PECULIARITIES

ON THE CONTINENT,

AS REPRESENTED FOR THE BENEFIT OF THE LOCAL CHARITIES,

IN THE DRAWING ROOM OF THE CLUB HOUSE, HONGKONG,

ON

SATURDAY EVENING,

THE 25th SEPTEMBER, 1858.

The Lecture will commence at Half-past Eight precisely, and occupy about two hours.

Price of Admission, Two Dollars-and-a-Half.

NOTICE. The Audience are respectfully but earnestly requested to be in their places by the time fixed for the commencement of the Lecture, which will be kept very punctually.

PART I.

OFF TO SWITZERLAND.

With a few words about the Old Diligence. The start by the South-Eastern Railway, *via* Dover, Calais, Lille, Malines, and Cologne, to the Rhine. Of BROWNE and his peculiarities abroad, especially his mistaken powers of illustration.

SONG, "THE YOUNG ENGLISH TRAVELLER."

THE RHINE,

Of the four Miss SIMMONDS'S—ANNIE, who loves Tennyson so; FLORENCE, the fast; JANE, the neither-one-thing-nor-the-other; and BABY, the unpleasantly candid. Also, of Mr. PEABODY TAYLOR, an American Traveller; and of Mr. MUFF, a London Swell, who is bored.

SONG, THE "BELLE OF THE BALL."

ZURICH.

The Fair Time, and its wonders. The Showman's description of *Kasperl* (the German Punch), and his wonderful adventures. A Swiss Cheap Jack.

A NOVEL DESCRIPTION OF COURTSHIP.

END OF THE FIRST PART.

Between the Parts an Entr'Acte of a quarter of an hour, during which, some Gentlemen Amateurs, who have kindly given their assistance on this occasion, will perform some favourite Glees, &c.

PART II.

THE RIGI.

Of Mr. PARKER,—the unfortunate Gentleman, who never knew his own mind; and more especially of the PRANCER, and her influence on Society in England. Mr. Parker and the Prancer attempt a

DUET—CORNET A PISTON AND PIANO.

THE GREAT ST. BERNARD,

Of Mr. PRINGLE and His Great ST. BERNARD Dog. Also of his wonderful Photographs. Of Miss POTTLES, the Literary Prancer. Mr. HOWARD, the quick Traveller, and his

PATTER SONG, "BROWN ON HIS TRAVELS."

AT SEA.

The Story of the English Engineer, in the service of the Austrian Lloyd's Company.

PARIS,

The Troubles of an Englishman, who does not speak French very well, at a Restaurant in the Palais Royal.

SONG, "GALIGNANI'S MESSENGER."

at bamboo-work, to whom I gave some orders.

In the afternoon, went with Rozario to inspect a bankrupt joss-house, up by the Hollywood Road. Round the interior were many small figures, representing the tortures of the Buddhist hell. Some were being sawn in half between two boards; others burnt, or boiled in oil; others rung to death inside large bells. This was a purely Chinese quarter of the town, swarming with a native population, and bearing a terribly bad character.

At 7.30 to dine with Mr. John Dent, whose French cooking sent up one of the best dinners I ever sat down to, in London or Paris. A claret cup was also a thing to recollect. Bets, and horses, and yachts formed the topic of conversation: and Hong Kong races were already on the *tapis*.

Saturday, 25th September.—Early this morning, Mr. Martin, of the Police Court, came with the Chinese carpenters to put up my platform [for his performance] in the Club Drawing-room, which they did in an uncommonly short space of time, making it, as they do everything, all of bamboo. Then two pianos arrived, one from Mr. Green, and another from Mr. Kingsmill, the latter of which I used. . . .

I never had so good an audience, and literally everybody was there, from Sir John Bowring and Sir Michael Seymour downwards. Some of my attacks on the routine of conventional society appeared to startle them a little at first, and they looked at one another with that expression, which I know so well with my London morning audiences from the suburbs, of 'Good Gracious! what will he say next? Ought we to laugh at this, or not?' But I had evidently a few old Piccadilly friends in the room, to tell them it was all right and perfectly well received at this Hall; and then, of course, they entered into it.

The whole thing went off capitally; and when I put a leader from one of the Hong Kong papers, about Sir Michael Seymour, into verse, there was a roar of approbation that almost knocked me off my legs. When it was all over I had some gingerbeer and brandy down stairs at the bar, but the whole club was swarming with fellows, so I crept quietly off to bed, about eleven. We cleared £200 by the show, which was left with Mr. Tudor Davis and Mr. Mitchell, to distribute *à discrétion*.

Sunday, 26th September.—To breakfast with Mr. Chambers, to talk over last night with Mr. Henry Dent and Mr. Scarth. Then went off fast asleep in the balcony on a bamboo chair, and when I awoke found myself all alone.

To lunch with Mr. Bridges, meeting Mr. Caldwell. . . . Mr. Bridges said that an Australian man had made an offer for all the hills about Hong Kong, now perfectly useless, to rear sheep upon, but that his offer had not been accepted. He also told me that the Chinese had made a great to do and met in the Temple about cutting through the spur of Victoria Peak to the west of Hong Kong, because they believe, when it is finished, the joss will send legions of white ants to eat up the city. The Bowring Praya, a waterside esplanade, is being finished towards the west, but there is great quarrelling about it. The resident English say, for the same sum of money that it will cost, Hong Kong could be permanently supplied with water, from the want of which, the common people, at times, suffer severely.

To dine with Mr. Dent, meeting the Governor of Macao.

Tuesday, 28th September.—. . . . As I left the club, all the fellows gave me a good English 'Three times three.' I could hardly fancy that it was all real. . . . All the balconies at Lane and Crawford's, the Commercial Hotel, Mrs. Marsh's Millinery Rooms &c., were crowded with people, and my heart was up on my mouth all the time. . . .

The feeling that my object is over: and that I am going home again, is very strange—but uncommonly pleasant. We went up nearly to East Point, round the *Calcutta,* and then back again to the western entrance of the harbour, and out into the sea. And as evening came on, the coast gradually faded away in the sunset. Good night to China!

PART IV

THE PURSUIT OF LUXURY
1860s-1880s

'Hong Kong presents perhaps one of the oddest jumbles in the whole world. It is neither fish, flesh, fowl, nor good red-herring.'
A. B. FREEMAN-MITFORD, 1866

'Drastic changes are now taking place in the way of life in Hong Kong. People are beginning to pursue luxury.'
WANG TAO, 1860s

Hong Kong used to enjoy the reputation of being the kind of place—distant, disagreeable, and very hot—to which one's worst enemies ought to be consigned.'
JOHN THOMSON, 1872

'Hong Kong, however, is a colony of which we have every reason to be proud.'
SIR CHARLES DILKE, 1867

'All Hong-Kong is built on the sea-face; the rest is fog.'
RUDYARD KIPLING, 1888

15

MY SOJOURN IN HONG KONG

WANG TAO

Wang Tao encouraged Western studies among the educated Chinese. Originally, he translated the Bible into Chinese while working for British missionaries in a Shanghai publishing firm. In the 1860s, after a run-in with the Qing government, Wang Tao moved to Hong Kong where he collaborated for many years with James Legge, the missionary, publishing Chinese classics in English.

The afternoon of the next day I arrived in Hong Kong. The hills all around are rather bare of trees, and nothing but water meets the eyes. The people appear rather stupid and speak a dialect that is quite unintelligible. The experience was so exasperating when I first arrived that I felt that I could hardly stand it.

My residence was halfway up the mountain, surrounded by banyans. Several large plantain trees could be seen outside the window, greeting the eyes with their luscious green. In the evening I was just dashing off a letter to my family by lamplight when the sound of a Chinese fiddle arose in the neighbourhood. Someone was singing sonorously to the accompaniment of the instrument. The sound of music in a foreign place only makes one sad.

Hong Kong was originally a barren isle. There is very little flat land between the mountains and the sea, perhaps a few yards altogether. Here the Europeans have made painstaking efforts in planning and building. Their persistence reminds one of the mythical *jingwei* bird that endeavoured to fill up the sea with pebbles, and the 'foolish old man' who tried to move mountains. Land in this area is now so costly that even a few square feet can command a fantastic price.

The district near the shore is the commercial district. It is divided into three so-called 'rings', the 'Upper', 'Central' and 'Lower' Rings, named in accordance with the topographical features of the hillside. Later, another Ring was added, so there are now four of them. The local people often refer to this last Ring as the 'Apron-string Road', an appellation which evidently derived from the way it circuits the hillside.

The people of Guangdong province have always had something of a monopoly on commerce, and thus Hong Kong has proved to be attractive to craftsmen from far and wide. Business flourishes here, and trade relations have been established with many places.

The people of Hong Kong depend mainly on mountain springs for their drinking water, which is pure and refreshing. Chickens and pigs are inexpensive, but are not as delicious as those from Jiangsu and Zhejiang provinces. The ocean fish have a pronounced fishy flavour. Most fresh-water fish come from Guangzhou, but cannot be kept for very long.

The streets in the Upper and Central Rings are closely lined with imposing shops. Passers-by are so numerous that they are constantly jostling against each other, and it is both noisy and dusty. The Lower Ring, by contrast, is more tranquil and shady with plenty of trees. It is less densely populated and retains a rural atmosphere. Many Europeans have built their summer houses in the district known as Pokfulam. This picturesque neighbourhood is a fit place for those who seek solitude and relaxation. The district beyond the Lower Ring is mostly inhabited by the fishermen, many of whom spend their entire lives on boats.

Central Ring has St. Paul's College, and Ying Wah College stands at the junction of Upper and Lower Rings. Great College is located in Upper Ring. In all these institutions students are taught Western languages so that they can render useful service to the government upon graduation. Ying Wah College has an automated typesetting machine and printing facilities.

The highest point of Upper Ring is Tai Ping Shan. Here the streets are neatly lined on both sides with gaudy houses sporting brightly painted doors and windows with fancy curtains. These are the brothels, which are literally packed with singsong girls. It is a pity that most of them have large natural feet, and that those with tiny bowed feet account for a very small percentage, perhaps only one or two out of a hundred. About half of the girls can be considered attractive. There is a class of girls called 'salt-water maids', most of whom live in Central Ring. As many of them are kept by Europeans, they have become quite wealthy and own houses of their own. The finest among them are attractive in their own way with roundish faces and seductive eyes. At a friend's request, I have improvised the following verse about Hong Kong:

A long isle displays its splendour on the sea
Magnificent buildings everywhere to be seen.
Yet outlandish are the singsong girls
Who put new lyrics to old tunes.

Drastic changes are now taking place in the way of life in Hong Kong. People are beginning to pursue luxury. When I first arrived there, merchants generally wore short jackets and put on a cotton overcoat when the weather got cold. The women paid little attention to their dress. Even the singsong girls wore plain cottons when entertaining their visitors, and rarely wore jewellery of any sort. But then the people became more wasteful and corrupt. Since the founding of the Tung Wah Hospital, the members of its board of directors have begun to hold an annual gathering to celebrate the lunar new year. For the occasion they don all sorts of fine headgear and gowns, as if they were illustrious officials having an audience with the emperor! Sartorial splendour has supplanted the plainer styles of the past. At fashionable social gatherings, some spend tens of thousands of dollars on a single dinner. Bright lamps burn through the night, and loud music is heard until the small hours. Hong Kong's prosperity now exceeds that of Guangzhou, and it is all the result of fate and chance. ▨

16
HOW THE RICH LIVE

A. B. FREEMAN-MITFORD

Renowned authors Nancy and Jessica Mitford's propensity for lively,
accurate descriptions has family precedents in The Attaché at Peking,
the travel book of their diplomat-grandfather, Lord Redesdale, from
which this extract is taken.

Hong-kong presents perhaps one of the oddest jumbles
in the whole world. It is neither fish, flesh, fowl, nor
good red-herring. The Government and principal people
are English—the population are Chinese—the police are Indians—
the language is bastard English mixed with Cantonese—the currency is the Mexican dollar, and the elements no more amalgamate
than the oil and vinegar in a salad.

The Europeans hate the Chinese, and the latter return the
compliment with interest. In the streets Chinamen, Indian policemen, Malays, Parsees, and half-castes jostle up against Europeans,
naval and military officers, Jack-tars, soldiers, and loafers of all
dominations. . . .

In this island of contrasts none is greater than that between the
European and Chinese quarters of the town. In the former the
houses are large and well built of gray slate-coloured bricks and
fine granite, and others, some of which will be real palaces, are in
course of construction. In the latter, on the contrary, the houses
are low and mean. They are generally built with one story: on the
ground floor is the shop with its various goods and quaint perpendicular inscriptions and advertisements; on the first floor, which
is thrown out over the footway and supported by wooded posts, so
as to form a covered walk, the family live, and here the ugly old
women—uglier in China than anywhere—and queer little yellow
children may be seen peering out of their dens at the passers-by.

Towards evening, when the paper lanterns are lighted and the shops are shut up, not by doors and shutters as with us, but by sort of cage and bamboo poles, through which the interior is visible, the Chinese house looks very fantastic and strange. This quarter of the town bears a very bad name. It swarms with houses of the worst repute, and low grog-shops which are largely patronised by the sailors. The coolies in the street are a most ruffianly looking lot, not pleasant to meet in a by-road alone and unarmed.

It is rather hard on a man when he first comes to these parts to have to learn a new dialect of his own language more bizarre than broad Somersetshire, more unintelligible than that of Tennyson's northern farmer. . . . An English gentleman from Shanghai went to call at a friend's house in Hong-kong. The door was opened by the head Chinese boy.

'Mississee have got?' said the gentleman. 'Have got,' answered the boy, 'but just now no can see.' 'How fashion no can see?' The boy answered, grinning from ear to ear. 'Last night have catchee one number one piecee bull chilo!' The lady of the house had been safely brought to bed during the night of a fine baby boy!

Life at Hong-kong passes away pleasantly enough. The residents are very rich, and they spend their money like princes. Their hospitality is boundless, and open house is the rule. I can fancy no better quarters for a naval or military man. The climate is very different from what it used to be, and has become very healthy; but if a man should fall ill he can get away north to Peking, or run up to Japan, or choose between a dozen trips nearer at hand. The usual daily routine here at this season of the year is as follows:— At six your boy wakes you with a cup of tea; you rise and bathe, and read or write till it is time to dress for breakfast at twelve (the merchants, of course, go to their offices at ten or even much earlier). Breakfast, as it is called, is a regular set meal with several courses, and champagne or claret; any one comes in who pleases, and is sure of a cordial welcome, and probably an invitation to return to dinner. After a cup of coffee and a cheroot, office work begins again, and goes on until about five, when every one turns out to ride, drive, or walk until seven, which is the hour for gossip, and sherry and bitters at the club, a first-rate establishment to which strangers are admitted as visitors, and where a man may put up if he pleases. Dinner is at eight, and a very serious affair it is, for Hong-kong is fond of good living and fine vintages; and this rule does not apply only to the heads of houses, for their clerks are lodged and boarded exactly on the same scale as themselves, and a boy who has been content to dine for a shilling at a London chop-house, sits down here to a dinner fit for a duke, criticises the champagne and claret with the air of a connoisseur, and rattles in his pocket £300 or £400 a year for his *menus plaisirs*. Which shows the superiority of vulgar fractions to genteel Latin and Greek.

The rides and drives about Hong-kong are in their way very pretty, though the almost entire absence of trees presents a violent contrast to the rich tropical vegetation of Singapore and Penang. On the other hand, both on the mainland and in the island itself, there are bold, rugged mountain outlines, often shrouded in a mist that reminds one of Scotland and Ireland; huge boulders of rock from which beautiful ferns of every variety (fifty-two species have been classed) grow in profusion; a bay studded with wild barren islands; and to the east, where the colony is only separated from the mainland by about a mile of sea, the picturesque peninsula of Kowloon. The racecourse in the Happy Valley is a lovely spot. It is surrounded by hills on three sides, and from the fourth, which is close to the bay, one looks up a blue glen such as Sir Walter Scott might have described. Here on the slope of the hill is the cemetery, and here and at Government House there are some trees, among which the graceful bamboo is conspicuous.

But it is the south-west of the island that is most affected by the residents. At a place called Pok Fo Lam, about four miles off, several of the rich merchants have built bungalows to which in summer-time, after stewing all day in their offices, it is their wont to resort of an afternoon, and let the fresh seabreeze clear their brains of tea, opium, silk, rises and falls, and such-like cobwebs. On a fine evening these gardens are a very pleasant lounge. At the back rises the Peak, a fine bold rock some 1700 feet high; all around are sweet-scented tropical flowers teeming with strange, many-coloured insects and gorgeous butterflies; while in front the view stretches to the mainland hills across the brilliant sea rippling against little islands, and covered with flotillas of native boats, peaceful enough to all appearance, but ever ready for any little piece of light piracy that may turn up.

I was very anxious before leaving the south of China to see Canton, and accordingly on the 28th April I started with a friend in one of the huge house-steamers that ply between Hong-kong and Canton, and are of themselves curiosities. They are divided into separate parts for Europeans, Parsees, and natives of the poorer class with loose boxes into which bettermost Chinese families are put. You may form some idea of their size when I tell you that three weeks ago, on the occasion of a festival, our boat the *Kin Shan* took up 2063 Chinamen to Canton whither they were bound to 'chin-chin' the graves of their ancestors. In all American steamers—and this is a Yankee venture—speed is the great object, and we accomplished the distance, between 80 and 90 miles, under the six hours.

We had a bright sunny morning for our expedition, and the harbour of Hong-kong appeared to great advantage, for there were plenty of fleecy clouds in the sky throwing fantastic shadows over the hills around. The sea was as calm and transparent as a lake, and we could sit in the best cabin, which is a huge building on the forecastle, catching every breath of air, and enjoying the scenery. ▨

17
ENGLISH ARROGANCE

SIR CHARLES WENTWORTH DILKE

Sir Charles Dilke, as a true Victorian, was eager to spread the assumed superiority of British culture. One copy of his book, Greater Britain: A Record of Travel in English-speaking Countries, *is now in the University of Hong Kong Library. Dated Christmas 1901 and inscribed 'To Father from Cades', the book includes an ode which begins as follows: 'Greater Britain! Greater Britain! How the heart leaps at the name, Never lived an Empire greater...' Well, you get the idea.*

The detestable climate of Southern China is a drawback to the strength of English influence. Anyone who sees the clean and beautiful island-city of Hong Kong in its lovely winter season, will think that its residents have nothing to complain of; but the breathless summer of many months of a still and damp heat, ten times worse than that of Australia, is as exhausting as is the summer climate of Calcutta itself. Hong Kong, however, is a colony of which we have every reason to be proud. While the Portuguese settlement at Macao, which lies close at hand, enjoyed a short-lived prosperity, founded on the infamous Coolie traffic, the prosperity of Hong Kong is founded upon free-trade. In the matter of the Chinese Coolie traffic we have cause for congratulation. In this, at all events, we have helped the Chinese Government with representations, and with action, which they never could have made or taken for themselves. It was time indeed that England should speak out, although it is to her honour that she should have spoken. The Chinese Coolie traffic was worse than the African slave-trade, to put down which we made such sacrifice. Happily Macao is ruined, while Hong Kong thrives. If we were to believe some of the Hong Kong merchants we should have to echo their complaint that Hong Kong is ruined too. I received the greatest kindness and hospitality from many of these gentlemen, but I feel bound to speak out with regard to their political ideas. . . . The Hong Kong merchants assured me with grave faces that the colony had been 'ruined by a Chinese blockade'. Trade is dull throughout the East, but the Hong Kong merchants protest that there is no cause for its dullness at Hong Kong, except this Chinese blockade. Chinese gunboats cruise around the island of Hong Kong and board the junks. . . .

There is still much smuggling of opium, and by our treaty we seem to have taken away the natural right of the Chinese to fine the smugglers, and as they can only seize the goods, they are bound to be doubly strict. What then is the complaint? The merchants say that the gunboats 'levy squeezes on the junks'. . . . I found that in spite of the general dullness of our Eastern trade the trade of Hong Kong had not at that time decreased. Our export trade to China will disappear, and its disappearance is but a matter of time. The day will come when the Chinese, with cheap labour, will make for themselves all, with the exception perhaps of woollen goods, that we can make for them more dear. They have cotton, coal, water-power, and clever fingers: and we shall be lucky if they only supply themselves, and do not also rob us of foreign trade. . . .

The value of Hong Kong as a door for the admission of English influence into China has been diminished by one act of Mr. Gladstone's First Administration. All Englishmen in the East regret what they believe to have been the folly of abolishing our mint at Hong Kong, which was giving an English coinage to all China. China has no real coinage for purposes of trade. Little bits of silver assayed and weighed, and dollars of the Mexican Republic, battered out of shape—this is the ridiculous 'coinage' of the coast. In Hong Kong itself, when I took my letters to the post and gave a dollar to the clerk to pay for stamps, I had to wait while he bit it, tried it with an acid, weighed it, and gave me change, not as though my dollar were a dollar, but according to its weight, which was 96/100ths of what it should have been. This was no exceptional case, but was the practice gone through in every instance. ▣

18

AT HOME IN HONG KONG

LETTERS FROM MATILDA & LUCILLA SHARP

The Matilda Hospital on Hong Kong's Peak—long an established institution—was named for Matilda Sharp, wife of Granville Sharp, a successful nineteenth-century banker, businessman, and land speculator. Matilda's sister, Lucilla, arrived in Hong Kong as a young widow, and eventually married Edmund Sharp, Granville's cousin. The sisters were prolific Victorian letter-writers. Some of the descriptions of pistols at picnics and prayer, make Hong Kong sound like the Wild West! The photograph on the following page shows Matilda and Granville Sharp on the left with Lucilla and Edmund on the right.

Matilda writes—

December, 1858

Granville took a boat and went on board for all our luggage and I came to Mr. Neaves's residence in Hollywood Road. But how? In a Chinese bamboo chair carried by two men, supported by long bamboo rods placed on their shoulders. This chair is the usual conveyance in Hong Kong where carriages are utterly useless. They are pretty little things covered in cloth usually, a comfortable cushioned seat inside and a cushioned back to lean against; a brush hangs on one side to keep off mosquitoes and a looking-glass on the other. In front your curtain is looped up and, there are venetians all around, you can see everything that is passing. I took my seat and convulsively caught hold of my chair as I was hoisted up by the men. They went very smoothly and fast, Mr. Fox walking by my side and chatting.

Sometimes they have no cover and are quite open. Mrs. Fox and I have gone out thus together every day, our men marching

together and keeping our chairs so close that we converse most comfortably ... except when going up or down a very steep hill, or rather flights of stair. Then the chair is almost upright and all you can do is keep your seat.

And so here we are, my beloved family, treated kindly and liberally, but oh we feel more than ever that the spirit yearns to be fed more than the body—that meat and drink do not satisfy man. Never have I so longed for a house of my own. Granville and I always seek God's blessing night and morning in our room.

Matilda writes—

January, 1860

You would have smiled to see us sit down to dinner at seven, Granville at one end of the table and I at the other; a servant behind each and a pigtail behind each servant. First soup, then fish, then six dishes, then various puddings, then dessert dishes and wine. Mr. N [Neaves] prides himself on his servants and his table. My favourite Chinese soup is one made of shark's fin. I have not yet tasted bird's nest nor rats that I am aware. Pray for us both, for the health of soul and body, for both are jeopardized here. Some ladies have to leave after a few months' residence only. . . .

We rise and walk before breakfast—that and family worship at nine, down to business at ten. Then I finish my private devotions, go to the store closet, give out to cook and settle accounts of the previous day, write journal etc., and find amah her work to do; visits at noon, either receiving or going out. Tiffin at one-thirty, when I see husband and Mr. Davis again for half an hour, alone again till five, either writing or something else. Then a walk with my precious husband, meet at dinner at seven, and spend the evening together either reading, tatting [related to lace-making] or netting. I use my pen much more than my needle—indeed I cannot bear to sit and sew by myself. . . .

Then my accounts are quite elaborate. I must compare mine with cook's, and his with the daily market list to see that he does not overcharge. I read so little and am very vexed on this account, yet Mr. Davis has so many nice books I want to get thro'. There, now amah tells me the washerman is come and I must go. . . .

I came back; before I could write a word I was told the milk-woman was come. Good milk is a great rarity, and, as we fancy cook overcharges, we are going to make an arrangement with this woman and see what we can do. The woman came to speak to me with long ear-drops and a large green bracelet on each hand.

After this transaction I called the amah. 'Amah go talky boy, talky Mr. Sharp and Mr. Davis tiffin ready, talky me when they come.' For I am quite hungry. The boy comes and says 'Mr. Davis down-side, come top-side', which is 'below and will come up'!

This morning I received as a present a brace of pheasant from Shanghai, where there is famous shooting. What would dear fa-ther say to this piece of Foochow [Fuzhou] bacon which adorns our breakfast table? I forgot the price but it is enormously dear, and on being boiled is hardly anything but skin. I was so disap-pointed as we had it purposely for my husband, who seemed quite to pine for a piece of bacon for breakfast. . . .

It is far cheaper to send for your stores from England. I have a large store-room which I long to see filled. Our sugar here is very nice, but what do you think it is? Sugar candy pounded. I have just bought half a picul, 66lb. It came in large lumps and my servants have been busy pounding it in a pestle and mortar for our daily consumption. I had some pieces brought up for my private delectation—it so reminded me of my girlish love for that same sweet. . . .

I look from my window and see that I am in China. There are the brown hills soon to be made green by the expected rains and again to be browned by the fierce angry sun. There is Government House where Sir John Bowring will soon terminate his career, having gained the esteem of few and indignation of many. There is the church with its four white spires and its many green venetians to keep us cool if possible; there is the water smooth as glass, with the great ships and their shadows lying on the surface; the wall before me is covered with a luxurious creeper, whose smiling lilac blossoms have often made me glad, and the Chinese lilac now being in bloom sends its sweet breath into my window and tells me God is good—even here where man is so vile.

Two little Chinese boys are playing together in the dusty road, and as the urchins roll over, their pigtails become enriched by the public dirt. . . . Two negresses are coming down the road; they remind me of Aunt Chloe with their black skins, thick lips and their partiality for pink, red or yellow print of the largest possible plaid pattern. They wear over their heads a gay coloured shawl or white handkerchief and look altogether Africa's daughters.

And there sits a group of poor coolies eagerly looking out for a job. They know 'tis our usual time for a walk, when our chairs follow us that we may sit down or ride when tired; as we have but two coolies, they are hoping to have the pleasure of carrying us. Poor fellows, they are out with us for an hour and the pay is ninepence for their work, and this is ample as they feed on rice at twopence a day. . . .

Indians live in bark huts outside the town. Yesterday I saw a funeral of one of their companions. The body was placed in a coffin with a vaulted top, like one of our travelling trunks; this was covered with a yellow pall, and the whole encircled with five or six green wreaths; a great many Hindoos in their picturesque turbans followed the bier while two preceded.

The other evening we both woke up hearing a noise; I started up, my hair on end looking as wild as Hogarth's 'Idle Apprentice' when he was disturbed at night. We saw a bright light through the door crack and it did not tend to my peace of mind when Granville whispered he had forgotten to bolt the door. You would have felt somewhat awestruck, as I did, when he crept out of bed and I heard him cock his fowling-piece which he had just drawn from under his pillow. He stealthily opened the door and I saw him creeping along towards the drawing room, his pistol ready pointed! There he found Mr. Davis fast asleep, having sat up late to read *Little Dorrit*—which he had no business to do as we are reading it aloud, but we were just in the midst of Mr. Merdle's history and his curiosity was excited. The lamp was flaring away, our windows and venetians wide open and he in a blissful state of ignorance as to our excitement. . . .

Many make the speedy departure of the mail an excuse for doing business on the Sabbath. Granville is very anxious now about business; he says his position here involves constant anxiety and thought. Hong Kong is so small a place yet contains a large population all crowded together, and all as eager and striving for business and as ceaselessly energetic as animalculae in a drop of water.

In 1865, Matilda's widowed sister, Lucilla arrived to live with them and married Edmund Sharp. Soon she, too, was penning long, lively letters home—

I am never tired of the view from the house. We are above everyone else and look down on the blue waters of the harbour and the distant hills, while the grand old Peak rises behind us. On the balcony outside the window stands a pot of English field daisies, now in full blossom. Mr. Davis brought back the seed and it is very much valued here, being the only specimen of the flowers in Hong Kong.

The first morning one bloomed, Matilda tells me, they all looked at it in rapture, and as it was a Sunday morning she gathered it just before going out, that she might still enjoy it. As soon as the service was over, Mrs. Legge said to her 'Mrs. Sharp do give me that daisy; it is the first one I have seen since I left England.' When ladies visit her they take away one as a great treasure and she has made various promises as to the seeds.

You would greatly have enjoyed being with us a few days ago when we all, with the addition of a few friends, made an excursion up to the Peak. We did not go to the very top, that was too far, but about half way, to a place called the Gap. We really looked quite a formidable party, twelve in number, each person in a chair and four coolies to each person, which you will find sixty in all.

The scenery was splendidly wild and as we wound higher and

higher up the Peak the ships in the harbour looked like small boats, though many of them were men-of-war. We had to pass through wild ravines, down which rushed foaming streams. Wild flowers and ferns grew around us in profusion . . . and amongst them were many of the English garden flowers. We had several revolvers with us for, beautiful as the scenery is, Chinese thieves abound and several more violent and daring robberies have been committed lately.

I have learned to load Matilda's revolver. I see that she carries it with her whenever we go out for a walk or ride, quite as a matter of course. The other Sunday evening, as we were starting for Chapel, I was amused to find myself asking her 'Have you got the pistol?' as cheerfully as if I had said 'Have you got the hymn book?'

You cannot economize here as in England . . . your servants always know your income and make you pay accordingly. All the market people know it also. There is not an Englishman in Hong Kong the amount of whose income is not soon found out by his servants and the market people, who decide upon the price he has to pay for each thing and divide the profits between them. For instance, our milk costs just about the same as our sherry; the latter we can do without, the former we cannot. The milkman knows this and makes you pay in proportion to your income.

In 1866, Matilda writes—

Men drink and take no care as to the sun. . . . Soldiers and sailors are worse than any—sailors are constantly seen lying intoxicated in the streets in the blazing sun. Granville is always putting them into chairs and sending them to hospital. Yesterday morning he saw four sailors before the office with a bottle of gin from which they were drinking by turns. He went out and begged for a drop for himself, but as soon as he had the bottle in his hands he dashed it onto the pavement. He then spoke to them of the danger they incurred and gave them money for what he had done, on condition that they would not buy any more. But, of course, he could not trust them; who knows what they did with it?

In 1866, Lucilla writes—

Ah Lui's room was attacked by a party of ten men who burst the door panel with stone hammers. When one man crept in, the four boys, all being petrified with horror, opened the door to the others and in a twinkling everything was taken away, even to the mosquito curtains and a bed.

While this was going on the other men of the party stood at different coolies' doors with long spiked bamboos to prevent assistance being given. All this was done quicker than I can write it; they climbed about like cats, so agile and quick.

Of course, we in the house were wide awake in a moment and quickly out with the lanterns, pistols and life-preservers. The moment, however, that Granville began to unfasten the great door, an enormous stone was thrown against it as a warning. . . . So the gentlemen went around to the front and fired off their pistols to bring the police—who, as usual, made a point of not coming. So sudden and rapid was the attack that long before this the thieves had decamped.

Since then we have been determined to allow no strange men on that part of the Peak behind our home. I was writing in our little study when I saw a man on the boulders. I ran and called Matilda and we two, Matilda with her pistol, and the two house coolies went onto the verandah and started a parley. Matilda said 'I've got too muchie thievesmen just now; any man come this side chop-chop.' This awful threat Matilda enforced with two shots from her revolver. Whereas the man, thinking discretion the better part of valour, made off. . . .

Now about our picnic. It was a moonlight one given by Mr. Whyte, our second judge, and Dr. Cane. It was an immense affair, over eighty guests and three hundred coolies, so you can fancy the imposing show we all made as we wound our way up the sides of the Peak. The dinner had been sent up by the French hotel and all was most tasteful and elegant. It was great fun, for the long table was set out in the open air and completely encircled by fanciful Chinese lanterns. Round it we ladies seated ourselves and as many gentlemen, with the host, the boys and the waiters, flew about to wait on us. They had cleverly improvised a type of kitchen so that everything was delightfully hot or deliciously cool.

Afterwards we adjourned to the sanatorium, a large building close by that had been built and intended for our sick soldiers until, when it was finished, with our usual military wisdom it was found to be in a very unhealthy situation, so it is now only used at picnics. Then we had some merry dancing to the music of the band. About 11 p.m. we all left and our large party came winding down the hill.

Matilda writes to her sister, Marian, in September, 1866—

We now have a piano here. Fancy moving a grand piano up a mountainside 1700 feet high. It required twelve coolies and a head coolie to superintend them, and a pianoforte tuner followed behind. They accomplished the journey in two hours. Our friends were greatly surprised.

The next year, Lucilla wrote home after an 'at home' at Government House with Sir Richard and Lady MacDonnell—

I danced with the Governor, and in mortal terror I was too, for the old fellow is never very firm upon his feet and the floors were polished to the last degree of slipperiness. Thought I, suppose he were to slip and drag me down with him—an idea to make me turn livid. As we stood up he said 'Now Mrs. Sharp, I never yet have been able to master the quadrille, so you must make up your mind to put me and push me and trick me and pummel me with your fists till you get me right,' enforcing all he said with the most vigorous gesticulations. However, he was not half as bad as he represented himself to be and I put him through triumphantly without having to resort to any such extreme measures.

But life for wealthy Westerners was more than elaborate picnics and 'at homes.' In September, 1874, the worst typhoon for decades struck. Matilda writes—

The servants had made everything tight, putting up typhoon bars and big shutters. We went to bed, but awoke about 11.30 p.m. with the shaking of this big three-storey house. We were as in a cradle or a boat—wind roaring outside, rain pouring and tiles crashing, water coming through here, there and everywhere. There was no more sleep for us. . . .

Our first task was to barricade the doors and windows by piling against them all the heaviest articles of furniture. By each door and window stood two men pushing against it with all their might . . . they stood there hour after hour for all that weary night.

The eastern half of the roof was so quickly gone that the heavy drops, like the first of a thunderstorm, began pouring in, so we had hastily to move all the perishable furniture. Just as we had got it in place in the hall, we found that the roof was going from there also and had again to put it in the morning room.

How I wish it were possible to describe to you the wind all through the night—it was fearful, howling in wild shrieks. When we wanted to speak to each other we had to shout at the top of our voices. . . .

Several of the principal clocks in town all stopped at the same time. It is supposed that there must have been a slight shock of earthquake to add to all the other terrors. A fire also broke out in part of town, but flames were actually put out by the force of the wind.

The little room in which our lamps and crockery are kept is a perfect ruin, and my nice double dinner set. Can't you fancy my feelings as I heard shelf after shelf go down and knew it was utterly impossible to save it? We were four at dinner last night and I had only three soup plates.

At 4 a.m. the blessed rain began to pour which showed us the worst was over. We were all completely exhausted and unnerved. Lu mixed mild portions of gin and water and made each coolie take a little. I then distributed to them some dry bread and sugar—our provisions were in the safe outside. I made them lie down in the hall.

At last the fearful storm abated and light dawned on the town, almost roofless and looking like a bombarded place. The harbour was almost empty save for the numerous wrecks floating about.

Lucilla was diagnosed with cancer in 1886, travelled to England for an operation, then sailed back to Hong Kong, her adopted home. Shortly afterwards she returned again to England for medical reasons where she died in March 1888. Her husband donated a stone font to St. John's Cathedral, the site of their marriage in 1865. The font survives today. Matilda caught pneumonia and died on 22 August 1893, at the age of sixty-four. Her memory has long been commemorated at Matilda Hospital. ▨

19
HONG-KONG PHOTOGRAPHERS

JOHN THOMSON

John Thomson, a professional photographer from Scotland, took some of the most artistic photographs of nineteenth-century Hong Kong. In this extract first published in 1872 in the British Journal of Photography, *he leads us to a Chinese photographer's establishment on Queen's Road. The first photograph shows a Curio shop, and the second an artist's studio. Both were taken by John Thomson.*

Hong-Kong used to enjoy the reputation of being the kind of place—distant, disagreeable, and very hot—to which one's worst enemies ought to be consigned. It was truly a vile place at one time—the resort of pirates and the worst class of vagabonds of the south of China, and even now it can hold its own in crime and vagabondage with its dark competitors in other parts of the world. It is, however, gradually throwing off its old bad habits under the liberal and enlightened government of our land.

It is not the safe and agreeable resort it used to be for the scum of Canton, as it possesses great stone institutions that frown on and furnish slender fare to evil-doers. Above all, it utilizes the camera to register the faces of its convicts—a thing which the Chinese do not take to, as they fancy that this process deprives them of a certain portion of their vitality. This is a very wholesome superstition if they value their lives; and, as they know if they do not contrive to look like somebody else when being photographed, it places a dangerous weapon in the hands of the law, as Chinese faces are not all alike, but sufficiently different to impart a marked character to each.

It may not be generally known that the Chinese in Hong-Kong and other parts of China have 'taken kindly' to photography. In

Queen's Road, the principal street of Victoria, there are a score of Chinese photographers, who do better work than is produced by the herd of obscure dabblers who cast discredit on the art in this country. There is something about the mystery of photographic chemistry and the nicety of manipulation implied in its various processes which suits the Chinese mind.

There is one Chinaman in Hong-Kong of the name of Afong, who has exquisite taste, and produces work that would enable him to make a living even in London. Afong is, however, an exception to the general run of his countrymen, as their peculiar views of what constitutes art in a picture are quite opposite to our foreign prejudices and to all that we have been taught to recognize as art.

I will now give a description of one of these celestial studios.

There is a seedy individual at the door having a strong suspicion of grease or blacklead about his hat, and whose graceful duty it is to waylay customers from the country. There are a few ghastly pictures in black and white in a frame at the doorway. Some of them have the cheerful expression of victims whose heads had been spiked to secure the necessary degree of steadiness.

There is a narrow ladder or staircase leading to the artist's quarters. Now we must mind our limbs, as a false step might land us in the carpenter's shop below. The pungent smell first encountered is that of collodion; the other more noxious odours are native.

Look round; we are now in the reception room, and the gentleman with the queue and without his shirt who advances to meet us is A-hung, the operator. He immediately puts his shirt and jacket on, as we are foreigners, remarking—'Too muchee long time my no have see you. Come in.' Allow me to interpret A-hung's pidgin English. 'You have been a great stranger,' he says. 'Are you busy, A-hung? We want to have our portraits taken.' 'How fashion?' says A-hung. But I had better give his conversation in ordinary English as the pidgin is embarrassing.

'You foreigners,' says A-hung, 'always wish to be taken off the straight or perpendicular. It is not so with our men of taste; they must look straight at the camera so as to show their friends at a distance that they have two eyes and two ears. They won't have shadows about their faces, because, you see, shadows form no part of the face. It isn't one's nose, or any other feature, therefore it should not be there. The camera, you see, is defective. Our artists know better, for they give you the features complete, without the shadows.'

'No,' I replied, 'Look at these card pictures of yours. They are not complete so far as the figure is concerned. Why not photograph the back and queue and stick it to the back of the card, so that your customers might leave no doubt in the minds of their friends as to their having a back and a queue?'

'Very good suggestion,' says A-hung. 'I will propose it. But come.'

We are in a small room, the walls of which are hung with portraits, some in oil and of a large size, for the firm paints on canvas. There are ships, too, and fairly well done. Oh, the portraits. They are chiefly of foreigners—seafaring men—and they form a kind of gallery of horrors.

There are four or five artists at work in the light part of the room and verandah copying photographs on a large scale in oil. How very lightly these limners [miniature-painters] are dressed—only a pair of silk trowsers and a pipe each. And how they smoke and chat and seem to enjoy themselves! That is a favourite starling of one of them that is singing so sweetly in the sunshine on the verandah.

A-hung produced a number of his masterpieces for our inspection, representing natives of both sexes in holiday dress. They were all taken in the same pose, seated at a very square table. On the table, there is a vase containing artificial flowers — gaudy caricatures of nature. The background of plain cloth is adorned with two curtains, arranged so as to form part of an isosceles triangle above the sitter who is posed as if his figure were intended to demonstrate a proportion in Euclid.

The faces of A-hung's choice samples are generally very white, and look flat and round, with the features well marked on the blank surface, like the mountains on a chart of the moon.

We remark to A-hung, 'The faces are as white as if your sitters' heads had been dipped in whitewash before being operated on.'

A-hung's face beams with satisfaction as, in reply, he says, 'Yes, I thought you would like them. They are very fine, and obtain the pure white by applying powder to the face of the sitter. The glass house is hot, you know, and he perspires at once when he sits down, so that the powder sticks admirably. Malays and negroes come under the same treatment, and it gives great satisfaction and costs nothing to speak of.'

The glass house is a small den at the back of the waiting room, lighted from above only. The glare is blinding and the heat stifling. We keep our hats on, to avoid the risk of sunstroke until we are seated at the posing irons. A-hung arranges our limbs after the fashion of his race until they ache with constraint. The small camera is then brought to bear upon us. We have to stare at the operator's head, all aglow with native polish or perspiration until the camera, stand, and his moving figure are jumbled together like the shifting form of the kaleidoscope. The minute of exposure seems to dilate into an age. Like drowning men, the incidents of our past lives are passing rapidly in review, when we hear the click of the cap, and rise to find we have been photographed by a Chinaman. A-hung vanishes into the dark room, and from a small window pronounces the plate 'number one'.

We will now have a look at our friends the limners. There is an old man in this establishment, or, rather, a man who looks twenty years older than he ought—he of sallow, deep-lined visage in the corner. He is a miniature painter, whose work is held in high estimation for its delicacy, careful drawing and beauty of colouring.

This individual is never able to work more than from two to three hours a day, the rest of his time being occupied with the opium pipe and siestas. Opium has been the curse of his life. As his occupation is a profitable one in his skillful hands, he can always command time and money for the excessive indulgence of his vice.

There is a degree of refinement and beauty about his mini-
atures which is rare and surprising when one considers his most
inartistic surroundings. His work is done chiefly from photographs.
A master hand paints in the head, an inferior the hands, and an
apprentice the costume and jewellery, the latter being generally
profuse, as it costs nothing.

It would be difficult to describe wherein these painters fail in
rendering the human face. I shall be best understood by saying
that, like the figures in a wax-work exhibition, in their delineation
they come so near the object intended to be represented, and yet
want the divine modelling and soul of the original so utterly as to
render the picture perfectly hideous.

The cost of a painting measuring about eighteen inches by one
foot is about thirty shillings. They are the delight of the foreign
sailors frequenting the harbour, who invest their savings in these
momentos of dear or dead friends. There is the traveller now
going off on his morning rounds to visit the ships in the harbour,
with his portable collection of samples. We will descend with him
to the street. A-hung is busy with new customers, who are engross-
ing his attention.

Mark the polite salutation of this photographer of the Flowery
Land as we bid him adieu. 🔲

20

AROUND THE WORLD IN EIGHTY DAYS

JULES VERNE

Jules Verne's 1873 novel has long entertained readers with its tale of a wager between Phileus Fogg and the gentlemen of the Reform Club over whether Fogg could fulfill the boast of the book's title. At this point in the story Fogg arrives in Hong Kong on his way to Japan. Passepartout, his manservant, accompanies him, and as well as Aouda, an Indian princess rescued in their travels whom Fogg hopes to leave with her cousin in Hong Kong. In the meantime, Mr. Fix, a detective, receives an arrest warrant for Fogg, whom he erroneously suspects of being a fleeing British bank robber. However, Passepartout believes that Fix has been sent by the Reform Club.

*I*n Which Phileas Fogg, Passepartout, And Fix Go Each About His Business.

. . . The *Carnatic* was announced to leave Hong Kong at five the next morning. Mr. Fogg had sixteen hours in which to do his business there, which was to deposit Aouda with her wealthy relative.

On landing, he conducted her to a palanquin, in which they repaired to the Club Hotel. A room was engaged for the young woman, and Mr. Fogg, after seeing to it that she wanted for nothing, set out in search of her cousin Jejeeh. He instructed Passepartout to remain at the hotel until his return, that Aouda might not be left entirely alone.

Mr. Fogg repaired to the Exchange, where, he did not doubt, every one would know so wealthy and considerable a personage as the Parsee merchant. Meeting a broker, he made the inquiry, to learn that Jejeeh had left China two years before, and, retiring from business with an immense fortune, had taken up residence in Europe,—in Holland, the broker thought, with the merchants of which country he had principally traded. Phileas Fogg returned to the hotel, begged a moment's conversation with Aouda, and, without more ado, apprised her that Jejeeh was no longer in Hong Kong, but probably in Holland.

Aouda at first said nothing. She passed her hand across her forehead, and reflected a few moments. Then, in her sweet, soft voice, she said, 'What ought I to do, Mr. Fogg?'

'It is very simple,' responded the gentleman. 'Go on to Europe.'

'But I cannot intrude—'

'You do not intrude, nor do you in the least embarrass my project. Passepartout!'

'Monsieur.'

'Go to the *Carnatic*, and engage three cabins.'

Passsepartout, delighted that the young woman, who was very gracious to him, was going to continue the journey with them, went off at a brisk gait to obey his master's order.

In which Passepartout Takes a Too Great Interest in His Master, and What Comes of It.

Hong Kong is an island which came into the possession of the English by the treaty of Nankin, after the war of 1842; and the colonizing genius of the English has created upon it an important city and an excellent port. The island is situated at the mouth of the Canton River, and is separated by about sixty miles from the Portuguese town of Macao, on the opposite coast. Hong Kong has vanquished Macao in the struggle for the Chinese trade, and now the greater part of the transportation of Chinese goods finds its depot at the former place. Docks, hospitals, wharves, a Gothic cathedral, a government house, macadamized streets give to Hong Kong the appearance of a town in Kent or Surrey, transferred by some strange magic to the antipodes.

Passepartout wandered, with his hands in his pockets, towards the Victoria port, gazing as he went at the curious palanquins and other modes of conveyance, and the groups of Chinese, Japanese, and Europeans who passed to and fro in the streets. Hong Kong seemed to him not unlike Bombay, Calcutta, and Singapore, since, like them, it betrayed everywhere the evidence of English supremacy.

At the Victoria port he found a confused mass of ships of all nations, English, French, American, and Dutch, men-of-war and trading vessels, Japanese and Chinese junks, sempas [sampans], tankas, and flower-boats which formed so many floating parterres. Passepartout noticed in the crowd a number of the natives who seemed very old, and were dressed in yellow. On going into a barber's to get shaved, he learned that these ancient men were all at least eighty years old, at which age they were permitted to wear yellow, which is the Imperial colour. Passepartout, without exactly knowing why, thought this was funny.

On reaching the quay where they were to embark on the *Carnatic*, he was not astonished to find Fix walking up and down. The detective seemed very much disturbed and disappointed.

'This is bad,' muttered Passepartout, 'for the gentlemen of the Reform Club!' He accosted Fix with a merry smile, as if he had not perceived that gentleman's chagrin. The detective had, indeed, good reasons to inveigh against the bad luck which pursued him. The warrant had not come! It was certainly on the way, but as certainly it could not now reach Hong Kong for several days; and this being the last English territory on Mr. Fogg's route, the robber would escape, unless he could manage to detain him.

'Well, Monsieur Fix,' said Passepartout, 'have you decided to go on with us as far as America?'

'Yes,' returned Fix, through his set teeth.

'Good!' exclaimed Passepartout, laughing heartily. 'I knew you could not persuade yourself to separate from us. Come and engage your berth.'

They entered the steamer office, and secured cabins for four persons. The clerk, as he gave them the tickets, informed them that, the repairs on the *Carnatic* having been completed, the steamer would leave that very evening, and not the next morning, as had been announced.

'That will suit my master all the better,' said Passepartout. 'I will go and let him know.'

Fix now decided to make a bold move; he resolved to tell Passepartout all. It seemed to be the only possible means of keeping Phileas Fogg several days longer at Hong Kong. He accordingly invited his companion into a tavern which caught his eye on the quay. On entering, they found themselves in a large room handsomely decorated, at the end of which was a large campbed furnished with cushions. Several persons lay upon this bed in a deep sleep.

At the small tables which were arranged about the room, some thirty customers were drinking English beer, porter, gin, and brandy; smoking, the while, long red clay pipes, stuffed with little balls of opium mingled with the essence of rose. From time to time one of the smokers, overcome with the narcotic, would slip under the table, whereupon the waiters, taking him by the head and feet, carried and laid him upon the bed. The bed already supported twenty of these stupefied sots.

Fix and Passepartout saw that they were in a smoking-house haunted by those wretched, cadaverous, idiotic creatures, to whom the English merchants sell every year the miserable drug called opium, to the amount of one million four hundred thousand pounds,—thousands devoted to one of the most despicable vices which afflict humanity. The Chinese government has in vain attempted to deal with the evil by stringent laws. It passed gradually from the rich, to whom it was at first exclusively reserved, to the lower classes, and then its ravages could not be arrested.

Opium is smoked everywhere, at all times, by men and women, in the Celestial Empire; and, once accustomed to it, the victims cannot dispense with it, except by suffering horrible bodily contortions and agonies. A great smoker can smoke as many as eight pipes a day; but he dies in five years. It was in one of these dens that Fix and Passepartout, in search of a friendly glass, found themselves. Passepartout had no money, but willingly accepted Fix's invitation in the hope of returning the obligation at some future time.

They ordered two bottles of port, to which the Frenchman did ample justice, while Fix observed him with close attention. They chatted about the journey, and Passepartout was especially merry at the idea that Fix was going to continue with them. When the bottles were empty, however, he rose to go and tell his master of the change in the time of the sailing of the *Carnatic.*

Fix caught him by the arm, and said, 'Wait a moment.'

'What for, Monsieur Fix?'

'I want to have a serious talk with you.'

'A serious talk!' cried Passepartout, drinking up the little wine that was left in the bottom of his glass. 'Well, we'll talk about it to-morrow. I haven't time now.'

'Stay! What I have to say concerns your master.'

Passepartout, at this, looked attentively at his companion. Fix's face seemed to have a singular expression. He resumed his seat.

'What is it that you have to say?'

Fix placed his hand upon Passepartout's arm, and lowering his voice, said, 'You have guessed who I am!'

'Parbleu!' said Passepartout, smiling.

'Then I am going to tell you everything—'

'Now that I know everything, my friend! Ah! that is good. But go on, go on. First, though, let me tell you that these gentlemen have put themselves to a useless expense.'

'Useless!' said Fix. 'You speak confidently. It is clear that you don't know how large the sum is.'

'Of course I do,' returned Passepartout. 'Twenty thousand pounds.'

'Fifty-five thousand!' answered Fix, pressing his companion's hand.

'What!' cried the Frenchman. 'Has Monsieur Fogg dared—fifty-five thousand pounds! Well, there's all the more reason for not losing an instant,' he continued, getting up hastily.

Fix pushed Passepartout back in his chair, and resumed: 'Fifty-five thousand pounds; and if I succeed, I get two thousand pounds. If you'll help me, I'll let you have five hundred of them.'

'Help you?' cried Passepartout, whose eyes were standing wide open.

'Yes; help me keep Mr. Fogg here for two or three days.'

'Why, what are you saying? Those gentlemen are not satisfied with following my master and suspecting his honour, but they must try to put obstacles in his way! I blush for them!'

'What do you mean?'

'I mean that it is a piece of shameful indelicacy. They might as well waylay Monsieur Fogg, and put his money in their pockets!'

'That's just what we count on doing.'

'It's a conspiracy then,' cried Passepartout, who became more and more excited as the liquor mounted in his head, for he drank without perceiving it. 'A real conspiracy! And gentlemen, too. Bah!'

Fix began to be puzzled.

'Members of the Reform Club!' continued Passepartout. 'You must know, Monsieur Fix, that my master is an honest man, and that, when he makes a wager, he tries to win it fairly!'

'But who do you think I am?' asked Fix, looking at him intently.

'Parbleu! An agent of the members of the Reform Club, sent out here to interrupt my master's journey. But, though I found you out sometime ago, I've taken good care to say nothing about it to Mr. Fogg.'

'He knows nothing, then?'

'Nothing,' replied Passepartout, again emptying his glass.

The detective passed his hand across his forehead, hesitating before he spoke again. What should he do? Passepartout's mistake seemed sincere, but it made his design more difficult. It was evident that the servant was not the master's accomplice, as Fix had been inclined to suspect.

'Well,' said the detective to himself, 'as he is not an accomplice, he will help me.'

He had no time to lose: Fogg must be detained at Hong Kong; so he resolved to make a clean breast of it.

'Listen to me,' said Fix, abruptly. 'I am not, as you think, an agent of the members of the Reform Club—'

'Bah!' retorted Passepartout, with an air of raillery.

'I am a police detective, sent out here by the London office.'

'You, a detective?'

'I will prove it. Here is my commission.'

Passepartout was speechless with astonishment when Fix displayed this document, the genuineness of which could not be doubted.

'Mr. Fogg's wager,' resumed Fix, 'is only a pretext, of which you and the gentlemen of the Reform are dupes. He had a motive for securing your innocent complicity.'

'But why?'

'Listen. On the 28th of last September a robbery of fifty-five thousand pounds was committed at the Bank of England, by a person whose description was fortunately secured. Here is this description: it answers exactly to that of Mr. Phileas Fogg.'

'What nonsense!' cried Passepartout, striking the table with his fist. 'My master is the most honourable of men!'

'How can you tell? You know scarcely anything about him. You went into his service the day he came away; and he came away on a foolish pretext, without trunks, and carrying a large amount in bank-notes. And yet you are bold enough to assert that he is an honest man!'

'Yes, yes,' repeated the poor fellow, mechanically.

'Would you like to be arrested as his accomplice?'

Passepartout, overcome by what he had heard, held his head between his hands, and did not dare look at the detective. Phileas Fogg, the saviour of Aouda, that brave and generous man, a robber! And yet, how many presumptions there were against him! Passepartout essayed to reject the suspicions which forced themselves upon his mind; he did not wish to believe that his master was guilty.

'Well, what do you want of me?' said he, at last, with an effort.

'See here,' replied Fix. 'I have tracked Mr. Fogg to this place, but as yet I have failed to receive the warrant for which I sent to London. You must help me to keep him here in Hong Kong—'

'I! But I—'

'I will share with you the two thousand pounds reward offered by the Bank of England.'

'Never!' replied Passepartout, who tried to rise, but fell back, exhausted in mind and body.

'Monsieur Fix,' he stammered, 'even should what you say be true,—if my master is really the robber you are seeking for,—which I deny,—I have been, am, in his service; I have seen his generosity and goodness; and I will never betray him,—not for all the gold in the world. I come from a village where they don't eat that kind of bread!'

'You refuse?'

'I refuse.'

'Consider that I've said nothing,' said Fix, 'and let us drink.'

'Yes, let us drink!'

Passepartout felt himself yielding more and more to the effects of the liquor. Fix, seeing that he must, at all hazards, be separated from his master, wished to entirely overcome him. Some pipes, full of opium, lay upon the table. Fix slipped one into Passepartout's hand. He took it, put it between his lips, lit it, drew several puffs, and his head, becoming heavy under the influence of the narcotic, fell upon the table.

'At last!' said Fix, seeing Passepartout unconscious. 'Mr. Fogg will not be informed of the time of the *Carnatic*'s departure; and, if he is, he will have to go without this cursed Frenchman!'

And, after paying his bill, Fix left the tavern. ▩

21

A VISIT TO THE HONGKONG RACES

LADY ANNE BRASSEY

This passage comes from one of the most popular books of the Victorian age, A Voyage in the Yacht Sunbeam. *But this extract was found in a local library's copy which hadn't been borrowed since 1940. The 1876 to 1877 trip around the world involved forty-three people on the yacht, together with assorted dogs, cats, and parrots. The boat suffered a fire, frequent flooding, and other mishaps, but also aided rescues at sea—all cheerfully managed by the Brassey family and crew. The fascination of the book comes from the vicarious excitement of the sea voyage and the colourful descriptions of the ports. Lady Brassey died of malarial fever off the coast of northern Australia in 1886 and was buried at sea—four days after her final journal entry.*

*M*onday, February 26th 1877.—At four a.m. we found ourselves close under the light on the eastern end of the island of Hongkong. We were surrounded by islands, and the morning was dark and thick; so we waited till 5.30, and then steamed on through the Kowloon passage up to the city of Victoria . . . Off the town of Victoria the crowd of shipping is immense, and it became a difficult task to thread our way between the fleets of sampans and junks. The latter are the most extraordinary-looking craft I ever saw, with high, overhanging sterns, and roll, or rather draw, up sails, sometimes actually made of silk, and puffed like a lady's net ball-dress. . . .

The sampans are long boats, pointed at both ends, and provided with a small awning. They have deep keels; and underneath the floor there is one place for a cooking fire, another for an altar, and a third where the children are stowed to be out of the way. In these sampans whole families, sometimes five generations, live and move and have their being. I never shall forget my astonishment when, going ashore very early one morning in one of these strange craft, the proprietor lifted up what I had thought was the bottom of the boat, and disclosed three or four children, packed away as tight as herrings, while under the seats were half a dozen people of larger growth. The young mother of the small family generally rows with the smallest baby strapped on to her back, and the next-sized one in her arms, whom she is also teaching to row. The children begin to row by themselves when they are about two years old. The boys have a gourd, intended for a life-preserver, tied round their necks as soon as they are born. The girls are left to their fate, a Chinaman thinking it rather an advantage to lose a daughter or two occasionally. . . .

After breakfast we landed on the Praya, a fine quay, extending the whole length of the town. . . . Soldiers and sailors abound in the streets; and if it were not for the sedan-chairs and palanquins, in which everybody is carried about by Chinese coolies with enormous hats, one might easily fancy one's self at dear old Gib[raltar], so much do these dependencies of the Crown in foreign countries resemble one another, even in such opposite quarters of the globe. . . .

From the Praya we went up the hill to write our names in the Governor's book. It was a beautiful road all the way, running between lovely gardens and beneath shady trees. Government House is a fine building, situated on a high point of land, commanding extensive views in every direction. After a pleasant chat we descended the hill again, and proceeded to the Hongkong hotel for tiffin. It does not seem a very desirable abode, being large, dirty, and ill-kept. At one o'clock a bell rang, and the visitors all rushed in and took their places at various little tables, and were served with a 'scrambly' sort of meal by Chinese boys.

After this, a carriage was sent for us, and we drove to the race-course. This is the fourth and last day of the races, and there is to be a ball to-night to wind up with, to which everybody seems to be going. The drive was a very pleasant one, the road presenting a most animated appearance, with crowds of soldiers, sailors, Chinamen, Parsees, Jews, all hurrying along by the side of the

numerous sedan-chairs and carriages.

We were puzzled to imagine where, on this rocky, hilly island, there could possibly be found a piece of ground flat enough for a racecourse. But the mystery was solved when we reached a lovely little valley, about two miles from town, where we found a very fair course, about the size of that of Chester, but not so dangerous. The grand stand is a picturesque object, with its thatched roof, verandas, and sunblinds. The interior, too, looks comfortably arranged, and certainly contains the most luxurious basket-chairs one could possibly desire. There are a lawn and paddock attached, and very good temporary stables, over many of which are private stands and tiffin-rooms.

Hongkong races are a great event, and people come down from Canton, Shanghai, Macao, and all sorts of places for them. Everybody knows everybody, and it seems to be altogether a most pleasant social meeting. Many ladies were present. Some of the races were capital, the little Chinese ponies scuttling along at a great pace under their big riders, whose feet seemed almost to touch the ground. There was also a race for Australian horses. But the most amusing event of all was the last scramble for Chinese ponies ridden by Chinese boys, in which horses and riders seemed to be exactly suited to one another.

The sun went down, and it grew cold and dark before all was over. The gentlemen walked back to the town, and I went down to the landing-place in solitary state, in a carriage driven by an Indian coachman, attended by a Chinese footman. I was immediately surrounded by a vociferous crowd, each individual member of which was anxious to extol the merits of his own sampan. The carriage having driven off, I was quite alone, and had some difficulty in dispersing them, and being allowed to enter the sampan I had selected. However, I did succeed at last, and making my boatman understand that they were to take me to 'the white ship', as the yacht is generally called, returned on board to rest. 🪷

22

AN ARTIST'S IMPRESSION

CONSTANCE F. GORDON-CUMMING

Equally well known as an artist as a writer, Constance F. Gordon-Cumming travelled the world, combining her skills to produce A Lady's Cruise in a French Man-of-War, Granite Crags of California, *and* At Home in Fiji, *as well as* Wanderings in China *from which this extract comes. Her paintings are avidly collected today. One of them, 'Hong Kong from the East', 1879, forms the central image on the front cover of this book.*

Care of Mrs. Snowdon,
City of Victoria,
Isle of Hong-Kong.
Christmas Day [1878].

C ertainly fortune has favoured me, for we reached this most lovely city early this morning, and have had a most enjoyable Christmas-day. . . .

In short, I have already seen enough to convince me that it would be difficult to find more fascinating winter-quarters than this oft-abused city. . . . I am told that this is a fair sample of the whole winter at Hong-Kong, and that for five consecutive months there will probably not be even a shower! Only think what a paradise for an artist! Every day at the same hour the identical lights and shadows, and any number of willing and intelligent coolies ready to fetch and carry him and his goods, and save him all physical fatigue!

We arrived here in time to find Mrs. Snowdon waiting to welcome me to cosy five o'clock tea in the pretty English drawing-room. In short, everything is so pleasant that already I have begun to feel myself quite at home in this British isle of Hong Kong. Now it is time to dress for dinner. Everyone here seems to have a dinner-party to-night.

*

Wednesday, 19th Feb. 1879

Hong-Kong certainly has good reason to appreciate its own race-course, for a prettier scene could not possibly be imagined. . . . This morning I determined to devote the day to sketching the scene, so I resolutely forsook the many kind friends, and went off by myself to a hill in the 'Happy Valley', the peaceful cemetery for all nations and sects, whence I could overlook the whole scene; and truly it was a pretty sight with the amazing crowd of Europeans and Chinamen seeming no bigger than ants—blue ants—and such a swarm of them!

From this high post I saw the races to perfection, and especially enjoyed the excellent music of the 74th band and of their seven pipers, headed by Mackinnon, a Speyside man. The music gained vastly as it floated up to me, every note clear, instead of the ear being distracted by all the jarring sounds of the racecourse. . . .

But, truly, looking down from this point, it is a strange combination to see the semicircle of cemeteries and mortuary chapels, just enfolding the racecourse, and, as it were, repeating the semicircle formed by the Grand Stands!

Two days ago I chanced to wander into this silent God's Acre, just in time to witness a most lonely funeral. It was that of a European who had died unknown at the hospital. Four Chinese coolies carried his coffin, and the only other persons present were the parson and the sexton, neither of whom had known the poor fellow in life. It was the funeral of 'somebody's darling', but not one mourner was near.

To-morrow night there is to be the usual great race ball, but ere that I expect to be far away at sea, as I embark for Foo-Chow [Fuzhou] early in the morning. ▓

23

LETTER TO JARDINE, MATHESON & CO.

FROM HENRY J. ANDERSON EDWARDS

Some people were far less enamoured with Hong Kong than others. The writer of this letter would rather have been anywhere else. Unfortunately, a continuation of the saga was not available.

Top Floor,
Beaconsfield Arcade,
Queen's Road
September 23, 1886

Jardine, Matheson & Co.
Hong Kong

Dear Sirs:

I am a Medical Practitioner from Sydney N.S.W. at present by accident in Hong Kong together with my wife and family, having just arrived from the Caroline Islands by way of Manila. By false representation on the part of a Trader in those Islands, I was fraudulently advised to take up a position as Medical Officer and Resident Manager at this Station and in consequence we are in Hong Kong today.

Hong Kong seems to have quite a sufficiency of Medical Practitioners without my staying here, besides it would appear useless to set up an independent practice on one's own account in so small a place where so many men are already established in practice unless one had this as a stand by for a good time which, unfortunately, I have not.

I am desirous of getting back to Australia (where I had a very fair practice indeed for a young man) or of getting to America unless something suitable presents itself.

Please note that I am open to engagement on any of your vessels requiring medical services or elsewhere and inform me whether you have anything to offer me.

In return for my service on the *Australian* or *American* Lines I ask only a passage for my wife and family (2 little children, one aged 2 years and the other a babe in arms) and nursemaid (aged 12). On any other line I ask only a sufficiency wherewith to maintain them fairly comfortable until opportunity offers of getting to Australia, America or something better presents itself.

Yours truly,
Henry J. Anderson Edwards
late of Sydney, N.S.W.

24

HONG-KONG NIGHTLIFE

RUDYARD KIPLING

In From Sea to Sea *Rudyard Kipling recorded his thoughts, as well as his strong opinions as he travelled to Hong Kong. Visiting with a professor guide in 1888 he takes his readers on a unique tour through the Colony, including its dubious night life.*

When you are in the China Seas be careful to keep all your flannel-wear to hand. In an hour the steamer swung from tropical heat (including prickly) to a cold, raw fog as wet as a Scotch mist. Morning gave us a new world—somewhere between Heaven and Earth. The sea was smoked glass; reddish grey islands lay upon it under fog-banks that hovered fifty feet above our heads. The squat sails of junks danced in the breeze and disappeared, and there was no solidity in the islands against which the glassy levels splintered in snow. The steamer groaned and grunted and howled because she was so damp and miserable, and I groaned also because the guide-book said that Hong-Kong had the finest harbour in the world, and I could not see two hundred yards in any direction. Yet this ghost-like in-gliding through the belted fog was livelily mysterious, and became more so when the movement of the air vouchsafed us a glimpse of a warehouse and a derrick, both apparently close aboard, and behind them the shoulder of a mountain. . . .

All Hong-Kong is built on the sea-face; the rest is fog. One muddy road runs for ever in front of a line of houses which are partly Chowringhee and party Rotherhithe. You live in the houses, and when wearied of this, walk across the road and drop into the sea, if you can find a square foot of unencumbered water. So vast is the accumulation of country shipping, and such is its dirtiness as it rubs against the bund, that the superior inhabitants are compelled to hand their boats from davits above the common craft, who are greatly disturbed by a multitude of steam-launches. These ply for amusement and the pleasure of whistling, and are held in such small esteem that every hotel owns one, and the others are masterless. Beyond the launches lie more steamers than the eye can count and four out of five of these belong to Us. I was proud when I saw the shipping at Singapur, but I swell with patriotism as I watch the fleets of Hong-Kong from the balcony of the Victoria Hotel. I can almost spit into the water; but many mariners stand below and they are a strong breed. . . .

When I went into the streets of Hong-Kong I stepped into thick slushy London mud of the kind that strikes chilly through the boot, and the rattle of hansoms. A soaking rain fell, and all the sahibs hailed 'rickshaws—they call them 'ricks' here [the full name is 'jinricksha']—and the wind was chillier than the rain. It was the first touch of honest weather since Calcutta. No wonder with such a climate that Hong-Kong was ten times livelier than Singapur, that there were signs of building everywhere, and gas-jets in all the houses, that colonnades and domes were scattered broadcast, and the Englishmen walked as Englishmen should—hurriedly and looking forward. All the length of the main street was verandahed, and the Europe shops squandered plate-glass by the square yard. (*Nota bene.*—As in Simla so elsewhere: mistrust the plate-glass shops. You pay for their fittings in each purchase.)

The same Providence that runs big rivers so near to large cities puts main thoroughfares close to big hotels. I went down Queen Street, which is not very hilly. All the other streets that I looked up were built in steps after the fashion of Clovelly, and under blue skies would have given scores of good photographs. The rain and the fog blotted the views. Each upward-climbing street ran out in white mist that covered the sides of a hill, and the downward-sloping ones were lost in the steam from the waters of the harbour, and both were very strange to see. 'Hi-yi-yow,' said my 'rickshaw coolie and balanced me on one wheel. I got out and met first a German with a beard, then three jolly sailor boys from a man-of-war, then a sergeant of Sappers, then a Parsee, then two Arabs, then an American, then a Jew, then a few thousand Chinese all carrying something, and then the Professor. . . .

I met one horse, very ashamed of himself, who was looking after a cart on the sea road, but upstairs there are no vehicles save 'rickshaws. Hong-Kong has killed the romance of the 'rickshaw in my mind. They ought to be sacred to pretty ladies, instead of which men go to office in them, officers in full canonicals use them, tars try to squeeze in two abreast, and from what I have heard down at the barracks they do occasionally bring to the guard-room the drunken defaulter. 'He falls asleep inside of it, sir, and saves trouble.' The Chinese naturally have the town for their own, and profit by all our building improvements and regulations. Their golden and red signs flame down the Queen's Road, but they are careful to supplement their own tongue by well-executed Europe lettering. I found only one exception, thus:—

Fussing, Garpenter
And Gabinet Naktr
Has good Gabi
Nets tor Sale.

The shops are made to catch the sailor and the curio hunter, and they succeed admirably. When you come to these parts put all your money in a bank and tell the manager man not to give it you, however much you ask. So shall you be saved from bankruptcy.

The Professor and I made a pilgrimage from Kee Sing even unto Yi King, who sells the decomposed fowl, and each shop was good. Though it sold shoes or sucking-pigs, there was some delicacy of carving or gilded tracery in front to hold the eye, and each thing was quaint and striking of its kind. . . . I was studying these things while the Professor was roaming through carved ivories, embroidered silks, panels of inlay, tortoise-shell filigree, jade-tipped pipes, and the God of Art only knows what else.

'I don't think even as much of him (meaning our Indian craftsman) as I used to do,' said the Professor, taking up a tiny ivory grotesque of a small baby trying to pull a water-buffalo out of its wallow—the whole story of beast and baby written in the hard ivory. . . .

I continued, sorting a bundle of cheap china spoons—all good in form, colour, and use. While big-bellied Chinese lanterns above us swayed in the wind with a soft chafing of oiled paper, but they made no sign and the shopkeeper in blue was equally useless.

'You wanebee buy? Heap plitty things here,' said he; and he filled a tobacco-pipe from a dull green leather pouch held at the mouth with a little bracelet of plasma, or it might have been the very jade. He was playing with a brown-wood abacus, and by his side was his day-book bound in oiled paper, and the tray of Indian ink, with the brushes and the porcelain supports for the brushes. He made an entry in his book and daintily painted in his latest transaction. The Chinese of course have been doing this for a few thousand years, but Life, and its experiences, is as new to me as it was to Adam, and I marvelled.

'Wanchee buy?' reiterated the shopman after he had made his last flourish.

'Yes,' said I, in the new tongue which I am acquiring, 'wanchee know one piecee information b'long my pidgin. Savvy these things? Have got soul, you?'

'Have got how?'

'Have got one piecee soul—allee same spilit? No savvy?'

'Two dollar an' half,' he said, balancing a cabinet in his hand. . . .

Is there really such a place as Hong-Kong? People say so, but I have not yet seen it. Once indeed the clouds lifted and I saw a granite house perched like a cherub on nothing, a thousand feet above the town. It looked as if it might be the beginning of a civil station, but a man came up the street and said, 'See this fog. It will be like this till September. You'd better go away.' I shall not go. I shall encamp in front of the place until the fog lifts and the rain ceases.

From a genuine desire to see what they call Life, with a capital Hell, I went through Hong-Kong for the space of a night. I am glad that I am not a happy father with a stray son who thinks that he knows all the ropes. Vice must be pretty much the same all the round world over, but if a man wishes to get out of pleasure with it, let him go to Hong-Kong. 'Of course things are out and away better at 'Frisco', said my guide, 'but we consider this very fair for the Island.' It was not till a fat person in a black dressing-gown began to squeal demands for horrible stuff called 'a bottle of wine' that I began to understand the glory of the situation. I was seeing Life. 'Life' is a great thing. It consists in swigging sweet champagne that was stolen from a steward of the P. and O., and exchanging bad words with pale-faced baggages who laugh damnably without effort and without emotion. The *argot* of the real 'chippy' (this means man of the world *Anglice*, a half-drunk youth with his hat on the back of his head) is not easy to come at. It requires an apprenticeship in America. I stood appalled at the depth and richness of the American language, of which I was privileged to hear a special dialect. There were girls who had been to Leadville and Denver and the wilds of the wilder West, who had acted in minor companies, and who had generally misconducted themselves in a hundred weary ways. So they cursed and they drank and they told tales, sitting in a circle, till I felt that this was really Life and a thing to be quitted if I wished to like it.

Then there was an interlude and some more shrieks and howls, which the generous public took as indicating immense mirth and enjoyment of Life; and I came to yet another establishment, where the landlady lacked the half of her left lung, as a cough betrayed, but was none the less amusing in a dreary way, until she also dropped the mask and the playful jesting began. All the jokes I had heard before at the other place. It is a poor sort of Life that cannot spring one new jest a day.

'Are we going to hold these dismal levees all through the night?' I demanded at the fourth house, where I dreaded the repetition of the thrice-told tales.

'It's better in 'Frisco. Must admire the girls a little bit, y'know. Walk round and wake 'em up. That's Life. You never saw it in India?' was the reply.

'No, thank God, I didn't. A week of this would make me hang myself,' I returned, leaning wearily against a door-post. There were very loud sounds of revelry by night here, and the inmates needed no waking up. One of them was recovering from a debauch of three days, and the other was just entering upon the same course. Providence protected me all through. A certain austere beauty of countenance had made every one take me for a doctor or a parson—a qualified parson, I think; and so I was spared many of the more pronounced jokes, and could sit and contemplate the Life that was so sweet. The worst of it was, the women were real women and pretty, and like some people I knew, and when they stopped the insensate racket for a while they were well behaved.

'Pass for real ladies anywhere,' said my friend. 'Aren't these things well managed?'

Then Corinthian Kate began to bellow for more drinks—it was three in the morning—and the current of hideous talk recommenced.

A night's reflection has convinced me that there is no hell for these women in another world. They have their own in this Life, and I have been through it a little way.

Once, before I got away, I climbed to the civil station of Hong-Kong, which overlooks the town.

There in sumptuous stone villas built on the edge of the cliff and facing shaded roads, in a wilderness of beautiful flowers and a hushed calm unvexed even by the roar of the traffic below, the residents do their best to imitate the life of an India up-country station. They are better off than we are. At the bandstand the ladies dress all in one piece—shoes, gloves, and umbrellas come out from England with the dress, and every *Memsahib* knows what that means—but the mechanism of their life is much the same. In one point they are superior. The ladies have a club of their very own to which, I believe, men are only allowed to come on sufferance. At a dance there are about twenty men to one lady, and there are practically no spinsters in the island.

The Inhabitants complain of being cooped in and shut up. They look at the sea below them and they long to get away. They have their 'At Homes' on regular days of the week, and everybody meets everybody else again and again. They have amateur theatricals and they quarrel and all the men and women take sides, and the station is cleaved asunder from the top to the bottom. Then they become reconciled and write to the local papers condemning the local critic's criticism. Isn't it touching? A lady told me these things one afternoon, and I nearly wept from sheer homesickness.

'And then, you know, after she had said *that* he was obliged to give the part to the other, and that made *them* furious, and the races were so near that nothing could be done, and Mrs.— said that it was altogether impossible. You understand how very unpleasant it must have been, do you not?'

'Madam,' said I, 'I do. I have been there before. My heart goes out to Hong-Kong. In the name of the great Indian Mofussil I salute you. Henceforward Hong-Kong is one of Us, ranking before Meerut, but after Allahabad, at all public ceremonies and parades.'

I think she fancies I had sunstroke; but you at any rate will know what I mean. ▩

PART V

LATE VICTORIAN DAYS
1890s

'I am fit and like the place.
The weather is delightfully cool and the people interesting'
HERBERT ELLISON RHODES JAMES, 1892

'Hong Kong looks small and insignificant, but its importance is
not to be estimated by its size alone.'
MRS UNSWORTH, 1890s

'The Chinese are a most interesting people and there is much
that is excellent about them if you comprehend them.'
JUDGE GOODMAN, 1890s

THE STEAMER WITH THE BUFF-COLOURED FUNNEL

'DOLLY'

The following is a late Victorian period piece by a male journalist who uses the pseudonym 'Dolly'. While winning no prizes for literary genius, it evokes a type of long-vanished woman, married but living alone in Hong Kong while her husband sails from port to port. And perhaps, should you find yourself on the Peak on a windy November day, you will feel the presence of her billowing skirts as she searches for a buff-coloured funnel on a ship that will never touch shore.

'Pardon me! Would you mind telling me if that steamer down there has a buff-coloured funnel?'

I had heard a light footfall behind me, and swung round in astonishment to find a pair of wistful grey eyes fixed eagerly upon my own. There seemed something strikingly strange about the figure of the woman who stood hesitatingly before me, that riveted my attention. Her face, that appeared at one time to have laid claim to considerable beauty, was lined and haggard with care, and from beneath the natty sailor hat, gay with a bright ribbon, the hair showed forth white as the driven snow. And yet I felt convinced that, in spite of the white hair and careworn lines, the face before me was a young face.

Her figure appeared bent and shrunken into itself, yet gaily attired, with touches of almost childish finery; and over all the large grey eyes, fringed with upcurling lashes, gazed now almost beseechingly into mine, as she asked again, 'Can you tell me if that steamer has a buff-coloured funnel?'

My eyes travelled from her face to the incoming steamer far below us, that was slowly threading her way among the islands toward Hongkong Harbour.

'No madam,' I replied after looking a moment, 'that steamer has a black funnel. A Douglas boat I should think by the look of her.'

'Strange!' she mused; a bewildered look crept into her eyes, as she drew from her purse a carefully folded scrap of paper and extended it toward me, 'they told me at the office, she would be in at one o'clock, and it is now half-past twelve. She ought to be in sight by now.'

I glanced at the sheet she held out to me. It was an ordinary office memo form, and on it was written in fading characters, 'Dear Mrs. Hesketh—The *Calyx* is reported as having passed Gap Rock at 10.40 a.m. and may be expected at Hongkong at 1 p.m.' As I cast my eyes over it again and looked up at the date, I saw with surprise that it was dated Nov. 21st 1891. It was then '97 and as I still looked at it in puzzled wonderment, she took it again from my hands, and saying hurriedly, 'Perhaps I shall see her from higher up,' passed on.

Toiling on my way to the summit of the Peak, I passed her again, seated by the path-side, her hands clasped on her knees, gazing with a yearning look of expectation out to the sea.

Almost involuntarily, I turned and followed her gaze. Not a ship was in sight. Away below and around us, the panorama stretched its vivid beauty like some tessellated pavement worked in sapphire and emerald, and out beyond the last emerald patch, with a stretch of blue sea sleeping sunnily around it, and the limitless ocean behind, now calm and docile as a sleeping child, stood Gap Rock, a mere speck on the distant horizon. The ship we had seen approaching from lower down had got under the land, and, with the exception of a few junks lazily beating their way out to the fishing grounds, no moving thing was in sight to mar the fancy that the scene below was ought but some fairy-woven picture, that existed but in the imagination.

As I gained the summit of the Peak, and entered into conversation with the presiding deity of the signal station, perched like the cherub whose duty it is to watch over the fortunes of poor Jack, aloft, I was awaiting an opportunity of introducing the subject that was uppermost in my mind, and endeavouring to learn more of the strange lady who had so powerfully exciting my curiosity, when a darkening of the doorway of the hut in which we were sitting, caused me to look up, to see the same person standing on the threshold.

She stepped in, and walked hurriedly up to the signal man, without betraying the slightest sign of being aware of my presence.

'Can you see anything of a steamer with a buff-coloured funnel, please?' she asked again, and there seemed to me an infinite gentleness in the signal man's voice as he answered, 'No ma'am, I can't see anything of the *Calyx* yet.'

'Strange!' she went through the same formula as before, offering him the note to read. He took it and scanned it carefully, taking advantage of the opportunity to gulp down a lump that was in his throat, before he handed it back.

'You see, ma'am,' he explained, 'it's a bit hazy out at the Rock, and we can't see very far. Maybe we shall see her later on.'

As a matter of fact, it was an ideally clear day, but she seemed to accept the explanation with childish faith. Saying patiently that she would go and sit outside and wait awhile, she passed out and sat on the bench a few yards from the door.

For two full hours she sat there, looking steadfastly out to sea, while we within smoked our pipes and spoke the few words we exchanged in a tone of hushed reverence. Then she rose with a great sobbing sigh and a slight shiver, and without another word, without a glance in our direction, passed drearily down the path.

I looked inquiringly at the signal man. 'Poor lady,' he said in answer to my look. 'It's a long time she'll have to watch and wait before she sees the *Calyx* comes sailing in again.'

'What was the *Calyx*?' I asked.

'The *Calyx*,' he said, after violently blowing his nose, 'the *Calyx* was a tank steamer engaged in the oil trade between here and Lankat. When she and her sistership, the *Carolla* were fixed steady on that run, the young captain of the *Calyx*, as nice a young fellow, I'm told, as ever commanded a ship, wrote home to his sweetheart, to whom he had been engaged for some years, only waiting for a decent chance to come out and marry him.

The *Calyx* used to come up here with oil from Langkat, and then take cargo in her tanks, and go round the ports: Saigon, Bangkok and so on, and then back to Langkat for more oil. She used to get into Hongkong here, about every three months.

Well, they had been married perhaps a year, and everyone who came in contact with the young wife of the captain, for the lady you saw just now is barely twenty seven yet, had come under the spell of the woman. She seemed to take all hearts by storm with her winning ways and bright smile, and the shipping clerk at the office deemed it a privilege to be able to send her a note the moment the *Calyx* had passed Gap Rock, saying when she would arrive in port.

It was the year before I came here that she received the note you saw her hand me and proceeded as usual to rig herself out in her gayest holiday dress to await her dear one's arrival.

But the ship never came in, and at two in the afternoon they wired out to Gap Rock asking if there had not been a mistake about the ship's arrival. But they wired back saying that she had passed there at 10.40 a.m. and hoisted her number. It was a dirty sort of morning with a strong N.E. wind and a driving mist, and the lighthouse keeper said afterwards that she had vanished into the fog again in the direction of Hongkong almost before he had sent the telegram off.

That's all they ever learned about her. After a further exchange of useless telegrams, they decided to send a boat out for her, fearing in the mist she might have come to grief on some of the outlying islands. It was blowing too hard, and there was far too high a sea running to have been able to send even the best of the harbour launches out for her. By the time a larger boat had got up steam and was ready for the search, it had grown dark.

She knocked about out there all night and came back in the morning with no news whatever of the *Calyx*. What had become of her? Where could she have got to in the short run of thirty-four miles that separates Gap Rock from Hongkong was a mystery.

Several days later, some odd bits of wreckage, principally deck fittings, were washed up on the shore at Aberdeen. A day or two later, the body of a Chinaman was washed up on Ai Chau [Centre Island] beach, which was thought to be the earthly remains of one of the firemen of the ship.

Then it was that wild theories began to fly around, that vainly tried to account for the ship's disappearance. Of course collision was the one that at first found most favour; but you see, Sir, it takes two to make a collision. A ship can't very well run into herself, and the only two boats that had left Hongkong that day were reported all well from their destinations.

Then they struck on the one theory that seemed to hold water. It was surmised that one or more of her tanks of oil must have exploded and blown the ship to atoms. Additional probability was lent to this by the discovery of a lifeboat off the beach of Great Ladrone Island [Lantau] with the name of *Calyx* on her stern. She was floating keel uppermost and when righted, it was found that the canvas cover was still laced on, and what was more, both davits were hanging to the boat by their tackles with the falls still neatly coiled up within the boat. That perhaps, sir, is one of the great failings of the Merchant Service. The prevalent idea seems to be that the boats are put on a ship for the sake of ornament, and the neater they can make them look, however unhandy in an emergency they may be in consequence, the better it is. Perhaps it saves a few dollars a year in rope by having them coiled up within the boat, even if it does mean the sacrifice of a few lives now and then.

However, everything being untouched like this was taken as showing that the vessel must have gone down before any attempt could be made to swing the boats out, and that as she sank, the boat had dragged the davits from their sockets and floated up with them to the surface again.

That was the last piece of news that was ever understood by Mrs. Hesketh, for she went down with brain fever. When, some time after the bodies of Capt. Hesketh, the chief officer and third engineer were found floating near the harbour, she was in no condition to understand the terrible calamity that had come upon her.

They say that when she recovered, her mind was a blank as to what had happened, and the first question she asked when she awoke from the sleep which had been the turning point in her illness was when the *Calyx* was expected.

When at last, very sorrowfully, they told her what had occurred, she simply refused to believe it. Not that she contradicted what they said, but her mind seemed capable of holding but one idea, and that was that the *Calyx* was expected shortly, and nothing else seemed to make any impression on her poor bewildered brain. Even when they took her to see his grave at Happy Valley, she looked down at it sadly and seemed for a moment to understand, as great tears gathered slowly in the stricken eyes, but no sooner had she turned away than she was speaking again with joyful anticipation of the *Calyx*'s impending return.

And now the poor young thing gets up on the morning of November 21st year after year, dons her gayest attire and toils patiently up here to watch for her husband's ship which, the letter tells her, is due her at one o'clock. The Flower Line boats have a buff-coloured smoke stack with a broad blue band round it, and in the old happy days, this was the mark by which she always singled out the ship.

Every year on the same date she comes up here and asks me if I can see a steamer with such a funnel approaching, and when I reluctantly tell her 'no', she sits down here and watches or wanders around the Peak trying to find a spot from which she can get a better outlook. And when, toward evening, there still is no sign of the steamer with the buff-coloured funnel, she goes down again and exchanges her holiday dress for the sombre-black gown that something impels her to wear for the rest of the twelve months. They say at the boarding house at which she stays that she seems quite quiet and rational enough until the month comes round for her to play through the same heart-rending farce.

Now and again she alludes with pride to her Jack, who is away in command of the *Calyx* and whom she expects home in November.

'God help her, poor soul!' The signalman's eyes held a suspicious moisture as he looked out through the door down to the ships scattered about the blue floor of the harbour like the toys of a tired child. They tried to get her to go home again, back to her own people, but she would not hear of leaving when her Jack might be coming back shortly. One kind-hearted old lady, who was going home to England, agreed to take the poor stricken thing with her. They almost had to force her to leave Hongkong, but when they started she fretted so much on board at being away that on their arrival at Singapore, the doctor decided that the only way to save her life was to let her return. So she was sent back and waits for the ship that will never come in.

'My God, it's hard!' The signalman's voice trembled. 'It's hard to see her come toiling up the path here, her that you wouldn't think could walk a hundred yards up this hill, without being knocked up, and to have those great, sad eyes looking right into you. They looked with such a world of dumb entreaty as though they dimly divined that there was something you were holding back from her, some elusive thought that the poor broken intellect could not grasp.'

'For five years now I've stood up here and told her that perhaps if we could see further, we might be able to see the *Calyx* coming in. Five years, and yet I could no more pain her to-day by telling her that there was no *Calyx* now to come in though I know that the poor thing would not believe me, than I could have done on that first November morning when she came up here to watch and wait.'

It was not until two years later that I learned more of the waiting lady. Then, on November 21st, as I came up at the close of a raw damp day to the Peak Hotel at which I had taken up my residence, a coolie came running in for assistance, saying that a lady had fallen down on one of the hills.

Four of us men, accompanied by an ambulance from No. 6 Police Station nearby decided to go out at once in the gathering dusk and ascertain what had happened. Half way up the steep sides of Mount Kellet, the hill that overhangs Aberdeen, we found her at the foot of a boulder. A blood-stained handkerchief was in her hand, and from the corner of her mouth trickled a small stream of blood. Her great love had demanded more from the frail body than it had been able to perform: she had ruptured a blood vessel in her eagerness to gain the summit.

One glance revealed to us that the spirit had lost its precarious hold of the fragile young body. But there was a look of peace, almost of gladness in the poor bewildered eyes that told us, as we stood there and reverently bared our heads, that she had at last seen the steamer with the buff-coloured funnel coming into that harbour from which she would sail no more, and where partings are not. ▨

114

26

DEGENERATE HONGKONG

'DOLLY'

Only in recent years has Hong Kong ceased to be known as a cultural desert. But a hundred years ago at least one person was so incensed by the cultural level that this poem was penned. 'Dolly' maintains his anonymity while expressing strong views on Hong Kong society—this time in verse.

Away with books! Nor let in Pleasure's train,
One single elevating thought remain;
What boots it, though in ignorance we live?
The human mind was made for naught but gain.

Away with books! Let Sport and Dollars rule;
What need of Culture? We who went to school,
Learned all required of us to fill a place,
In bank, or business on the office stool.

'Degenerate'? Why use so harsh a word?
From gaining dollars who would be deterred
By wish for knowledge, yielding no return
For time and trouble uselessly incurred.

Away with books! Let Pallas yield her place
To Comus, and the Terpsichorean grace;
Carlyle and Huxley? What care we for them?
Who once have pulled an oar, or won a race?

Away with books! Dash Wisdom's trophies down,
And Intellect in sparkling vintage drown;
Our servitude to Folly freely give,
And Bacchus with Athene's laurels crown.

This be our cue; to try to emulate
The lower brutes, in their contented state,
That strive for naught beyond their daily food;
And spurn with scorn the books that elevate.

Away with books! Yet stay, we fain would keep
The novel, so it's lesson be not deep;
The 'Deadwood Dick,' of blood-and-thunder strain,
That will not rouse us from our sottish sleep.

So we can boast that we in Hongkong here,
Are far without vain Learning's futile sphere;
And count, where 'ignorance is bliss,' that we
Are doubly happy in the larger share. ▦

27

THE VIEW FROM GOVERNMENT HOUSE

SIR G. WILLIAM DES VOEUX

Des Voeux Road runs parallel to Queen's Road near the Harbour on part of the massive land reclamation named after Sir William Des Voeux, Governor of Hong Kong between 1887 and 1891. Upon his return to England, Des Voeux, like many colonial governors, published his memoirs: My Colonial Service in British Guiana, St. Lucia, Trinidad, Fiji, Australia, New Foundland, and Hong Kong with Interludes. *They provide a look at the Colony from Government House with its then fabulous view, now partially blocked by the imposing Bank of China Building. The Victorian love of pomp and ceremony surfaces in the Jubilee celebrations, as well as at the Governor's inauguration.*

A s I left the ship in the large steam-launch *Victoria*, which is in Hong Kong provided for the Governor's use (and, like many others used there, is really a small yacht), the usual salute of seventeen guns was fired from the man-of-war hulk *Victor Emmanuel*, which was then the headquarters of the Commodore. As we passed to the wharf guards were turned out and presented arms to the other warships in harbour, and as I landed a shore battery also saluted. On the wharf were the General and his staff, the whole of the Legislative Council, the foreign consuls, and a large number of public officials. After shaking hands with a considerable number whom the General presented to me by name, and inspecting the guard of honour, behind which was a dense mass of Chinese, I drove off with the General to the public buildings, where I was shortly afterwards 'sworn in' before the Legislative Council, and made a very brief speech on the occasion.

Accompanied by the General, I then proceeded to Government House, which at once struck me as particularly convenient in design and a model residence for a tropical climate. It was far superior, indeed, as regards comfort, to other Government Houses of a more pretentious character, which have been since built at much greater cost. The roof was flat, and offered a magnificent view of the town and harbour, thus permitting of agreeable exercise in illness or at other times when seclusion was desirable. The grounds were not very large, hardly exceeding two acres in extent, with flowering trees at the sides. . . .

An effective supplement to the somewhat restricted grounds of Government House was the Botanic Garden, separated only by a road. Situated in a climate barely tropical, it was inferior to the Trinidad garden in luxuriance of foliage, but had nevertheless a beauty of its own which could hardly be surpassed. . . .

Looking out at night from the front gallery of Government House, before the moon had risen, I witnessed an effect which was quite new to me. The sky, though clear of clouds, was somewhat hazy, so that the small-magnitude stars were not visible, though some of the larger ones were plain enough. Beneath, however, the air was quite clear, and consequently, though the vessels in the harbour were invisible in the darkness, their innumerable lights seemed like another hemisphere of stars even more numerous than the others, and differing only as being redder.

Official work occupied me immediately after my arrival. Social duties also began at once.

General Cameron had rightly anticipated my wishes in inviting to stay at Government House the Siamese Prince who, with three nephews and a retinue of some fourteen persons, was on his return from Her Majesty's Jubilee, where he had been representing his Sovereign. Lack of bedrooms, the only defect of the house, prevented me from 'putting up' more than four of the party. The others were therefore of necessity quartered at the hotel, though occasionally coming to meals. . . .

The celebration of Her Majesty's Jubilee, postponed because its occurrence during the hot months would have rendered less effective the intended display of enthusiasm, took place in November. On the morning of the celebration the band of the regiment and a large guard of honour marched into the grounds, and my reception began. I 'received' in the hall, the leading officials and some sixty military and naval officers in uniform standing on either side of me.

The first arrival was a large deputation of Chinese, bringing a splendidly embroidered address to the Queen, containing a striking recognition of British justice. You will see in the papers my speech on the occasion. What you will not see, however, is that these very rich Chinese brought me a present of food (analogous, I suppose, to the bread and salt of other countries), consisting chiefly of two hams and a dozen of porter!! An English address was presented by Mr. Bell Irving, a member of Council; with the committee of the Chinese temple called 'Man mo' brought a tablet to adorn Government House with Chinese words on it, signifying 'Everlasting Prosperity'. All the principal ladies of the place came, and altogether I shook hands with four hundred people. I had speeches to make to two other deputations, and if I may judge from what was said to me and from accounts in the papers, the affair was a great success.

At five o'clock, attended by an escort of twelve Sikh mounted police, I went down in my eight-coolie chair to review the troops. Three other Government House chairs followed, the string of bearers looking extremely well in their new bright-red liveries, white gaiters, and 'mutton-pie' hats with red tassels, a sort of European adaptation of Chinese dress, the invention of some former Governor. As I had never gone through such a function before, General Cameron gave me the necessary hints, and all went off satisfactorily. . . . Mrs. Cameron and a number of ladies stood near me at the saluting flag, and the ground occupied by the troops was surrounded by a dense mass of Chinese, some hundreds of whom had climbed into the neighbouring trees. ▧

28

REMINISCENCES OF A
COLONIAL JUDGE

SIR WILLIAM MEIGH GOODMAN

Sir William Goodman served as Chief Justice of Hong Kong at the turn of the century. His observations, privately published, are the unabashed views of a very colonial official. Ah, the inscrutable East!

We reached Hong Kong on March 15th, 1890. . . . When we arrived, only the town and the lower spurs of the hills were visible; all the rest was shrouded in dense mist. It was not till we had been two days in Hong Kong that the fog yielded to a strong breeze, and revealed all the grandeur of the mountain masses, glistening with dew and damp in the glorious sunshine. It has been said that Hong Kong blends 'the wild scenery of Scotland with the classic beauty of Italy', and I do not think this is an exaggeration.

The enterprise of the residents is wonderful. What, on my arrival, was a muddy and somewhat smelly foreshore, has been filled in and faced with huge blocks of granite and cement. Broad roads, shaded with charming trees, have been made; and what is known as the New Praya West Reclamation (finished in 1903) has done for a large part of the harbour frontage of Victoria (Hong Kong Island) what the Thames Embankment has done for London. New and handsome buildings have been erected, and the Hong Kong Club is not only a fine edifice, but one of the best Clubs in the East. . . .

On March 31st, 1890, the Duke and Duchess of Connaught arrived in the *Kaiser-i-Hind*, one of the P. and O. steamers, and were accorded an enthusiastic reception, and went to Government House to stay during their visit. There was an official dinner, to which my wife and I were asked 'to meet their Royal Highnesses', and a great reception afterwards. The Duke next day laid the foundation-stone of the Praya Reclamation Works, and in the evening was entertained by the Chinese community.

The entertainment consisted of a great Chinese dinner at the Ko Shing theatre, at which I was present as a guest, seated between two Chinese. During dinner, which included bird's-nest soup, shark's fin and many other Chinese delicacies, a weird play was being acted on the stage, to the accompaniment of noisy Chinese music. Dr. Ho Kai, acting as interpreter, explained the scenes to the Duke and Duchess, who seemed very much amused. Our ivory chopsticks were given to us as mementoes of the dinner. Personally, I do not appreciate a Chinese *menu* very highly.

I was most kindly received by all my brother officials, and after staying a while at the Hong Kong hotel, which is down in the town, my wife and I got very comfortable rooms at Cragieburn, a sort of private hotel at the Peak. We moved there at the latter part of April, when the hot weather was beginning. My official chambers, as Attorney-General, were in the Court House. I had a large and somewhat gloomy room on the ground floor for myself, and a smaller one for my clerk. The Court House was one of the most unsatisfactory of all the public buildings. . . .

While I was in Hong Kong there was always 'going to be' a new Court House, and I saw the plans of it many years ago. However, before I left, the work had actually been in progress for four years, two of which were taken up in completing the foundations, which proved a more difficult task than had been anticipated, owing to the site being situated upon newly reclaimed ground. How well I remember the thud of the heavy pile-drivers as they drove home, foot by foot, deeper and deeper down, the enormous piles on which the concrete was to rest.

What patient folk these Chinese labourers are! What an endless work it seemed! When this splendid edifice, close by the Hong Kong Club, is completed, the Colony will have so much cause to be proud of its Court House building as of the honest, impartial justice which is administered within it. . . . [Now the offices of the Legislative Council, the building still stands in Statue Square.]

On the first arrival of an official in the East, he cannot but realize that he is face to face with a people whose thoughts, in many ways, are not his thoughts. It takes him some time to familiarise himself with his surroundings and to understand the point of view from which the Oriental regards a question.

The Chinese are a most interesting people, and there is much that is excellent about them if you comprehend them. If, when you are introduced to a Chinese gentleman, he asks you, How old are you? Are you married? How much money do you make a year? How many children have you? and so on, you must not think him an ill-mannered person. It is quite the correct thing, and shows his interest in you and yours.

If you ask a witness whether he is certain of such and such a thing, he may reply that he is seven-tenths certain. If you want to know when an event occurred, you may be told that it happened in the last decade of the second month. Probably you will not get the witness to fix the date more precisely. The month is regulated by the moon, and the same word does duty for both.

A counsel in England pressing a witness as to how long he saw a person, would be surprised to receive such an answer as 'the time it would take to drink a cup of tea', or again, 'the time it would take to eat a bowl of rice'. These are replies I have often received in Court. Of course, as the Chinese have no Sundays, they have no weeks. They do not seem to attach so much important to time as we do. Indeed, except in the Treaty ports and where foreign clocks are used, the Chinese hour is twice the length of ours. ▨

29

A MILITARY DOCTOR WRITES HOME

HERBERT ELLISON RHODES JAMES

In 1973, this delightful bundle of letters was presented to the Hong Kong Collection at the University of Hong Kong. Written by a military medical man in the 1890s, they are spontaneous and illustrated with informal pen and ink sketches.

Portobello Barracks
Dublin
7th August, 1892

My Dear People,

I have got my warning for China! which is as good a station as there is from a money point of view, and a 4 years one only. I am informed that 'I may be required to proceed to China on short notice'. So I am getting leave now and you will probably see me in the course of next week. I shall most likely be in these climes until September, but I mean to run over for a short time at once, and put the finishing touches to my outfit. Short notice might be three months. November is the usual trooping season for China. I will answer Mother's letter in detail! You might tell Sydney.

Queen's Gardens, Hong Kong
Tuesday [November 1892]

My Dear People,

I am settling down here, and like the appearance of the place very much. The weather is cool and nice, and the people seem hospitable. My duties are at present to take charge of the Shropshire Regt. and the Casualty ward where all the bad cases are congregated. I like this. I hope you are all fit. I did not get letters from you last mail but no doubt shall this time. I am setting up my dark room, and hope to send you some photos shortly. We live up a very steep incline and the only way to avoid perspiring through one's clothes is to be carried up in a chair. Some have four coolies but the hired ones generally only two. In summer a chair is indispensable.

I have been having lessons in Chinese Canton dialect from my boy. He is married and has a child. He looks about 18. My quarters are very comfortable but I expect to go on board the *Meeanee* next month for one month. April will be the next time, and in the typhoon season it is rather unpleasant sometimes as one can't get ashore. The last big typhoon that struck Hong Kong was in 1874. I wish you all a very happy New Year and heaps of them. I have called on Mrs. Barker and presented Miss Lathbury's card. She seems a nice woman. I met the General at dinner. He's a miniature man with a considerable carpet-bag but pleasant. The Medical officers here are none of them Irish, which is also an advantage. When coming from Kowloon we came across a tiny junk with an orange as an offer-ing to the Water god, and a man in it. It was a most delightful arrangement. None of the Chinese boatmen would touch it. The sampans are the ordinary small boats, and the entire family lives on one. The father, mother and children all row or steer and they sleep and eat and are born and die there.

If anybody falls overboard they may not be picked up as the water god would be annoyed, but they are at liberty to get out by themselves if they can. They assist foreigners sometimes as the water god does not want any but Chinese proper. There are supposed to be about 1200 pirates in Hong Kong in Chinatown. The police are Scotchmen, Sikhs or Chinese and they are most efficient, I believe. I saw a big Sikh with two Chinese prisoners marching them by their pigtails. The Sikhs are very handsome as a rule and most of them are six feet high and more.

One sees very few oblique eyes and eyebrows here, but I believe they are more common further north. All servants have to wear a cap when waiting and not to tie up their pigtails.

There are a good many women with crumpled up feet.

For the present, goodbye,
    best love to all
        ever your affectn
            HERJ

A. M. S. Mess
Queen's Gardens, Hong Kong
7.12.92

My Dear People,

I received your letters and news. I am very fit and like this place. The weather is delightfully cool and the people interesting. My whole time has been taken up this week in paying necessary calls. The place is full of people and too much so in my opinion. My boy continues his lessons in Chinese, and I now am competent to write at least 20 hieroglyphics but have not yet caught on to all the suppressed vowels and aspirates. I am to dine at the General's next Monday. The Governor was very civil and Miss Robinson is very pretty. I have not yet been introduced to her but no doubt that will happen on the 8th. I have run this too fine for the mail as it goes in ten minutes and I had to retire last night.

Better luck next week.
    Love to all
        ever your affectn
            HERJ

Queen's Gardens, Hong Kong
13th December 92

My Dear People,

I hope you are all fit. I am very well and enjoying the most lovely weather. Bright sun and cold air and all sorts of flowers and blossoming trees. I like this place so far. Dined with the General last night and P. Phillipps, Clare Horton's cousin, dined with me tonight. He is a very good chap with a large moustache. He is a subaltern in the Marine Artillery on the *Impérieuse*. I suppose Fred Walker will come out in the *Tamar* as she brings the relief crews to this station. She is expected to sail in a few days from Portsmouth or Plymouth. There is a frightful lot of calling to be done here on the various men of war and private individuals. I am going to Canton on the 23rd for 3 days to see it and shoot snipe. The Chinese are said to be decent quiet people, but try to get shot so as to get money out of the shooter. There has been a tiger in one of the villages near here but several people have had unsuccessful tries at it.

I have got a fox terrier puppy at last from one of our men going home on expiration of his service. A very promising little dog and bred out here so not very likely to die of fever as some imported ones do.

My Chinese progresses well and my boy continues satisfactory.

I interviewed Cantlie and he is very pleasant and has given me a standing invitation to come to his hospital and consulting room which is an immense advantage. I am to become a freemason on Friday next as it appears that this is the most economical lodge in existence. The ordeal is very alarming to one of the candidates who has been led to believe that a red hot poker comes into the ceremony.

Miss Robinson is very pretty. H. E. the Governor is a Suffolk-looking man with a beard and whiskers.

There are about 11 British, 2 Chinese and 1 Spanish man of war in harbour.

Dark room nearly finished. I work on it on my days of orderly duty. Am going to Stonecutter's Island for artillery gun practice on Thursday. 12 inch guns. We go in rickshaws here and the coolies wear the regular grass coats that one sees pictures of on Japanese fours. They are not allowed to wear their lounge hats on the pavement.

Now goodbye. Love to all, ever your affectn
HERJ

126

Hong Kong
21st December 1892

My Dear People,

I got your letters, some forwarded from Bombay and some direct. Today I have been to Stonecutters Island to take care of some artillery who were doing their annual firing. They nearly sank a junk which insisted on crossing at the wrong moment. Afterwards I went for a long walk to a place called Aberdeen on the south side of the island and shot some specimens. There are very beautiful butterflies here. I went to a meeting of the British Medical Association, Hong Kong branch, and a somewhat feeble paper and somewhat more feeble discussion afterwards. Did I tell you that I have got a fox terrier puppy 3 months old and he will be a very good dog I think. It is useful to have one as a watch dog. He barks at almost every Chinaman and if their pigtails are very long they tickle his fancy immensely. Parts of the island are extremely pretty. They keep their haystacks up trees which is a somewhat original plan. They are a very saving people and understand the value of manna to a nicety.

My boy is carrying on very well up to the present time and is intelligent. I am going to lunch with Picton Phillipps on Friday on board the *Impérieuse*.

She has some very nice and dependable guns and can go 16 knots, which is satisfactory. The buffalos here are very quaint beasts. I believe they are vicious at times. They are somewhat like the Scotch with very massive bodies and heads in a line with their necks. They milk them. The jungle is quite a new thing to me, and I got a thorn today 5 1/2 inches long and could not go through a thicket on account of the creepers. There are a good many sorts of orchids here on trees. The Canton expedition is all off as far as I am concerned as one of our people has become sick and three cannot be spared at once. Christmas day is the day after tomorrow and I go on the *Meeanee* then. It will be rather a nuisance but not so very bad. The *Meeanee* is about 500 yards from shore, perhaps more. I suppose Fred Walker will come in the *Tamar*.

Goodbye for this week
best love to all
ever your affectn
HERJ

30

FESTIVITIES AT THE MAN-MO TEMPLE

CHARLES J. H. HALCOMBE

Charles Halcombe was one of the many British members of the Imperial Maritime Customs of China. As the author of books with exuberant Victorian titles such as Tales of Far Cathay *and this excerpt from* The Mystic Flowery Land: A Personal Narrative, *he offered romantic descriptions of the exotic Orient, capturing the colours and bright lights of Hong Kong in the 1890s. The Man-mo Temple on Hollywood Road continues today to be high on the list of traditional tourist attractions. This photograph shows him with his wife.*

A t the western end of Hollywood Road, in Hongkong, and on the left-hand side, stands a temple called the Man-mo which was originally—at least, before the occupation of the island—a shrine where poor fishermen and travellers in that locality used to pay their respects and make their humble offerings to the God of the Fishermen and other deities there.

It had latterly fallen into an almost ruinous state, and in the middle of 1893 a subscription was made amongst the native population of the colony to effect repairs, rebuild a portion of the same, and add an extra sanctuary to it. The money having been liberally supplied for this purpose, the work was commenced, and was completed for the China New Year in 1894. The old temple now looked really imposing—its interior resplendent with huge brass vessels, incense brasiers, giant candlesticks, all highly polished, banners, scrolls and other ecclesiastical ornaments; and the exterior magnificently and tastefully embellished with square-shaped panels of artistically moulded scenes comprising animals, mountains, lakes, bridges, temples and palaces, all done in plaster and afterwards carefully painted over with specially prepared pigments, which resist the action of wind and weather for ages. The roof was covered with quaint and elaborate designs after the same style but on a much larger scale.

In celebration of this important event in the history of the temple, and to propitiate and congratulate its deities, another large fund was raised among the Chinese for the purpose of having a grand pageant and erecting a reception-house for the mighty Sky Dragon who would come down on earth to see the improvements made in the temple.

Great preparations went forward, and a magnificent spectacle was eagerly anticipated—thousands of sight-seers crowding into the colony from Canton and all parts of the surrounding country.

Outside the temple piles of long poles and bamboos of all sizes and lengths were brought—the former being fantastically painted in various bright-hued designs. With these a lofty scaffolding was soon raised to a height of one hundred or more feet, as the Chinese are particularly dexterous and rapid in this work. When this gigantic though fragile looking framework was complete, huge chests full of light mat-work panels, ornamented with effectively painted designs, appeared on the scene. These were soon emptied and the contents taken aloft and fitted, each into its proper place, forming a complete and gorgeous covering and lining for the framework—thus transforming it into a fairy-like fane [temple] of enormous dimensions from the roof of which flower-decked crystal chandeliers and silken-tasselled lamps of all sizes and descriptions . . . were suspended. Round the walls of the interior costly scrolls, some of great antiquity and value, pictures by native painters, and autograph verses and proverbs by famed poets, philosophers and dignitaries, were hung in artistic profusion.

In the centre and at the corners of the enclosure were ornamental stands for the musicians, around which were placed cages with bright-plumaged birds and pots of choice flowers and plants—many containing complete miniature trees, curiously stunted, and other cultivated freaks of nature.

At the beginning of the First Moon, in our February, festivities commenced in earnest. A splendid procession, costing thousands of dollars was formed. It was fully a mile in length and passed through every thoroughfare in the colony. First came the musicians headed by an enormous drum, beating cymbals and gongs and playing flutes, trumpets and other instruments too numerous and noisy to mention; then came hundreds of standard and screen bearers with vari-coloured silken banners, followed by gorgeously apparelled boys bearing arms and trophies. After these came fantastic stands with artificial trees upon whose branches were fixed young and beautiful girls in silk and satin star-spangled robes to represent heroines of history and romance. Behind these little 'Celestial' demoiselles came the younger sons of Han, also exquisitely dressed, carrying spears and bows and mounted on gaily comparisoned ponies which were led by male attendants clad in red cloth and bunting. Following these were miniature temples with clockwork figures, the former being made with remarkable skill and ornamented with the highly prized plumage of the king-fisher. Behind these came miniature 'flower-boats' each with its complement of enchanting demsels; and in their rear came huge monsters—animals with moving jaws and wagging tails, and reptile heads of great size, accompanied by boisterous clowns and lithesome acrobats who pleased the public greatly.

Following these were more musicians, models, figures, soldiers and standard-bearers; and finally the 'Sky Dragon' himself appeared in all its pomp and splendour—with jaws distended and glaring red eyeballs rolling in a fierce and truly hideous manner about their wide sockets. This monster was constructed with wonderful ingenuity—its scaly body, nearly two hundred yards in length . . . on either side the forms of the numerous bearers were partially hidden by folds of yellow bunting, only their legs being visible as they carried it along, from time to time being relieved by relays of strong coolies.

Onward went the gigantic monster, its side-bells ringing and its myriad of legs scuffling along, to the intense delight of the spectators upon whose closely packed heads one could have easily walked for miles, so dense was the crowd.

In front of the advancing dragon, danced two energetic harlequins carrying long ball-mounted poles with which they were supposed to direct the movements of this unearthly prodigy whose immense horned head moved impetuously from side to side in a most diabolical manner which must have impressed the awe-inspired spectators with its power and majesty; for they followed its every movement with staring eyes and gaping mouths. It was a sight they would never forget and might never see again.

In D'Aguilar Street some thrifty housewife had hung her washing out of a front window to dry; and as the procession advanced towards the house a great cry of rage and indignation was raised. The vast concourse came to a standstill and every eye was angrily fixed upon those fluttering clothes aloft there. They were a dastardly insult to the dignity and power of the mighty Sky Dragon and those accompanying it, and an omen of bad luck; and the procession could and would not proceed until they had been removed.

The poor guilty woman was nearly frightened out of her senses and wept bitterly that she should have thoughtlessly offended so great a deity. It is needless to say that her washing was soon taken in, and the procession moved on its course—the dragon's legs seeming to move all the merrier for the short rest.

The poor country folk were simply wonderstruck—they had never beheld or even imagined anything so grand and beautiful before; and would remember it to the end of their days. But the greatest surprise of all had been prepared for the evening. On the newly reclaimed spare ground facing the harbour, another lofty scaffolding had been raised, and this was covered from head to foot with every conceivable kind of firework. A spacious stand had been prepared for His excellency the Governor, Sir William Robinson and Lady Robinson, and the Chief English and Chinese officials. ▦

31

A LADY'S IMPRESSION OF HONG-KONG

MRS UNSWORTH

A speech by an intrepid lady traveller, first name not noted, read, it is stated, to the Manchester Geographical Society on Saturday, 30 June 1900. One can almost imagine the late-Victorian lady, probably with a large, plumed hat, sharing her experiences in the distant Colony with her eager listeners.

There has been within the last twenty years a growing interest taken in our own colonies. It may be that travelling has become so much cheaper and better, that we see more of one another. Formerly a person going out to Australia or the East seemed lost to his friends and relatives for the rest of his life, only a small percentage returning. If we look at a map of the world, the British colonies being marked in some vivid colour, Hong-Kong looks small and insignificant, but its importance is not to be estimated by its size alone. It is the position which makes it so valuable—first as a naval station, and secondly as a distributing centre for trade.

Being a British colony, the Chinese are not allowed to build such narrow streets or crowd together as much as they love to in their own cities. They are compelled by Government to observe some rules of sanitation; but they try to evade these as much as they can, and make their streets as narrow as they dare, and crowd them up with massive signboards hanging down, lines of clothing, and other obstacles. One can step out of Queen's Road into a dirty narrow street where the poorer Chinese are living in a miserable condition and keeping up all their unsavoury habits and customs.

The crowds in the streets are of all nationalities; of course, the Chinese predominating. On first impressions, the lower classes seem to have no difference of sex; men and women look the same, and one person the exact resemblance of another. But by and by you find out the men wear the long pigtail, whilst the women have a little knot of hair behind; and also, on closer observation, they begin to observe different features and expressions, some faces more attractive and some more repellent than others.

A Chinaman dearly loves a crowd, and to jostle and push, and there being so many of them, it would be impossible to get through some parts of the city if it were not for the policemen; some of them are Chinamen, some British; but the latter are mostly on duty at night time, whilst during the day the streets are kept in order by the Sikhs, very picturesque-looking individuals, with their coloured turbans and white uniforms, fine looking men, six feet high and more; these put the fear of men into the Chinese and keep the streets passable.

There are other national elements in Hong-Kong besides Europeans and Chinese. There is a large community of the Macao Portuguese, and there is also a Parsee community. With all these different nationalities, the streets present a very interesting spectacle. ▦

PART VI

AN ESTABLISHED COLONIAL CENTRE 1900s-1920s

'The fragrance of the East, essence of the Orient. . . . They call it Hong Kong—the Fragrant Port.'

HILARY METCALFE, 1900, IN *DYNASTY*

'And go you east or west, go always you must to Hong Kong, for it is a part that lies ever in your path, not obtrusively, but as a calling-place on your way to somewhere else.'

MARY A. POYNTER, 1914

A VICTORIAN INNOCENT

ROBERT ELEGANT

Robert Elegant spent many years in the Far East as a journalist. His novel, Dynasty, *covers the entire colonial history of Hong Kong to the 1970s. This opening chapter captures many of the attitudes prevalent among early Westerners, attitudes which happily have disappeared. In its entirety, this novel continues to be the most comprehensive and readable history of colonial Hong Kong in a single work of fiction.*

28 May, 1900

Mary Philippa Osgood was four weeks removed from the twentieth birthday that would, by the rigid standards of the late Victorian era, transform her from a young woman into a spinster. Never during the preceding nineteen years and eleven months had she been as acutely aware of her own body as she was at 8:15 on the morning of May 28, 1900. Dancing across the ruffled Pearl River Estuary, the gusts that swelled the vestigial sails of the *Orion* moulded her ankle-length dress to the curves of her bosom, her hips, and her legs.

Before leaving England seven weeks earlier, she had bought a new dress for £5, her Aunt Margaret's generous going-away gift. The motherly wife of the major commanding the home depot of the Royal Wessex Fusiliers had helped her select the long-wearing dark blue serge the Stepney mercers recommended as 'eminently suitable for summer'. But the 'lightweight' fabric was a sackcloth torment in the 92° heat and 93 per cent humidity when *Orion* left the fresh sea air behind on entering the western approaches to Hong Kong.

She had daringly discarded her camisole along with two of her three petticoats, and she wore her lightest stays. The major's wife had confided that the corsets suitable for the English summer could be agonizingly confining in the faraway, subtropical Crown Colony. . . .

'Miss Osgood, there it is, just over the horizon. You can see the loom against the clouds.'

Hilary Metcalfe's deep voice recalled her to a reality different from any she had known. *Orion* was steaming among rocky islets veined with emerald vegetation, which lay upon the wind-brushed sea like meteorites. In the distance on her left a wisp of smoke rose, and a dark shape that might have been a small craft bobbed beneath an elongated, vertical shadow that might have been a sail. She saw no other sign of human life. Yet her nostrils were assailed by unfamiliar odours that overcame the clean tang of the sea: wood-smoke and incense; an unpleasant mustiness and the reek of corruption; a nauseatingly fecal stench and a garlic-laden, many-spiced scent.

'The fragrance of the East, essence of the Orient,' Metcalfe rumbled in her ear. 'They call it Hong Kong—the Fragrant Port. There's the stench of decay, of course, but mainly the effluvia of the chief Chinese occupation—eating. There's wood-smoke, garlic, coriander, anise, vinegar, oyster sauce, dried fish, and barbecued pork. And, over all, dark brown, pungent soy-sauce.'

She had learned early in the voyage that Mr. Metcalfe was a pedant. She knew the type well, for she had earned her keep as a governess since her mother's death two years earlier. As she would not have a few months earlier, she applied the word to a man who seemed venerable at fifty-six. The journey had taught her that she was quicker, more forceful, and more perceptive than most young women in the sixty-second year of the reign of Her Most Excellent Majesty, Victoria, By the Grace of God of the United Kingdom of England, Scotland, Wales, Ireland, and of Her Other Realms and Territories over the Sea, Queen; Empress of India; Defender of the Faith. She guarded her knowledge of her capabilities, and she could flutter her eyelashes as fetchingly as the most hapless Victorian miss. Besides she had learned much from Hilary Metcalfe, who was neither patronizing nor importunate. She had also learned that she could bend Metcalfe and the ship's officers to her wishes, not only by feminine-guile, but by calm persistence.

'Perhaps the Chinese don't have enough to eat, Mr. Metcalfe,' she teased.

'Sometimes, Miss Osgood. But they're devoted, religiously devoted to their bellies—pardon an old man's directness. More than family, more than their gods, more than their Emperor, more than their—anything else, they're devoted to their bellies.'

'And to nothing else, Sir?'

'I didn't say that. The Chinese are also devoted to gold, and acquire wealth in many devious ways. They'll also labour hard— if they must. They are an ingenious race and a desperately industrious race, when all else fails. But they are also different from all other races.'

Hilary Metcalfe paused to formulate his words precisely, straining instinctively to give his best to his eager pupil.

'We have moved slowly over the seas and through the weeks from one pole of civilization to another. The curious sights you saw in the Mediterranean, the Near East, India, and the Straits Settlements were but a gradual transition. You have now arrived at the true Antipodes. Even the Japanese are not more strange.'

'How so, Mr. Metcalfe?' she asked.

Orion's captain had told her that the Metcalfes possessed much wealth amassed in the India trade. But Hilary Metcalfe worked as a clerk-interpreter in the Hong Kong trading house of Derwent, Hayes and Company, rather than tending his fortune in fashionable state. His occupation afforded him both opportunity and leisure to study the culture, the history, and the language of the Chinese. Though he might have taken a swift Peninsular and Oriental mail steamer that guaranteed passage to Hong Kong in just thirty-four days, his eccentricity had led him to sail on *Orion*, which was finally closing port on the fiftieth day after leaving the Pool of London.

Mary had been granted no such choice. The War Office, reluctant to disburse £60 for her passage on *Orion*, had flatly refused to pay a surcharge of ten guineas for a mail steamer. Only the cajoling of the major's wife had spared the lonely girl the rigours of a troopship, since her father was no more than the Bandmaster of the Regiment.

'How', Mary persisted, 'are the Chinese different?'

'How?' Hilary Metcalfe echoed her question. 'It's not just the clap-trap you've heard—men wearing skirts and women trousers, soup at the end of the meal, brides wearing red, mourners wearing white—though all true enough. Their minds are made different . . . antipodean, the other pole from ours. They'll scramble for a handful of coppers today, but disdain to plan to gain a bag of gold tomorrow. Hong Kong was a barren rock before we made it the world's third busiest port—soon, perhaps, the second.'

Mary gasped in pretty wonder, though she was as much concerned about commerce as she was about the dark side of the moon.

'We had to force the Chinese to trade,' Hilary Metcalfe continued, 'though they could've made Hong Kong or Canton their own goldmine. But they virtually compelled us to seize Hong Kong. And we get the lion's share. Some don't do badly, too shrewd not to. But the ruling classes, the Mandarins, profoundly despise trade—and despise us too.'

Hilary Metcalfe pondered the inner resonance of his own words. The broad head beneath his checked deer-stalker cap withdrew like a turtle's into his heavy shoulders. He gestured towards the surrounding islands.

Two objects bobbing on the water caught Mary's eye. One was pale grey, and its swollen curves glittered repellently. The other, equally distended, was a livid black. From each four small posts thrust upright like warped tables abandoned to the sea. She caught her breath, when a rising wave displayed the bloated carcasses of a pig and a dog keeping strange convoy in death.

The horizon was speckled with islands. Some barren grey, others richly green, all seemed to appear from the depths as the broom of the wind dispersed the morning mist. The *Orion* was winding through a narrow channel. On her right two shoe-shaped boats lay on a dun-brown beach. On the left, a cliff loomed on the verge of a large land mass.

'Hong Kong?' Mary asked. 'Hong Kong, finally? No it can't be. It must be China, the mainland, there.'

'Neither, Miss Osgood,' the Sinologue answered. 'That's Lantao, Rocky Mount. It's bigger than Hong Kong, the biggest island.' The Portuguese, who settled Macao three hundred and fifty years ago, called these islands the Ladrones—the Thieves. They were home for a nest of pirates until we began cleaning them out sixty years ago. Pirates are still about, though they'll not bother us. But these islands are still the Ladrones. The big thieves've driven out the little thieves. Haphazard Chinese theft's given way to organized European theft.'

'You sound as if you too hated the English. Do you really despise us?'

'Despise the English, Miss Osgood?' Mr. Metcalfe rallied. 'Hardly. It would hardly do to despise myself. We've done fearful deeds here, but we've also done some magnificent things.'

'Fearful *and* magnificent things, Mr. Metcalfe?' Mary prompted.

'Yes, both. Hong Kong was a barren, fever-ridden island of a few hundred fishermen and pirates, no more. We made it a great port. But we taught the people to hate us—and to fawn on us. We forced opium on them. The mansions you'll see aren't built on rock, but on the noxious juice of pretty poppies.

'You know, Miss Osgood, at this moment in Peking, the Chinese are rising. The Boxers, we call them. The Righteous Harmonious Society, they call themselves. A devil-worshipping sect that claims esoteric powers is stealthily backed by the Court of the Empress Dowager. The Boxers claim they can't be killed by our bullets. Nonsense, of course. But they know what they want. No nonsense about that. They're sworn to expel us from China. They want our blood.'

'*Our* blood, Sir?'

'*Our* blood, *your* blood, Miss Osgood. We've forced their hands, forced the Chinese to trade with us when they wanted only to be left alone. We've done so with guns and arrogance, with rapine and destruction and slaughter.'

'My father wrote we had to keep the upper hand or they'd be at our throats.'

'He's right, perhaps. So most people believe. But why? In part, because we've always kept them apart in Hong Kong, even farther apart than they wanted to keep us in China—the Chinese and the British are two different species, not different races. Between the two—a few Chinese we've won over, a few who co-operate for gain, a few *déclassé* Portuguese, and some Eurasians . . . mixed bloods, your pardon, Miss Osgood. We've driven the Chinese, but they've done the work. They've sweated to build this British paradise in the Orient.'

'You feel very strongly.'

'That I do!' Mr. Metcalfe forced a chuckle. 'Your father tells you we must keep the upper hand. He'll probably tell you the

Chinese all hate us, that we can't trust one of them. He may tell you that a single drop of Chinese blood in a great Eurasian gentleman like Sir Jonathan Sekloong or that promising young man, Robert Hotung, makes him less than a man—neither proper Chinese pagan nor good British Christian.

'But such men have served us well—and served China well. Ten centuries ago, their ancestors were living with civilized grace on the mainland just over to the north. No hive of bandits, thieves, and pirates, the mainland was a cultivated community. Yet I grow too heated—and there is Hong Kong.' . . .

Mary shuddered involuntarily as the vista of the harbour opened before her. She would, she knew, stay no longer than a year before the Regiment was posted home to England. But her blood throbbed as if she had come to a long-awaited rendezvous in a place that was outlandishly strange, yet fragrant with ancient memories. She was, at once, exhilarated and terrified.

'Quite different from what you pictured, but still somehow familiar, isn't it, Miss Osgood?'

Mr. Metcalfe's voice in her ear was almost drowned by the shrieking siren. She looked up half-fearfully at his blunt features dominated by the brooding grey eyes that had uncannily discerned her own feelings.

'I'll leave you now,' the deep, gentle voice said. 'It's better to see Hong Kong for the first time alone. Please don't forget you can reach me at Derwent's if you can find time from the round of gaiety—or if you need help.'

She nodded abstractedly. Why, she wondered, should she need Hilary Metcalfe's help? But the unease evoked by his remark was forgotten when she gazed upon the panorama of Hong Kong.

The harbour was forested with masts: the rope-and-wood tracery of sailing ships' masts crossed by square yards; the blunt masts of steamers; and the light-grey warships, tripod masts like little Eiffel Towers. Multitudes of wooden Chinese junks skittered through that forest under their fabric sails. The all-pervading medley of odours was already as warmly familiar as the aroma of new-baked bread. For the first time, Mary told herself self-consciously, she knew that she had come to China. ▩

33

JOHN CHINAMAN AT HOME

THE REVEREND E. J. HARDY

The Reverend Hardy, also the author of How to be Happy Though Married, *spent over three years in Hong Kong as chaplain to the British Forces. An irrepressible story-teller, Hardy knew Western society in Hong Kong well—and had opinions on everything else.*

When I went to China I had a great ambition. It was to gain the distinction of not writing a book on that country. I failed to do this because of the fascination of the subject. The population of Victoria, the capital of the island, and of Kowloon opposite it is 324,631 Chinese and 18,581 non-Chinese. Most of the Chinese are males; they leave their wives at Canton, from whence they come, because they do not trust European morals or because these ladies can live cheaper there. Do the grass widowers want their clothes mended? There are women wearing owlish spectacles who sit at street-corners and earn a living with their needle.

The Governor, the two Admirals, the General, and the Chief Justice lead society, and the Bishop blesses their doings as far as he conscientiously can. Of the civilians in Hong Kong, all that we shall say is that some are nicer than others. The number ones, twos and even threes of the great commercial firms are sometimes social successes. There are distinctions, however, that are not easy to understand. Why should pig-iron turn up its nose at tenpenny nails? To this distant land people come with double names that sound formidable until it is discovered that the double-barrelled ones discharge very small shot at home. The Service people call the civilians dollar-snatchers, and the latter think of the former as dollar-lackers.

Dancing days and nights begin with the three practice dances that precede the ball which is given by Scotch residents on each

St. Andrew's night. The great difficulty men have is to get partners, so few unmarried girls are in the colony. Here it is men and not women who are wall-flowers.

If men cannot get partners for a dance unless they bespeak them days before, it is even more difficult to get them for life. Owing to this scarcity of wife material, as well as to impecuniosity, young European men, instead of marrying, form themselves into bachelor messes. Just before leaving Hong Kong, I dined at one of these establishments. It was monstrous. There were six mere men daring to have as nice a drawing-room, as well arranged a table, and as good servants as any house I have seen run by that old institution—a wife. It was unnatural, and a committee of women should come out to break up the mess before the offenders get too much into the habit of celibacy and make a mess of their lives. The poor fellows are starved at heart, however, replete in stomach, and each starts a dog for companion. Alas! some of them go to the dogs in other ways. A ten-thousand-miles-away-from-home feeling has many temptations connected with it.

Polo is played all the year round, but the ponies do not appear to have their hearts in the work. Games can be found in the New Territory, and for those who can content themselves with clay pigeons there is a gun-club in Hong Kong.

The L. R. C.—that is, Ladies' Recreation Club, or, as some read it, Ladies' Recrimination Club, is managed with great care by ladies. Gentlemen are eligible as subscribers.

If England had taken all China in 1841 (considering her opportunities her moderation is wonderful!) instead of only Hong Kong, she could have made a Chinese army that would have held the world at bay.

34

INTERCEPTED LETTERS

FROM 'BETTY'

The author of these exuberant epistles, known only as 'Betty', clearly understood the foibles of Hong Kong society at the turn of the century. Frivolous? Absolutely. But deadly accurate, one suspects.

Brighton, Feb. 14th, 1905

T hese letters originally appeared in the *China Mail*, to the genial and courteous proprietor of which Journal I am indebted for permission to reproduce them.

I believe that the correct thing, in a stupendous work of this kind, is to put an index at the end giving the real names of all the people that appear in its pages. I have prepared such an index but have been advised to withhold it for the present. In the wildly improbable event, however, of the first edition selling like hot cakes, it is conceivable that the second edition may appear with an index attached. I make no promise.

I trust that the letters furnish a fairly accurate and not unpleasing picture of Hongkong life.

BETTY

The Peak
Hongkong, Sept. 14, 1903

MY DEAR NELL,

At last I find time to write and tell you that we have survived our honeymoon and the long voyage out here, and have arrived safely in this land of dragons and yellow devils, and I am glad to be able to say that, tho' we have been married for nearly two whole months, the other person is still as devoted as ever. . . .

My dear Nell, I'm simply dying to tell you what I started to write, and if I'd only left those three lines you'd have been dying to know the rest. But I had to blot them out because my short experience of Hongkong has already taught me that a married woman who desires peace and happiness must learn to control her tongue and must *never never repeat* nasty things about people. Now, my dear, I desire both peace and happiness, and I like to be on good terms with everybody—rather a difficult task in Hongkong, I must say—and it's no use holding the paper up to the light because I've already tried it and you can't make out one single word that way.

A full and faithful account of Society and its doings in Hongkong was what I promised you, Nell, but I hardly know where to begin—there is so much to tell. I think I had better send you a series of letters telling you of our various frivolities and odd ways of amusing ourselves in this far-off spot.

Well, to begin, Hongkong, as far as I can make out on so short an acquaintance, seems to be divided into—

1. The Peak, a would-be mountain dotted over with bungalows and villas, wherein live the elect.
2. The lower levels, inhabited by the great business population.
3. Kowloon, where the soldier-folk come from.

The Peak looks down on everything and everybody. The lower levels look up to the Peak, while Kowloon is supremely indifferent to both.

Personally, I cannot quite make up my mind whether I should like to be a Mrs. Taipan (a Taipan, my dear, is the head of a firm and his yearly income is something 'normous) or a Mrs. Service. In the first case, you have lots of money, and can walk about with your nose in the air like a high-born aristocrat and live like a hot-house flower; while in the second case you have a very good time and are only slightly patronized by the Taipans. It is quite easy, let me tell you, to be a Mrs. Service, for I am told, that if your uncle or your grandfather, or even your brother-in-law, was or is a soldier or sailor, you may lay claim to be included.

Just at this time of the year it is so awfully hot here that there is very little going on except bathing-parties, and they take place on every day of the week, each being run separately by some leading lady with a large capacity for management and business. This is the way it's done. The party meets at one of the piers, of which there are lots in Hongkong, takes a tea-and-cake-laden steam-launch to some remote quiet spot where has been built in anticipation a mat-shed divided into stalls, in which we women-folk disrobe. It is always pitch dark in these stalls, and the places between the floor-boards are so wide that you often run the risk of losing a necessary garment. Still, it's good fun, on the whole. . . .

One good lady nicknamed 'The Angel' is most persevering and energetic and carries all before her—especially the water. She is fair, fat and forty, and her efforts are most praiseworthy tho' perhaps a trifle painful. It may interest you to know why she is so named.

Some years ago, a big fancy-dress ball was given here in the City Hall, and the good lady of whom I'm writing decided to anticipate events and become an angel, of the type depicted on Xmas cards, before her time. Now wings and harps won't fit well into a rick-shaw or a chair, and our Angel, realizing this, made up her mind to walk to the Hall. To protect her spotless and snow-white feet, she drew over them a pair of black woolen stockings. On arriving in the ladies' dressing-room, the arranging to perfection of the wings and hair took so much time that she forgot all about her poor feet, and danced through the first set of Lancers before she discovered her mistake. It must have been a unique sight—*an angel with black legs!!!*

Well, Nell, I think I have written about as much as you will care to read this week, but I shall write again soon. William sends his remembrances; he has been badly bitten by a sea-urchin and it has tried his temper a bit.

—Yours,
BETTY

The Peak
Hong Kong, October, 1903

MY DEAR NELL,

Last week, the bathing season ended in a series of moonlight picnics—a most delightful form of entertainment. The first one I went to I particularly enjoyed. We started off in a launch at 5.30, and cruised about for some hours in a perfectly calm sea; all we women-folk made ourselves happy crowded together in the stern, and, as the men vanished to enjoy their cigars we were able to indulge in a little domestic conversation. I am a little out of the know in the matter of things domestic as yet—having only so recently arrived here and being still a bride—but one learns a great deal by listening.

I learnt, for instance, a great deal about Chinese servants: how your 'boy' only lives for the sake of 'squeezing'; the manner in which your cook makes pastry (too horrible for words, my dear) and how he washes his feet in the soup tureen; how your 'amah' wears your stockings and steals your handkerchiefs—in fact, from all accounts that night, your servants leave you your life and that is all.

Well, to return to the picnic, we landed at a place called 'Deep Water Bay'; had dinner; then a moonlight stroll and then returned to our launch *en route* for home. Somehow, on the return journey I did not feel that longing to possess domestic virtues which I'd felt on the outward journey, and so I managed without great difficulty to persuade—*William*—to take me to a peaceful corner where we could enjoy a quiet cigarette. I think, on the whole, I enjoyed the return journey most; the moonlight *was* so lovely and a cigarette is very soothing.

The dancing season will soon be here now; I hear St. Andrew's Ball is the great event of the season—I have never been to a 'St. Andrew's' yet, but I shall duly report on its fascinations later on.

My dear, I had nearly forgotten to tell you one thing: I've got the golf fever. There is a very fine links here with at least one natural bunker. This year, for the first time in the history of Hongkong, the members of the Royal Hongkong Golf Club have most kindly and generously allowed us poor down-trodden women one afternoon in the week—Thursday to wit, a day on which they can't get off early themselves on the links because of its being so near to mail day. On this day, we are allowed, not only to play round the course, but even to come inside the sacred enclosure of the Club House railings to drink a cup of tea. Before this magnanimous rule was made, we had to drink our tea standing outside the fence. Their generosity does not stop here—some men even condescend to play with us when their letters are written off early!! I *do* think men are *so* unselfish, don't you? Well, Nell, adieu for this time—more news next time.

—Yours,
BETTY

The Peak,
Hongkong, June 4th, 1904

MY DEAR NELL,

I have a confession to make. I had set my heart on such a gem of a jade bracelet, and I was awfully afraid some one else would snap it up, and I had been outrunning my allowance and I simply *dared* not ask William for the money. In despair I sent copies of my letters to you to the leading local paper, and, joy of joys! they are accepted and printed in due course. To see one's self in print for the first time is one of the most delicious and thrilling sensations that I know. When the second letter appeared I was not quite so excited. When the third letter appeared I was mercenary enough to calculate how much nearer to the jade bracelet I had arrived. I found I was exactly thirty cents nearer. As a matter of fact all the payment I had received was a complimentary copy of the paper each time my letters appeared.

Oh, Nell, I cried and cried and cried. It wasn't because of the bracelet; it was because the market value of my literary effort was presumably only *a farthing a yard*! . . .

Then the editor wrote again hoping I would accept 'the enclosed cheque' it was quite a substantial one, and after paying for the bracelet I bought a Panama hat with the change, and hoping I would continue to give his readers the pleasure of reading 'my charming letters to Miss Eleanor'. Very nicely put, wasn't it, Nell?

He went on to say that he had been afraid of offending me by sending a cheque in the first instance because his other lady contributors were all too proud to accept any remuneration for their literary services. I wrote back by return to say that I would go on writing, and that I wasn't at all proud. Then he sent me some instructions which he requested me to observe. Common-sense had already suggested them to me, all except the last. The last was silly, as you will see, and also rather impertinent. 'I want', he wrote, 'the maximum of description of Hongkong and Hong-kong life and the minimum of 'William' and your own domestic differences.'

I shall give it him and straight from the Guide Book. 'The population of Hongkong consists of 283,905, of whom 274,543 are Chinese.' The population of Hong Kong as far as I am con-cerned consists of William and about three hundred more, none of whom is Chinese. All of them, however, can read, while most of them *do* write—of course they all write, but I mean that many of them have by means of manuscript or print stamped their names on the literature of the age.

Unobservant critics have gone away and written that Hongkong thinks and dreams nothing but dollars. This is entirely wrong, because I have never been to any place where people were so free, with their money.

I believe, on the other hand, that this is the most prolific liter-ary workshop for its size in the whole world.

I know of heaps of manuscripts that are blushing unseen in their owners' desks. It makes my pulse beat quicker sometimes to think that 'one mute inglorious Kipling here may dwell—.'

Many more waste their sweetness on the limited air of Hongkong through the medium of the four daily papers. These papers aim at a very high literary standard; they cull the very cream of the World's contemporary journalism which they use merely as a set-ting for the local gem. I am sorry to say, however, that a five-dollar advertisement for my lost kitten once crowded out a sweet little poem written by a very clever and dear friend of mine. . . .

But *revenons a nos moutons*—l mean let us revert to William. I don't know whether I told you before, but, he first came out to Hongkong because some girl at home threw him over. On the voyage out he wrote a colossal and melancholy story of love unre-quited in which all the women were bad and died old, while all the men were good and die young—mostly by committing sui-cide. After William had been six months in Hongkong he had forgotten all about the faithless heroine, but when he saw the high esteem accorded to literary people here he began to examine the story from the point of view of a work of art.

After changing all the names of places and substituting Hongkong ones, he managed to persuade a local firm to publish it in book form 'on spec.'

It turned out to be about the worst 'spec' that this particular firm ever embarked on. Seventeen copies were sold at the Star Ferry bookstall to unwary globe-trotters; the rest of the edition hung fire and was finally given away in single copies 'with the author's compliments.' I remember receiving a copy in England and being awfully proud of it. . . .

I must finish—I think I must have written nearly a column by this time—in my next I shall tell you about our visit to Macao.

—Ever yours,
BETTY

THE 1906 TYPHOON

ABBAS EL ARCULLI

Abbas el Arculli wrote this essay as a fifteen-year-old student at Hong Kong's Queen's College. From a Sunni Muslim Hong Kong family of Indian origins, but with a Chinese grandmother, Abbas grew up to be a solicitor, a

Arculli Brothers,

MERCHANTS and COMMISSION AGENTS,

64, QUEEN'S ROAD CENTRAL, HONGKONG.

Telegraphic Address: "CURLY." Telephone No. 409.

SOLE AGENTS FOR:—

SEAMING TWINES of Messrs. Linificio & Canapificio Nazionale of Milan, Italy.

"ACORN BRAND" ELASTIC BOOT WEB and BOOT LOOPING of Messrs. Flint, Pettit & Flint, of Leicester, England.

Justice of the Peace, and the unofficial leader of the local Indian community. While some relatives stayed with the Arculli family business, his grand-nephew, Ronald Arculli has continued the legal tradition as a member of the Legislative Council in the 1990s.

O n Monday the barometers in the island fell slowly and there was nothing to warn the people in the Observatory that there would be a typhoon in a short time until eight o'clock on Tuesday morning when the barometers fell suddenly and fierce gusts of wind blew over the island. That was the beginning. The *Tamar* fired the Typhoon Gun at five minutes past eight o'clock, but it was too late. Ships could not get up steam quickly enough nor could junks and sampans find shelter in so short a time. Between the hours of nine and ten, the storm was at its height. The sea was white with foam, and the waves were as high as mountains.

After the typhoon, the harbour presented a terrible appearance. Near Jardine's Pier the sea was covered over with wreckage and even now people can walk over it. Dead bodies can be found there, and the smell arising from them is intolerable. The reason for this enormous damage is that the boating population was unprepared for the storm: when the typhoon came, those boats that were out at sea were sunk, and those that were near the shore had not enough time to find safe anchorage. Some of the boats, while trying to find shelter, smashed into one another or into vessels greater than themselves, such as men-of-war.

The King has telegraphed his sympathy, as well as the governors of Macao, Singapore, Mauritius, etc. Launches are still sent out daily to recover dead bodies, and yesterday, two Chinese gunboats were sent by the Viceroy of Canton to help in the search.

As proof of the havoc wrought by the typhoon, a naval officer says that though he had seen cyclones, tornadoes and other storms, he never saw such damage done by a storm as that done by the recent typhoon. The first warning that their ship had of the typhoon was the blowing away of the wireless telegraphy apparatus.

When the sea was rough, some of the boats smashed onto the sides of the man-of-war, and the sailors had hard work to effect rescues. The first boat that smashed into the vessel contained an old man and an old woman. The sailor threw ropes to them, but instead of tying themselves to them, they tied some old clothes and banknotes to the ropes. Then a sailor seeing this, jumped down to the boat, tied the couple to some ropes and had them hauled up on board the man-of-war. ▩

36

A LADY'S TRAVEL JOURNAL

MARY A. POYNTER

Back in the days when sea voyages consumed weeks and months, writing was a suitable occupation for well-bred ladies. Here, in her journal published as Around the Shores of Asia *are the Hong Kong entries from one such trip. Mary Poynter accompanied her husband, a British official, on a trip to the Middle and Far East in connection with the Turkish Salt Monoploy. She appears to have made good use of her time.*

March 27th, 1914

The wild monsoon continues, and our captain, realizing he cannot make Hong-Kong harbour in time to disembark his passengers, kindly goes some miles out of his course to get into quieter waters near shore; giving those who had suffered acutely from *mal-de-mer* a chance to come on deck (their chairs being placed in quiet shelter in the captain's own corner) and to revive, after the storm and stress of much pitching and tossing and twisting of our miniature boat where the rather primitive passenger accommodation was all placed aft.

Hong-Kong, March 28th, 1914

We were in a way unprepared for and most pleasantly surprised with Hong-Kong as seen from the sea and with the island-encircled, far-spreading harbour as seen from the land. It seems as if this fair port has a right to feel aggrieved that its praises have not been more widely sung—that somebody has not placed it alongside the harbours of Smyrna, Bombay and Naples for beauty. Its typhoons alone seem to be widely advertised, and they, now that science predicts the exact hour, force and direction of their coming from their haunts and places of brewing in the eastern islands of the China Sea, do not fill the breasts of navigators with quite so much trepidation as formerly. Then, too, typhoons have only restricted areas and seasons of their own; their visitations to the winding waters of the harbour of Hong-Kong are not of daily or even monthly occurrence. And Hong-Kong island sits for the most part in placid majesty and an even, damp temperature throughout the year. Whether you sail in by day or by night, it has a compelling attraction. By day its abrupt, almost perpendicular green heights,

with embowered houses nestling here and there, almost to the very summit of the Peak, with the city itself, Victoria by name (though seldom called by its rightful appellation), at its base in the foreground make immediate appeal. At night, with the thousands of ships' lights in the harbour, with the city's own illumination and the twinkling lights all along the Peak that make it difficult when looking up to tell where the stars on land leave off and those in the sky begin, it appeals perhaps still more.

And go you east or west, go always you must to Hong-Kong, for it is a part that lies ever in your path, not obtrusively, but as a calling-place on your way to 'somewhere else'....

If nature is generous on the Peak at Hong-Kong so is the hospitality within doors—and generous is the hospitality throughout all the East for that matter. We lunched on one side of the Peak with wide views of islands and far glimpses of the China Sea in the distance, and tea was served to us in a garden at the other side overlooking the mainland of Kowloon, that looked blue and impressive if somewhat barren of vegetation. Among the familiar family pets of the children in this latter garden was a turkey, destined originally for the Christmas feast, but saved from its fate by virtue of unusual turkey perspicacity and signs of devotion. He would strive forward with a friendly gobble to be spoken to and to have his feathers stroked as naturally as the two little woolly 'chow' puppies. When tea was forthcoming he waited in dignified silence near the tea table for the biscuit that was to be his portion; in this instance, his portion not being bestowed with the usual promptitude, he strode forth to the front, spread out his fine tail feathers in a circular fan, and gobbled for notice. He secured amused attention and his biscuit immediately, but I am sorry to have to add that when our backs were turned he marched to the tea table and purloined a sandwich without gobble or warning of any kind to announce his intention.

To add excitement to life on the Peak, word was about that a tiger's footprints, 'pugs' as they are called, had been seen in various places; that the originator of the pugs had even been seen by one of the Indian policemen, a stalwart Rajput with fierce black beard parted down the centre, and others, and a price was put upon the striped cat's head. He was supposed to have swum across from the mainland and was shy in his fresh surroundings, decoys of calves and sheep failing to attract him; but ladies living outside the city limits were a little timid about setting forth in their sedan chairs to festivities after nightfall as long as the island could furnish plain proofs of the mark of the beast!

37

GANGSTERS & HAT-SNATCHERS

KENNETH A. ANDREW

At the age of 101, Kenneth Andrews was still living on his own, exercising every day on his stationary bicycle, and reminiscing about his exciting days with the police force in Hong Kong. The writing style of his memoirs, Chop Suey, *is informal and direct, and the earthy feeling of 'this is how we caught the bad guys' is quite charming.*

My story can be said to touch upon the period between 1912 and 1938. Being young and of an adventurous turn of mind, I applied to the Crown Agents for a post in the Hong Kong Police Force, since honoured by Her Most Gracious Majesty Queen Elizabeth II with the prefix of 'Royal' and it is with very great pride that I now claim to have been a member of the Royal Hong Kong Police Force for over a quarter of a century. . . .

This gun-running business was a most serious and heinous crime because we never knew when we might be faced by an armed criminal holding in his hand one of these very weapons that had been smuggled into the colony. I know from my own personal experience how very savage and cruel the Chinese gangster can be, for on several occasions I was obliged to tackle some of these gangs. On one occasion, acting upon information I set a trap for a gang of eight such men, and after a savage gun battle I and my party of police were able to account for the whole gang. These men attacked a distillery in Kowloon and from the start showed they were determined to shoot it out with us and not give in. The battle ended with a count of four dead bodies and the capture of four live gangsters; there were actually nine men in the gang, but one of them swam out to sea and was not seen again; his revolver was found on the beach and we presumed the man drowned.

PRISONERS WEARING WOODEN COLLAR.
They are thus paraded before the people.

Fortunately the only police casualties were one Chinese detective stabbed in the hand, and another who had a bullet hole in his hat, but this we did not discover until after we had returned to our station.

It is not the case that the police always have such luck in the matter of trying to arrest armed men; we have had some pretty awful tragedies. One gangster who tried to take my life was armed with a point four-five revolver; having filed his bullets across the nose, thus making them into what were virtually dum-dum bullets; it can be imagined the amount of damage such bullets would have caused me if I not had the good fortune to get my own bullets off first; I shot the man dead. The life of the Hong Kong policeman can be full of pleasant and unpleasant features, but still, life on the whole was interesting because one never knew what would crop up next.

It was not a case of arresting criminals all the time; there were many other things to occupy the time. In my early days in Hong Kong it was the custom to put convicted criminals in stocks as part of their punishment. The stocks were placed on the public footpath as near to the scene of the crime as possible; a Chinese or Indian constable would be in attendance. The prisoner would have a large placard hanging from his neck giving details of his offence, punishment, etcetera. He would spend four hours in the stocks on the first day of his sentence, and another four hours on the last day. The main object of the use of stocks was to cause the offender to lose 'face', as there is nothing a Chinese detests more than this.

One of the main methods of stealing was by snatching the gold jewellery from women. Chinese females are very fond of wearing gold ear-rings, hairpins and neckchains and the like, all of which to the expert snatcher are easy meat. It is sometimes difficult to tell whether such an offence is just 'larceny person' or the more serious crime of 'robbery with violence'. In snatching an ear-ring it is often the case that the victim will suffer damage to her ear. The snatcher will creep up behind his victim and with a deft movement will possess himself of the gold earring and will be off like a shot down a side street before the alarm can be raised.

I recall a case in the Wanchai district when a gold neckchain, together with a small gold crucifix was snatched from the neck of a prostitute by a thief who immediately ran off with his loot. The lady in question was standing at her doorway awaiting business, when her neckchain was snatched. She blew her police whistle (all Chinese carry one) and a crowd of onlookers soon appeared as is usual in such cases. Among those people there was a Chinese detective who gave chase, and within a few steps managed to capture the thief.

At no time was the thief out of view, but when the detective reached his man there was no sign of the neckchain. A search of the vicinity was made but no neckchain could be found. The thief was taken back to the woman, who at once identified the man. The thief resolutely denied knowledge of the affair and when asked why he ran away, he replied that when the police whistle was blown, he, with others, had run to see what was going on. The woman was adamant that this was indeed the man who had robbed her, and on this the detective had no choice but to arrest the man and charge him accordingly. At the time of the arrest the man was searched by the detective, and at the police station he was again searched, but no sign of the missing necklace could be found. Here surely was a case of 'one word against another' but upon the suspect's finger prints being taken it was found that this man had no fewer than six previous convictions for snatching jewellery. This was very promising from the police point of view, but of course we could not mention, or produce these convictions until such time as the magistrate trying this case was satisfied that the defendant was guilty as charged. . . .

The thief was sentenced to six months imprisonment plus 'six-of-the-best' on admission. Birching was included in the sentences of persons found guilty of using physical violence. During the trial the thief objected in no small voice to being found guilty; 'If I stole that neckchain and, as the detective says, I was kept under observation up to the time I was arrested why was the thing not found on my person? The police have made a very big mistake here.'

On admission to the prison the man was searched in the usual way, but nothing incriminating was found on him. Before the birching was carried out, the prison doctor inspected the prisoner to certify him as being fit to receive a birching. The inspection proved satisfactory, and the man was then placed across a bench for his dose of birching. On the very first stroke with the birch the man let out a loud yell and from his mouth there dropped the missing neckchain and crucifix intact. It had been under the man's tongue from the moment it had been snatched!

From the prison I received a somewhat friendly but slightly sarcastic note, suggesting that in future all prisoners should be properly searched before admission to gaol. All the same, it was good to be able to report 'property recovered'. It also pleased us because we now knew we had not got the wrong man after all.

A common form of larceny was what we termed 'hat snatching'. The hat thief would ever be on the look-out for a foreigner wearing a nice hat and riding in a ricksha. The snatcher would, with or without the connivance of the ricksha puller, set himself out to snatch the hat. He would simply run behind the ricksha and at the opportune moment snatch the hat from the passenger and disappear down a side street. Many a good Stetson went this way. There was always a ready market for stolen hats and no questions asked.

Another type of thief was the dishonest ricksha coolie who would rob a passenger who was the worse for drink. It was a common thing for a European, who after a good time at a local hotel would engage a ricksha to take him home or to the wharf. This type of robbery was simple to operate, the risk of capture or detection being small. The drunken passenger after having given instructions as to his desired destination would promptly fall asleep. The ricksha coolie would change course and take his passenger to the Happy Valley area or some similar spot, where at the right moment he would either tip his ricksha up backwards and deposit his passenger out on the roadway at the rear or else tip the vehicle forwards and throw his passenger out at the front. It did not really matter which method was adopted, for the result was the same. The poor passenger would be slightly concussed perhaps or was so stunned as to render him incapable of knowing what was going on. The ricksha coolie would quickly find the passenger's wallet and decamp with it, of course taking his ricksha along as well. . . .

Another serious type of theft was the stealing of children, mostly boys. In some cases it was just a kidnapping for ransom, but as often as not it was a case of stealing for re-sale. In the Po On district of what is now Communist China in Kwangtung [Guangdong] Province, many of the male population seek their livelihood in America, Canada and Australia and seldom go back to their motherland to visit their wives and families. This is bad because according to Chinese custom it is imperative that a male child shall carry on the family name for the purpose of ancestor worship. In Po On, therefore, there is a ready market for such stolen boys.

Nothing in this world is sacrosanct; there will always be somebody who will find a way to steal anything. The wardrobe thief is such a one; he does not steal wardrobes, but is satisfied with taking the contents. This fellow operates without even entering a house or flat. He does his work from the outside, his working tools being simply two very thin but very strong bamboo canes, at the end of one of which he inserts two nails. This thief confines his activities to ground-floor foreign style premises, and is a confounded nuisance. This fellow operates mostly during hot weather when occupants have to sleep with open windows. Most of these windows are protected by metal grilles but these do not deter the wardrobe thief. With the aid of his two bamboo sticks he can open a locked wardrobe and extract the contents with no trouble at all. With the stick with the two nails at the end he will open the wardrobe door, and with the other stick he will slide the coat hangers down to the window where he will be able to pull them through the grille and make away with the clothing he has purloined. If the alarm should be raised he will simply scamper off leaving his two sticks behind; a couple of bamboo sticks don't cost much. There have been instances where the wardrobe thief has actually operated in an occupied bedroom. The occupants did not discover their loss until daybreak. . . .

And finally, there was a very early morning in Kowloon when I received information that an armed gangster was sleeping at an address in Canton Road. I quickly drew up my information and a warrant, and took these along to the Kowloon Y.M.C.A. where there was a magistrate in residence.

It was around 7 a.m. when I awakened the magistrate and told him of my problem. He agreed to sign my warrant but did not have a Bible. I had not taken a Bible with me as I expected a Y.M.C.A. would have several copies. The magistrate asked me to go down to the library on the ground floor, and there I was sure to find a Bible. Believe it or not, after a thorough search I could find no trace of a Bible, and as time was so very important I sought out a likely looking volume which I took up to the magistrate. On this I swore that the contents of my information were, to the best of my knowledge, true. I got the magistrate's signature on my warrant which I duly executed, resulting with the arrest and conviction of the armed gangster.

The title of the book upon which I swore my information was *The Life of Nelson.* I know it was naughty of me, but there are times when you have to bend the rules a bit. I just could not allow my gangster to get away through a mere formality. ▨

38

OPIUM & INGENUITY

S. H. PEPLOW & M. BARKER

Ah, the mysterious Orient! Peplow, as a government official, collected
yards of exotica to entertain and educate (in that order) Westerners
in his book Hongkong: Around and About. *There was a fascination*
with the opium process, from smuggling to boiling, which did not
become illegal in Hong Kong until after World War II.

A great problem for the government of the Colony is the
opium question. By law opium is a government monopoly
and may only be imported and sold by accredited agents
under strict supervision, but there is a vast trade in illicit opium
which it is almost impossible to trace and control.

The illicit opium used in the divans [opium dens] is chiefly
composed of raw Chinese opium boiled in the Colony, in many
cases on the premises of the divan keeper. He is supplied with
small quantities, prepared or raw, generally not more than half a
tael of the former or up to six taels of the latter being stocked at
one time. Regular dealers send women and children to deliver
daily to the various divans, many of which are managed by paid
keepers, while the real owner keeps discreetly in the background
and is rarely caught.

After some time, a valuable good-will attaches to a floor or
cubicle which has become a popular divan, and although it may
have been raided, the keeper convicted, and his smoking apparatus
confiscated, it is not very long before the same place is opened
again under a new keeper. In some instances the tenant of a floor
charges a regular fee each night for allowing one of the cubicles
to be used as a divan; so one man may run it for a few days, and
then hand it over to another. In one case the same floor was
found to have been used as a divan no less than five times in

succession. The keepers were convicted and some sent to prison, but the only thing that put an end to the career of this place as a divan was the demolition of the house after a fire.

Sometimes children act as managers of divans, it being impossible to imprison them or make them suffer for doing what their parents or employers would punish them for refusing to do. A fourteen-year-old girl was recently charged with possession of thirty-six taels of opium, and the question of the disposal of the offender was raised. It seemed obvious that the child had been employed by a gang of opium smugglers as a carrier, and this, together with her youth, called for sympathetic consideration from the Bench. She was a waif without any relatives in the Colony and the Magistrate said to her, 'I know that you are working for a gang, so I am going to send you to the Po Leung Kuk Home' [for the protection of females].

Most curious receptacles are used for carrying the smuggled drug. A one tael tin has been used as a substitute for the heel of a shoe; a ten tael packet was secreted in the hollow shaft of a saw. A restaurant ham was cut and shaped to hold tins, and once the matronly appearance of a Chinese woman was found to be due to tins of smuggled opium swathed round her body. In one case, where a Chinese was charged with unlawful possession of thirty-four taels, an extra large pumpkin was produced. A small piece had been cut out in the centre, the heart had been scooped out, the opium stuffed into the hollow, and the cut piece carefully replaced. The ingenious smuggler was arrested as he came off the wharf carrying the vegetable on his shoulder.

On another occasion the opium was found concealed in eight pieces of wood which formed a bundle. There were five tins in each piece. One piece was exhibited in Court. It had been slit in two, the inside of each piece had been neatly carved and hollowed, and the halves rejoined, and fastened at the two ends with small nails which could not be seen unless the wood was very closely inspected. Forty taels were seized. The Revenue Officer stated that there was no doubt that a certain amount got through in this way, as firewood from Wuchow comes in loads of five or six tons at one time, and it would be impossible to examine every piece. . . .

The attitude of the uneducated Chinese to the mechanical inventions introduced by Europeans is illustrated by the arrival of the first traction engine to be used in the Colony. Cartage and hauling were done (as they still are to a large extent) by manual labour, but during the erection of some buildings on the Peak a traction engine was imported for hauling up stores and materials, as this was thought to be a quicker and surer method.

The coming of the engine caused considerable wonder and comment among the coolies who had never seen anything like it before, but when they were told that their services would be no longer required their wrath was unbounded. Next day the engine was put into use. It was watched by crowds of open-mouthed Chinese who wondered at the deep breathing of the 'English Devil'; but superstition soon gave way to anger as they realised that it was doing their work more cheaply and quickly.

During the day the coolies made various attempts to kill it, but without avail, and for the time being the idea was abandoned. After the day's work was done, the engine was taken back to the contractor's yard for the night. An English constable on his beat was staggered to see two coolies mounted on the engine, one sitting on the body while the other was standing on his companion's shoulders pouring a liquid from a can down the smokestack. The coolies were arrested and the engine examined, when it was found that about a pint and a half of spirits of salt had been emptied into the smoke box. On being questioned the prisoners stated that they had tried to burn the 'English Devil', they had tried to blind it with pepper, and they had tried to shoot it, but meeting with no success they had finally resolved to poison it. They were utterly amazed to learn that the 'Devil' was still alive and breathing strongly after its deadly drink. The attempt to introduce horses was also strongly opposed, and some years ago the suggestion that the Peak Tram should be used at night for carrying goods up the Peak, was defeated by the hostile attitude of the coolies.

Motor cars, were taken up quickly and joyfully by the Chinese, after some initial reluctance. In fact in 1912 'the increase in the number of motor cars let out for hire in the City and a certain number of accidents arising from reckless driving was the cause of a petition signed by some seventeen hundred of the Chinese gentry and merchants requesting the total prohibition of all cars at livery.' In addition to the accidents the common use of cars at all hours of the night for joy-rides (always with full accompaniment

of two or even three horns) was becoming a general nuisance, while the new opportunity for extravagance touched the resources of more than one family which owned a prodigal son.

Now, the streets and transport of the city are a mixture of the old and new. Rickshaws, sedan chairs, and the coolie-pole work side by side with the latest type of motor omnibus, car, and lorry, though gradually the new must tend to drive out the more leisurely and cumbrous methods of carrying both men and goods. . . .

There are tea-shops equipped with small tables to seat four persons. Here the villagers meet after the day's work for a chat and a game of dominoes or Ma Cheuk, for the shops often have electric lighting and are more cheerful and comfortable than the houses which are lighted only by small oil lamps. These tea-houses take the place of the small 'pub' in an English village. Very many different kinds of tea are used of which the following are the most popular: lotus nut kernel, water fairy, dragon-well, black dragon, white hair, red plum, 'peace and happiness', 'age and distress', 'Prince's eyebrows', and 'monkey gathered'. . . .

Barbers abound and are always busy shaving or cropping heads, and cleaning their clients' ears with long metal picks. Dentists' establishments are at once recognisable by their painted signs and by the long strings of extracted teeth which decorate their doors. . . .

One of the most interesting shops to inspect is that of the 'joss' maker who deals in all the paper articles used at funerals—houses, suits, chairs, junks, sampans, rickshaws, money, boots, even motor cars and the hundred and one things required by the dead in the other world. In other shops are sold thick red wedding candles, elaborately carved, while the pewter merchants provide wrought candlesticks and a variety of vessels needed for temple and house. There are shops which sell red paper for cards of invitation, and white paper for funerals. Others supply the fire-crackers and joss-sticks which are indispensable whenever a funeral or festivity is to be held.

Shoe-makers sell footwear of many kinds; wooden pattens for wet days, slippers of felt or satin with felt or leather soles, European shoes for men and women who can afford them, and poor man's shoes, sandal-shaped made from old car tyres.

The medicine shops exhibit jars of snakes, frogs, deers' horns, and other curious things. There are astrologers and palmists whose places of business are conspicuous for their quaint charts and diagrams hung at the entrance. Some shops are devoted to the selling of images and idols, handcarved on the spot in various shapes and sizes and painted with gold and vivid colours. These are greatly in demand for home worship, especially by the fishing population. In the smaller shops are vegetables, dried fish, peas, eggs black with age (the greater their antiquity the higher the price they fetch), and other foods raw and cooked.

All the shops have sign-boards hanging in front, the largest being ten or twelve feet long. These are painted red with gold lettering and add much to the picturesqueness of the street as do the large white door-lanterns with their coloured decorations and characters. Nearly every shop has a shrine to Tsui Po Tong, the god of wealth, who is generally shown as a visitor, with attendants who are laden with presents and treasure; but sometimes he is symbolised by a tree, the branches of which are laden with strings of gold and silver 'cash' (small copper coins worth about one-tenth of a cent).

Until recently it was common to see hung at the doors of shops or houses lanterns with riddles written upon them. The owner used to offer a prize to any passer-by who could solve the conundrum. The practice has died out now as far as private dwellings are concerned, but the lanterns can still be seen at places of amusement like the Lee Gardens, or the roof gardens of the Wing On, Sincere, and Sun Companies. ▨

39

CHILD SLAVERY IN HONG KONG

MRS H. I. HASLEWOOD

Many people were outraged by the mui tsai *system in Hong Kong in which children, predominantly girls, were sold as virtual slaves in homes and factories, and as prostitutes. Mrs Haslewood campaigned against the system and was instrumental in alleviating the situation.*

In the summer of 1919 my husband, a retired Lieutenant-Commander of the Navy, was appointed Superintendent of the Naval Chart Depot at Hong Kong. We reached the colony, travelling in the *Empress of Japan*, on August 15, 1919, in a blaze of golden light. Victoria is literally a 'city set on a hill,' physically, politically and spiritually. It commands one of the grandest harbours in the world, and is an immense shipping centre. It is the one bit of the British Empire in the whole of Far Cathay, and the flag beneath which, as Kipling has said 'the life-blood of a generation has been shed' floats proudly above it.

The Cathedral dedicated to the fearless forerunner of Christ, St. John the Baptist, stands high on the hillside of the Peak; and it is a city which cannot be hid, as it stands for the Christian faith, and for all that this faith entails in surroundings that are largely heathen; and it stands, or it should stand, for high ideals of administration, worthy of a great race.

One Sunday evening in October of that year, 1919, a sermon was preached by the Chaplain of the colony in the Cathedral of St. John. The preacher took the following text; the searching question of the prophet Micah: 'What doth the Lord thy God require of thee, but to do justly, and to love mercy, and to walk humbly with thy God?'

The preacher said: 'It has long been our boast that our British Empire brings freedom, and technically, of course, slavery is not recognized anywhere within it; but for all practical purposes slavery does exist here, as far as these poor little girls are concerned, and while such is the case, we have no right to boast that our flag is the symbol of freedom. In this colony there are probably many thousands of these little girls, some of them sold by their parents, some of them stolen from their parents, and sold into slavery. Some of them are no doubt kindly treated, but many of them are not; some of them are grossly ill-treated; and even if they were all well-treated, it would still be a cruel injustice that they should not be free.'

It was a proud shock to realize that beneath the flag of England small children and young girls were being sold and resold at a profit, bartered as human property; and yet this was a fact, vouchsafed for by responsible people. The worst feature in the case, in our opinion, being the fact that the governing officials in the colony allowed these practices to go unprotected, thereby concurring in them. To call the practice 'adoption' was really not honest. Children bought in infancy, and at the age of four or five years set to work for the household, and continuing so to work for years with no wages and no freedom, could not with any semblance of truthfulness be described as 'adopted daughters of the house'. Yet this was the evasion to which the Government resorted to clear themselves of guilt.

No doubt there were genuinely adopted children in the colony. The sermon did not refer to them; it referred to the *mui tsai*, the domestic slaves, and that was and is the only true description of them. If all of them were kindly treated and well-fed—and of course many were—the practice would still be wrong in principle. Human beings should not be purchasable as were these poor children, and nothing can alter that fact. It has since been admitted by the British Government that the system is tantamount to slavery, and it has been condemned by all right-thinking people.

The thought of it gave us no rest, and we were soon to be brought into closer contact still with this appalling evil. Below the hotel in which we lived there was a house owned by Chinese who had a number of these unpaid girl slaves, among them being a small child of eight years old. One evening we were on the balcony overlooking this house when we heard the most terrible screams from this child, in which pain and terror were dominant. I had heard her crying and moaning on a former evening, but these sounds were different. They were cries of absolute terror. The owner of the hotel informed us that he and his wife had heard similar sounds, 'as of someone in agony,' coming from this house.

We reported the matter immediately to the British Police Station, and the British sergeant on duty remarked, '*It is probably a slave girl.*' It was a Saturday night, and we were told that no steps could be taken to protect the child, nor anything done about the matter until the following Monday. We then brought the occurrence to the notice of the Chief of Police, the Secretary for Chinese Affairs, and the Chaplain who had preached the sermon.

The week following I made searching enquiries into the system among British residents, and learnt a great deal from an earnest-minded Chinese Christian who had the cause of the unhappy slaves closely at heart. He told me that, sorrowful as might be the life of the domestic slaves, it was the life of the wretched brothel slaves which haunted him the most. 'All my life I have wanted to help them,' he said, 'and perhaps my opportunity has come at last.'

It must again be repeated that whether well-used or ill-used, the *mui tsai*'s services have been obtained by purchase. They are paid no wages for their work, and at the death or the whim of their employer they are liable to be resold to the first comer willing to purchase them. This possibility being always present in their mind, who will contend that their lot is anything but a cruel one, the cruelty being usually of so subtle a nature as not to be easy to prove or discover?

Had the British Government from the very outset even prohibited *resale*, some of the worst horrors these girls have undergone in Hong Kong might have been averted, but no steps had been taken in this direction at any time by those responsible for the government of the colony. It is an undisputed fact that a large percentage of the girls and children sold in Hong Kong were bought as a Commercial proposition with an eye to their future resale at a large profit, and the Government were well aware of it.

The Government have persistently denied that there is any connection between the *mui tsai* system and the sale of girls for purposes of prostitution. The facts that the interport trading of girls for immoral purposes was one of its worst features.

The existence of this trade on an immense scale was vouched for by merchant captains engaged on the China coast runs. A British Government official was detailed, it is true, to question the girls who were being shipped off to the various ports, and the girls were taught what to answer for weeks beforehand, and threatened with horrible penalties for disobedience in this respect. The line of examination by the British official, put into plain English, was as follows:

'Are you a prostitute?'—'Yes.'
'At your own wish?'—'At my own wish.'
'Has anybody told you to say this?'—'No.'
No Chinese or British woman was stationed at the harbour

to interrogate these girls privately and assure them that they had nothing to fear if they told the truth. They were shipped off to a terrible life, its only mitigating feature being its early death, a merciful release from untold misery. These things were taking place in a colony composed largely of a Christian community who need not have been ignorant of what was taking place had they chosen to enquire. Recruits for the local registered brothels were obtained in exactly the same way.

Another fact was the utter absence of any legislation to protect these purchased children and girls from exploitation in factories and workshops, and in trades dangerous to life and limb. there was no law limiting the work of any children in the colony, nor any control over their enforced labour. They could be made by their employers to work for any number of hours day or night, weekdays and Sundays; there was nothing to prevent it.

Tiny *mui tsai* could be kept up all night to fan their mistresses fatigued by the game of *mah jong*; small boys and girls in factories would fall headlong into the machinery at night from sheer fatigue, to be killed or horribly mutilated. Little creatures from four to thirteen years of age could be seen any day toiling up the paths of the Peak carrying loads of sand and gravel loaded far beyond their strength. These burdens would sometimes be taken from them by disgusted citizens.

Two little boys, their ages given as eleven and thirteen respectively, were seen by an English doctor carrying baskets of lime and earth up the Peak one day early in April, 1920. One of them was crying. The doctor rang up the police, and on investigation it was found that one of the children was carrying two baskets of sand weighing 60 pounds, and the second had two baskets of earth of the same weight. Dr. Aubrey said it was 'a disgraceful scene'. ▨

HONG KONG

SIR CECIL CLEMENTI

Sir Cecil Clementi, an intellectual governor of Hong Kong, spoke fluent Chinese and wrote poetry. This poem comes from his 1925 collection which includes some passionate love poems to his wife. It was reprinted privately by his descendents.

L AMP-BESTARR'D, and with the star-shine gleaming
From her midnight canopy or dreaming
　　Mirror'd in her fragrant, fair lagoon:
All her streets ablaze with sheen and shimmer;
All her fire-fly shipping-lights a-glimmer,
　　Flitting, flashing, curving past Kowloon:

Oh, to see her thus! Her hill-recesses
Bright with household glow that cheers and blesses
　　Weary men and guides them home to rest:
And the criss-cross strings of light ascending
Round the Peak, a-sparkle, circling, ending
　　Where the roadways touch the mountain-crest.

Ending? No! For human aspiration
Passes here to starry consummation,
　　Mountain-roads into the Milky Way.
Earth is strewn with Danae's golden dower.
Grandly here the Master Builder's power
　　Crowns the work of England in Cathay.

Government House, Hong Kong.
1st November, 1925.

PART VII

SOCIAL CLIMBING
THE 1930S

'The deepest impression I am left with of Hong Kong is the cruelty of imperialism and the unbearable stink of the night bucket.'

AI WU, 1931

'Nights in Hong Kong are very beautiful. Don't miss them.'

BA JIN, 1933

41

THE P. S. O. C.

BELLA SIDNEY WOOLF

For Hong Kong's affluent citizens, much of life has always been concerned with social activities, from seeing friends off on ocean liners to worrying about whether the amah is over-charging. Bella Woolf, sister-in-law of Virginia Woolf, was part of the British social élite with her title of Lady Southorn, wife of Governor Clementi's Colonial Secretary. But between tea parties, she was well known in her time as a writer who depicted the social life of Hong Kong in Chips of China *(1930), and* Under the Mosquito Curtain *(1935) from which both these stories are taken.*

In England, farewells at stations and on ships have been whittled down to a minimum. Occasionally you see a small group at a station making heavy conversation round the carriage door when relatives or friends go East, but it is all very subdued and unemotional. It is, therefore, a revelation to enter into the 'farewelling' of Hong Kong. It is by funerals and home-leave that Flower Street lives. On the day of the departure of 'popular residents' it is as if a horde of locusts had passed over the flower stalls. A steady stream of flower bearers proceeds to Statue Pier and the Ferry. Others with nobbly parcels of chocolates, lavender water or books stray in on foot or by car. The departing female traveller embarks on the launch be-flowered like a Jack-in-the-Green and rejoices for once in her life in feeling like a prima donna or a film star while the long-suffering husband follows with the parcels. All the friends pour on to the launch or the Ferry and eventually transfer themselves to the P. & O. or Empress Boat which becomes a seething mass of humanity and herbage. Perspiring coolies endeavour to push their way up the gangway with countless baskets of flowers.

The grateful recipients of flowers and chocolates order drinks wildly, but often these do not appear until the 'see-ers off' have gone and the ship is under weigh. It is pathetic to see the stewards trying to force their way through the crowds which close in on them like treacle.

'But surely these aren't *all* friends,' I said, as I emerged flushed and panting on the jetty after my first experience of this orgy, feeling as if I had been involved in a dog-fight. Men, women and children were pouring down the gangway in an unending stream.

'Oh, no,' replied my friend, 'Many belong to the P. S. O. C.'

'The what?'

'The Professional See-ers-off Club'.

'Good heavens! What is it?'

'It consists of rival members of the World's Workers' Society who self-sacrificingly spend an hour or two on board the outgoing liners joining cheerful parties or giving drinks to lonely-looking passengers. There are many stories told of this great and good institution. A member went on board and saw a pale, disconsolate man sitting in a corner. "Have a drink, old chap," he said. "You'll feel all the better for it, and you'll be as merry as a grig once you're off."

'The melancholy man accepted two "pink drinks" and a cigarette.

Wyndham Street, where flowers are sold, Hongkong.

'"Yes, I hope to find dear Aunt Eliza still alive," he said with a sigh.

'Then came the cry:—"All friends ashore."

'The member of the P. S. O. C. wrung the pale man's hand.

'"Good luck to you, a good trip and may you find them all well at home and your good Aunt on the road to recovery."

'The other responded with a wan smile.

'The kindly hearty soul swung down the gangway. Once on the jetty he gazed up to see if the pale man was gazing over the side of the ship, but he was not to be seen. Passengers were expressing their *joie de vivre* by throwing streamers of coloured paper from the ship to the shore and in a short while everyone was tangled up in a web of pink, blue and yellow paper. The ship's band was playing jazz—the world seemed brimming with love and laughter.

'Our hero unwound twenty yards of pink paper from his neck and hastened to the Star Ferry. On the ferry-boat back to Hong Kong he read the paper, thinking between whiles of the lonely soul who had none to see him off, and of the good work done by the P. S. O. C. that day.

'He looked up as they neared the Hong Kong side and all prepared to disembark. Behold—beside him stood the tall, pale, disconsolate man. As their eyes met the latter turned a fishy unrecognizing eye and melted into the crowd.

'He is on the Black List of the P. S. O. C. now.' ▨

42

THE BORROWER

BELLA SIDNEY WOOLF

Neither a borrower nor a lender be
For loan oft loses both itself and friends.

HAMLET

I t was a pity that Mrs. Kettlewell had not studied her Shake-speare more assiduously. Unfortunately she had 'no use' for poetry, either Shakespeare's or any other and her life was moulded on lines which led to unpopularity. For these poets, though wild fellows in many cases, addicted to conviviality in taverns, and bawdy company have been the mouthpieces of great truths, which help us to negotiate the daily round and set us in the company of the Immortals.

'Neither a borrower nor a lender be—'

Mrs. Kettlewell had never heard that line, and even if she had heard it she would have dismissed it contemptuously.

Mrs. Kettlewell lived in a row of houses far up on the steep sides of the Peak. Each house had a row of steps up to the front door, a small patch of garden and then a paved piece of terrace ending in a wall. Over the wall was a view that took your breath away, a stretch of sea and islands and headlands shimmering on fine days in a magic woof [weaving] of turquoise and green.

But Mrs. Kettlewell, as she went about her lawful avocations, never looked at the view. She was busy wondering whether the cook had cheated her over that last leg of lamb, for she had had no time to weigh it—or whether the amah was selling the soap or the boy stealing a spoonful of marmalade every day.

By degrees a chill crept over her relations with her neighbours, until they were only just on speaking terms. No one would lend the garden roller or a 'tiny drop of milk as ours has run out' ('It has never run in,' said Mrs. Fulwell grimly) or 'a quarter of a pound of butter till ours arrives' ('It never will,' said Mrs. Gamble warmly) or 'Your sewing machine for an hour as ours is out of order' ('It never has been or will be in order,' said Mrs. Jones firmly).

The climax came when one day Mrs. Kettlewell's amah arrived at Mrs. Fulwell's house at the far end of the terrace with a request for the loan of a spoonful of castor oil for little Reggie as 'Mississy' had forgotten to order a new supply. Ah Wong, Mrs. Fulwell's trusty No.1 boy, refused the request coldly, as he had been informed by his mistress not to lend anything to Mrs. Kettlewell, whether she asked for a pin or a sewing machine.

'What for your Mississy no buy oil for self?' said Ah Wong sternly.

Amah was silent with that sullen expression which a Chinese woman assumes when it is a question of 'saving face'.

'My Mississy say no more give your Mississy garden roller—sew machine—milk—now you come ask oil?'

Amah's tongue was loosened:—

'Little master have big pain.'

'Maaskee—you more better go shop.'

'Little master muchee cly.'

Ah Wong's heart softened, but only up to a point.

He did not answer but went upstairs to the medicine chest.

Mrs. Fulwell, returning from her shopping in town, walked along the terrace. Midway between Kettlewell's house and her own she met a strange procession.

First of all came Ah Wong carrying a tablespoonful of some liquid. He walked slowly, deliberately his eyes fixed on the spoon. Behind him walked Mrs. Kettlewell's amah.

'Ah Wong, what *are* you doing?'

Startled, Ah Wong looked up, his hand shook and half the liquid in the spoon was spilt.

'That Mississy,' he said pointing with his disengaged hand to the Kettlewell house, 'she send this amah ask one spoon castor oil for little master. You tell me no send any more thing—She *say* one spoon, she *want* one bottle, I send one bottle—never see again. Little master have big pain—perhaps makee die—I take one spoon oil that Mississy.'

'Quite right, Ah Wong,' said Mrs. Fulwell in a loud voice, blissfully conscious that Mrs. Kettlewell was looking out of her window. 'Take the oil to Mrs. Kettlewell but wait for the spoon.' ▦

43

THE CLASH OF OLD AND NEW

LANCELOT FORSTER

Although vaccinations are now widespread in Hong Kong, traditional medicine shops continue to line parts of Queen's Road. Elderly women still burn offerings before small roadside shrines, but bullock carts have long been replaced. Also fading is the absolute belief in Western superiority and the assumption that the new is always better than the old. This extract comes from Forster's 1930s book, Echoes of Hong Kong and Beyond.

I t is always pleasing to stand at the confluence of two streams and watch the mingling of the two smaller volumes of water to form a stronger and more vigorous flow. . . . It is infinitely more interesting to watch and meditate on the junction and the mingling of two civilizations which outwardly are so separate and disparate as those of the east and west.

There is a very busy street in Hong Kong leading to Pokfulam. It contains a Sanitary Department Office, a Government School, a University Hostel, numerous shops, and, at the side of the road, a tree. Because the tree is tall and once fair to look upon, and especially because it grows upon the side of the walk and does not therefore interfere with the motorcar driver, it has been spared. Trees must not impede motor traffic. Through the street there pass the bullock carts belonging to the sanitary department, there are rickshaws, heavy motor-lorries, motor-buses, and many motor-cars. The street is busy at all times of the day, for the area is densely populated, and it is what the town authorities would call a main artery.

But to return to the other elements, not three hundred yards away is a modern university, with its three faculties, all very thoroughly equipped and producing teachers, engineers and doctors all trained and instructed on the latest Western lines. Nearer still is a secondary school recently established at a cost of about one million dollars, and containing the very latest improvements known to Western educational methods. These two institutions, like the Sanitary Department Office, let it be carefully noted, have their roots in Britain—the Britain of the present—but the old tree has its roots in the soil of China of the past.

The tree is important, though it is old and of necessity rather dusty, for round it there is enacted daily, after sunset usually, a scene which, when fully comprehended, is intensely moving in its pathos. The chief actors are a few Chinese women who, utterly oblivious of the surge of traffic and of the passers-by, perform their rites around the base of the tree as though the world about them did not exist.

In a niche of the tree are burning joss sticks, tended by one of the suppliants, another is uttering incantations with a sort of rhythm, in keeping with which another, with a long bamboo pole, beats the trunk of the tree. On the ground is an old woman turning about, on the pavement, a young child's garment, while another woman belabours it violently with a heavy bamboo mat to expel the devils of disease which are presumed to be lurking in it and to be the cause of the infant's illness and the woman's distress. The long-continued efforts of the woman with the mat are supplemented by the woman on the ground who holds some burning joss paper as she runs it rapidly over every portion of the garment in a restless, energetic way that betokens fear.

There is a sincerity and earnest concentration of mind on all these acts, which express the fundamental instinct of mother-love in its most intense form. No child's life could possibly be prayed for with greater fervour, no god in Nature ever heard more ardent supplications from the innermost recesses of the heart than these. If the prayers of a righteous man availeth much those prayers must prevail, for never was a ritual performed in any Western sanctuary with the same ardour and unity of purpose as is displayed by these five women.

And the tragedy of it is that probably it was smallpox from which vaccination might have saved it ... but such people are determined to know nothing of it, for they have no faith in it. Here is being fought out the real struggle between science and religion—science in its most recent form, and religion in its most primitive, a religion which attributes all ills to supernatural evil causes and seeks therefore to expel them by beating, by burning, and by prayer. It is only that a part of the theory is wrong.

The old tree of superstition still flourishes, somewhat bedraggled it is true, with the dust, but still hale and strong. It is really the old tradition springing up from the soil of China, flinging its arms wildly and defiantly against University, School and Sanitation, indifferent to the rush of motor-cars at its side, and the whirr of the 'Hermes' seaplanes overhead. It continues and will continue for many years to attract its devotees seeking relief in their distress. This tree will take an unconscionable time to die in China. ▓

44

HONG KONG PROSTITUTES

STELLA BENSON

When Stella Benson arrived in Hong Kong she was immediately shocked by the conditions of Chinese prostitutes. Her crusade to have prostitution banned in the Colony was ostensibly successful—measures were introduced between 1932 and 1935—but as a result compulsory health checks for the women ended, while prostitution still flourished illegally. Yau Ma Tei, now best known to visitors as the Jade Market area in Kowloon, was the site of a tour of legal brothels in 1931. Stella Benson visited both the more refined brothels of Miu-nam Street which entertained and served only Chinese men as well as the déclassé so-called 'Big Number' houses which served Europeans as well.

4 March 1931

Mrs. Forster and I spent the afternoon with Mrs. Mow Fung visiting the brothels of the Yaumati district on Wednesday, March 4th. While waiting for a Chinese girl, one of the pupils in Mrs. Mow Fung's school for prostitutes, we sat for an hour or so in the schoolroom, and noted the following facts, told us by Mr. Mow Fung.

The school had re-opened that day, after the New Year holiday, and that day, as it happened, the question of age having arisen between Mrs. Mow Fung and her pupils, two girls told her that they had been licensed as prostitutes at the age of fifteen; of these two, at least one is still under age. Mrs. Mow Fung takes for granted that this is a very common state of things among local prostitutes. The girls usually claim to be 22 years old when applying for licences; they treat this lie as a joke, saying that the government officials are easy to deceive.

The girls told Mrs. Mow Fung that it cost either them or the 'mother' (brothel-mistress) between thirty and forty dollars in bribes to get a girl a licence. This, I gather, was not cited as a grievance, but taken for granted by the girls, as indeed it is taken for granted by them that practically all the minor officials of the government with whom they came into direct contact—police, inspectors, clerks, doorkeepers, etc.—both English, Chinese and Indian—were corrupt. If payment of bribes is refused or delayed, the government employee follows the girls to the brothels, suggesting that if satisfaction is not given, adverse reports of the establishments will be made. Though not actually stated, it seems probable that this initial outlay in bribes, if paid by the 'mother' is chalked up to the girl's debt; it may be supposed then that in this respect, the Government's toleration of the brothel system adds to the hopelessness of the girls' enslavement.

Referring to the case of a small girl, daughter of a brothel-amah, a child known to Mrs. Mow Fung and seen by Mrs. Forster, the prostitute pupils told Mrs. Mow Fung that she actually has no home except the brothel in which her mother works—but has to stay out in the streets every night till 2 or 3 a.m. at least, in case an inspector should find her in the brothel during its time of business. It was attempted at one time to send this little girl to the ordinary school, but since lessons begin at 9, the child could not continue to attend school, since she had no time for sleep. Mrs. Mow Fung says that there are many children living in brothels; it is made worth the inspectors' while not to report this very common state of things.

The girls are not as a rule personally hampered in their freedom by the 'mothers'. One had gone away to the country for a short time to see her family. Much going out, however, is necessarily discouraged by the fact that if an inspector calls at any time and finds licensed girls absent, their licences are likely to be cancelled—again, unless it is made worth the inspector's while not to.

Girls tell Mrs. Mow Fung that police and other government employees use every possible means to dissuade girls from going to the Salvation Army home—which is supposed to be an alternative fairly offered to every girl who applies for a licence. It also seems that this alternative—very simple food, steady work and separation from the gay friends of the streets—has very little chance to attract a girl who has been attracted by the illusion of brightness and variety apparently offered by brothel life.

Asked how many licensed prostitutes there were in Hongkong, Mrs. Mow Fung said that she believed the number was nearer 3,000 than 2,000, and that the number of unlicensed girls in 'sly' brothels was no doubt greater.

After we had sat in the schoolroom for some time, two girls came in—one the pupil whom we had been expecting, who had promised to show us round some brothels, and the other a bright-looking girl who said she had been bought out of a brothel by a Chinese as 'Number Three Wife' and was being well-treated—though unfortunately (it appeared) at the expense of the Number One wife, who had practically been turned out of doors.

The first girl, a prostitute living in a brothel, who had come to show us round the streets, was a very modest-looking girl, very plainly dressed. She said that another brothel-mistress—(not *her* 'mother') had been offering her two thousand dollars to go to Singapore and be a 'waitress'. The girl was tempted, as she evidently didn't enjoy her present life, but Mrs. Mow Fung said that the offer was almost certainly a trap, and advised the girl against it. Asked what she would have done with the money, she said she would have sent it to her family. Mrs. Mow Fung says that many girls claim to have been sold into prostitution in order that their brothers' education might be paid for.

These two girls and Mrs. Mow Fung accompanied us to several brothels in Miu-nam Street. We went and sat in their cubicle while the girls talked. All the cubicles in this district were very much alike; all were tawdry but clean. One out of five or six we saw had a window. The others were simply like horse-boxes, partitioned off along the length of the landings, at a right angle to the street. Each cubicle was about half-filled by a large bed, the linen clean and in some cases decorated with crude embroideries, the work of the girls themselves. In each cubicle, there was also a table crowded with tawdry ornaments and a chair. The walls were plastered with bright posters and Chinese advertisement pictures, photographs and cheap coloured fancy things. None that we saw had any indecent suggestions.

All the girls were delighted to see us and many crowded into each cubicle in which we sat for a time. Some of them talked very freely. The girls pay fifty cents in every dollar to the 'mother', and twenty-five cents to the amah. An amah is provided for each girl, she sleeps on a trestle bed outside the girl's cubicle.

We saw many of these amahs. They seemed to me a mean and sullen type of woman, but only a few looked as if they resented our visit. Out of the remaining twenty-five per cent of her earnings, the girl has to pay for everything—theoretically—but actually the 'mother' provides practically everything, and enters it to the girl's account.

The girl who told us that her own mother had sold her, implied a weariness of the life she lived. We asked her if many other girls in that brothel had entered the life unwillingly too—she said that she and the other girls in the brothel live separately, 'like separate families', and never knew one another's private affairs.

The girls in these houses consider themselves—and are—superior to the girls in the Big Number houses, with whom they will not associate. These girls in Miu-nam Street are used by Chinese men only; the girls are often sent for to the Chinese hotel in that street, where they entertain men diners, singing, talking, etc., and afterwards bring the men back to their cubicles. The singing is an additional expense. The 'mother' will decide, perhaps, that one of the girls must learn a new song. The song is taught by a professional teacher and may cost—if a long song—as much as forty dollars, or, if short, about fifteen. These sums are of course added to the 'debts'.

There is the small sum Mrs. Mow Fung asks for attendance at her school. A few 'mothers', it seems, do not object to the girls having interests that do not interfere with their night work. Also, 'mothers' are alert for any opportunity of adding to the girls' indebtedness. In the majority of cases, the girls pay for their own schooling, and attendance at the school is often discouraged by 'mothers' owing to the danger of a visit to the brothel by an inspector while the girls are absent. In a few cases, a brothel-mistress will have her own actual daughter in her brothel. One girl, older and more brazen than the rest, said that she had entered this life with the encouragement of her own mother, who lived in Hongkong. Nearly all the other girls we spoke to had been brought to Hongkong from other parts of China (many from Macao) and had lost touch with their families.

There was the constant presence of male hangers-on of all kinds in the houses. Any man could come in at any time, said the girls, but no women could except those connected with the business. Coolies carrying water, pedlars selling food and other wares, idlers sitting eating and drinking with the amahs, were everywhere. The girls were in many cases wearing scanty underclothes only.

In Miu-nam Street we saw many small children apparently at home in the brothels. Those we inquired about were always said to live somewhere else and to have come there only to play during the day. But since many of them were obviously the children of the brothel-amahs with whom we saw them, it seems scarcely credible that this story was true. We saw several prostitutes who were nothing but children themselves, by the look of them. One wonders how such immature little girls get licensed however much they and the 'mothers' may lie about their age.

From this district of 'superior' prostitutes, reserved for Chinese men, we went to a street of Big Number houses, used by British and other soldiers and sailors and other Europeans. The girls who had guided us so far would not accompany us to the Big Number houses which are considered by them very inferior. It is evident at once that they *are* indeed strikingly inferior, both in the type of girl and in the condition of the house. The girls are obviously older, and though they were all very friendly to us and delighted to see us, they were very much more brazen in manner. They were all dirty, some were dressed in tawdry and soiled semi-European (unwashable) clothes. Some were out in the street in their underclothes, whereas in the first district we saw, all were modestly dressed when out of doors. Nearly all the girls in the Big Number houses had more or less unhealthy skins. None seemed to me to show those remnants of self-respect which the girls in the other district seemed to have retained in some cases. Many of the Big Number girls seemed to us to show signs of having European blood, and two were very evidently Eurasian. One of these last herself referred to the fact that she had 'English eyes'.

The entrance halls of the Big Number houses were larger and brighter and perhaps little cleaner than the 'Chinese district' houses, also the stairs were in better order and cleaner, superficially. But the condition of the cubicles was quite horrifying. In no cubicle was the bed made. It seems that the linen is not even straightened or smoothed from night to night. All linen was in the filthiest condition, the pillowcases literally black with greasy dirt and the sheets loathsomely dirty and in complete disorder.

On the landings, dirty clothes were lying on the floor. All this in spite of the fact that it was by now after five o'clock and the girls were beginning to expect visitors. (One English sailor went into the next brothel to the one we were visiting while we were there.) It was notable also that the girls did not seem ashamed or apologetic about the disgusting state of their cubicle. They did not seem to realize that they *were* dirty, though in the other districts the girls apologized even for the slightest and least perceptible disorder in their persons or their cubicles.

It is impossible to believe that conscientious inspection of these Big Number houses is effectively carried out. Yet these are the houses that are *recommended* to English soldiers. These houses are 'safe'. One girl said vaguely that once a year she had to see a doctor. At any rate, our observation emphatically showed is that in the matter of dirt alone—quite apart from any other sources of disease—the condition of those recommended houses would not bear a moment's honest inspection.

At the door of the last brothel, as we came out, we met a little half-caste boy—almost wholly English-looking—and dressed in European clothes—being carried by one prostitute and affectionately kissed on the mouth by three or four others. He was the son of a Chinese woman who kept a little 'café' between two brothels. She said his father was English. There were children everywhere in and out of the houses, as in the other district.

Two girls, quite drunk, were sitting with the English sailor before mentioned, in the entrance hall of the next brothel.

The impression of hopelessness and degradation made upon us by those Big Number prostitutes was unmistakable. It seemed to us that no honest observer could fail to be impressed by the fundamental spiritual and physical cruelty of the system or reconcile his conscience to the idea that a British government should seal with its approval such a system—against the opinion of civilised government all over the world, including the British home government. The only excuse usually given for licensed prostitution (and it seems to me at best a conspicuously one-sided excuse) is the safeguarding of the health of men. One necessarily comes away from a visit to these brothels' convinced that in such a filthy and degraded atmosphere such an excuse is wholly illusory. There can be no safety for men in such conditions, on the contrary, the tacit government recommendations of such houses is an additional danger since it engenders unfounded confidence. As for the girls themselves, I believe that their position as licensed public conveniences—a position which they have, in many cases, no choice of entering, and from which they know of no chance of escape—robs them of their human heritage. ▩

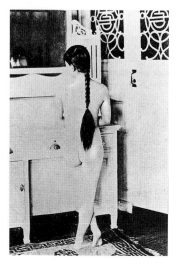

45

ONE NIGHT IN A HONG KONG GAOL

AI WU

After reading endless ecstatic descriptions of Hong Kong, this one, from a Chinese prisoner's point of view, is strikingly different. Ai Wu's writing displeased the British in Burma, and he was deported to China in 1931, spending this memorable night in Hong Kong on the way.

I had many fine fantasies about Hong Kong, though I had never been there. This time on my way back to China, quite unexpectedly, in this Hong Kong of which I had dreamed of so frequently, I became the recipient of special treatment by the English imperialists and stayed one night in a 'government courtesy hotel'. The next morning, some local British mandarin dispatched a 'yellow-skinned Westerner' to escort all of us who had enjoyed their hospitality the night before onto a ship departing for Amoy [Xiamen]. And so in this manner, I said farewell to my long-dreamed-of Hong Kong. I felt an indescribable sadness, as if I had been forced to join the army the day after my wedding night!

I like travelling around but my favourite pastime is to visit a big city for the first time. Of course I love the vast blue sea and luxuriant mountain ranges, but still I can't forget these metropolises with their fine gentlemen and beautiful ladies. Before coming to Hong Kong, I often compared China to a loving mother and Hong Kong to her young daughter. At the mere thought of this I could hardly resist the temptation to see this gorgeous young lady. When our ship, which had sailed across the Indian Ocean, arrived that drizzly day at dusk, the lights burning up and down the mountains made this bejewelled debutante look even more refined and enticing. We were fed up with prison life in Burma; we had little tolerance for our fortnight's 'exile' at sea. Hong

Kong was the designated place where we were to be set free. If the English imperialists chose to open our cages here, this was where we would spread our wings and fly up into the sky of freedom; if they chose this place to set the fish free as a demonstration of their love for all creatures, then we would flap our fins and swim into the boundless sea. So, Hong Kong was nothing less than a symbol of freedom restored! Just imagine how these prisoners rejoiced when they saw the enticing figure of this Goddess of Liberty decked out in all her finery.

We were told that we could not go ashore till the English imperialists completed their inspection. All the criminal offenders and political prisoners from South-East Asia before us were released this way. So we had to wait. Leaning on the rails we waited until late at night when a few English policemen, who had been drinking with the ship's owner, arrived with a set of identification photos provided by the government of Burma. They checked each of us against the photos, and then, without a word, took us ashore in an electric boat. We were herded into a police station which was about as comfortable as a pigsty, and quite unceremoniously slammed in the clink. With no hope of being freed now, we all fell into the abyss of misery.

As we peered around inside, a sixteen watt bulb illuminated six prisoners sleeping on the floor in the fifteen-square-metre cell. When we were told to enter, they all woke up with a start and looked up at us, revealing heads swollen with dropsy. With the two of us, there was scarcely enough space for everyone to sit down. In one corner stood a tin night-soil bucket. A large section of the floor around it was soaking wet, obviously with urine that had spilled from the bucket. There was also a couple of banana-shaped turds lying there conspicuously in the middle of the floor. The room stunk of a mixture of acrid disinfectant and fragrant piss and shit, and struck us new-comers as being quite out of this world. It was terrible on the other side of the bars too: the December wind was howling away outside, in a ghastly and blood-curdling way. An Indian cop wearing a black jacket was pacing back and forth with a rifle on his shoulder; he looked like the shadow of a ghost. Frustrated and angry, all of us started cursing out loud: Foreign devils! F– – – your mother! Red-headed barbarians!

Our detention house in Burma was a lot better than this place in Hong Kong. There at least you were fed a meal upon arrival, and got a blanket at bedtime. The room was spacious and there was fresh air to breathe. There was a Western style toilet: one pull of the rope and all the filth and stink was flushed to hell. But in Hong Kong no one gave a damn if you were hungry when you got there or cold at night. In place of a toilet, you were provided with a night-soil bucket, as if prisoners were expected to enjoy the fragrance of piss and shit. 'The red-headed barbarians treat us Chinese worse than slaves!' We all said things like this as a result of what we had gone through.

Later we talked to those six prisoners. They told us that they had been sent back to Hong Kong by the colonial government in Singapore because they were unemployed there, and had been here for a couple of days already. Does that make sense? Is it a crime to be unemployed? Sending them home would be enough, but on top of that they were locked up in a pigsty. Are the laws of this self-professed civilized country so cruel? It is thanks to the sweat and blood of these honest unemployed labourers that the Malay Peninsula and the Straits Settlements enjoy their current prosperity, providing those ungrateful imperialist pigs and dogs with a comfortable life. And in the end, these labourers were expelled by the thousands. The few of us who had been banished and sent back to China perhaps deserved the special treatment we were receiving at the Hong Kong government's free lodgings because we had ostensibly committed crimes, by either exposing in writing the sinister designs of the English imperialists in their deception and oppression of small and weak nations, or by digging a deep grave for British imperialism through some form of direct action. But what crime had been committed by these innocent unemployed workers that they should be treated like prisoners?

The next morning before I got up, I heard the sounds of my fellow prisoners taking turns moving their bowels in the bucket. The fetid stench in the room intensified. All this made me feel even sadder. All you could do was clench your teeth and silently curse the English imperialists.

It was not until breakfast time that the door was opened and we were allowed into the courtyard. The Indian guard was very nice indeed, and motioned me to come over and talk with him. Fortunately, I could speak a little Hindustani (the *lingua franca* of India), so that I managed to carry on a conversation with him, using English to fill in the gaps. The Indian policeman was so pleased to find someone who could speak his native tongue that he became even more amicable. Later that day the Hong Kong government moved us to another prison before putting us on a ship bound for Amoy, and it was there that I met another Indian policeman. We tried to get close to him, and at parting he gave us a salute and said, '*Salaam, Babu*' (an expression of respect for a superior). There we also met two Indian prisoners, who looked like well-educated men. They told us they had worked for the Labour Department in the British Concession in Shanghai. They were on their way back to Calcutta since they had been expelled from Shanghai, perhaps for political reasons. We wanted to take advantage of this rare opportunity to speak with them more, but we had very little time, as we were soon taken to our respective ships under escort.

So this is how I said good-bye to my beloved Hong Kong, with anger and sadness. The deepest impression I am left with of Hong Kong is the cruelty of imperialism and the unbearable stink of the night-bucket! This I will never forget.

When the ship had travelled a good distance, there seemed to be a low, plaintive call coming from the direction of the Colony. 'Will those who love me please forgive me? I'm being raped by the British imperialists!' 🁢

46

HONG KONG NIGHTS

BA JIN

Ba Jin, the pen name of Li Feigan, is one of the great modern Chinese novelists. After studying in France, he spent much of his long life in Shanghai, but viewed Hong Kong briefly in 1933 as his ship sailed through Victoria Harbour. This passage suggests the dream-like quality of Hong Kong for those who only visit.

My friend A. called to me from outside my cabin just as the boat was leaving. I came out and heard him say, 'Nights in Hong Kong are very beautiful. Don't miss them.'

Leaning against the railing outside my cabin I watched Hong Kong recede in the distance.

The sea was dark, as was the sky, and there were some stars out, but few were bright. In contrast, Hong Kong itself was an endless panorama of stars.

There were lights on the mountains, on the streets, and on the buildings. Each light was like a tiny star, but to me they seemed brighter and more splendid than stars. In their dense array they resembled a mountain of stars, shining endless beams of light in the night sky.

The night was still and soft. Not a sound was to be heard from the shore; Hong Kong seemed to have shut its great mouth. Yet when I gazed upon the scintillating mountain of stars, I could hear the lights whispering to each other. The rocking of the boat created the illusion that all the lights were moving. The headlights on the trams and cars darted about; I could see them winking like human eyes, or perhaps they were chasing or talking to each other. Sight and hearing became confused, and I seemed to be listening with my eyes. The mountain of stars was hardly silent; it was performing a great symphony.

I almost forgot where I was. The boat seemed to be turning. The mountain of stars was beginning to shrink. But I could still see the stretch of golden lights in my eyes, and hear that wonderful symphony.

When the boat passed through mountains (or islands, I am not sure), Hong Kong finally disappeared. There were no lights at sea, and our boat was shrouded in thick darkness. The mountain of stars had now become a distant and indistinct dream.

I stood there gazing into the distance, trying to find that mountain of stars again. But I could see nothing. It was rather cool outside, and the wind blowing on my head was uncomfortable, so I returned to the cabin. It was another world there, full of noise and excitement. The moment I stepped into the cabin, I asked myself: 'Was everything I just saw an illusion?' ▨

47

HONGKONG

W. H. AUDEN

In the late 1930s, Christopher Isherwood and W. H. Auden travelled to the Far East to record their impressions of hostilities in China. The resulting book, Journey to a War, *published in 1939, includes both poems and prose.*

The leading characters are wise and witty;
 Substantial men of birth and education
 With wide experience of administration,
They know the manners of a modern city.

Only the servants enter unexpected;
Their silence has a fresh dramatic use:
Here in the East the bankers have erected
A worthy temple to the Comic Muse.

Ten thousand miles from home and What's her name,
The bugle on the Late Victorian hill
Puts out the soldier's light; off-stage, a war

Thuds like the slamming of a distant door:
We cannot postulate a General Will;
For what we are, we have ourselves to blame.

195

PART VIII

WAR LOOMS AND DESCENDS THE 1940S

'Let's take whatever time we have left right here.
I like Hong Kong.'

EMILY HAHN, 1941

48

PREPARING FOR WAR

EMILY HAHN

As a journalist specializing in the Far East, Emily Hahn, an American (nicknamed Mickey), spent years on the China Coast. After the war, she married Charles Boxer, a writer, and the father of her daughter, Carola, born in Hong Kong. Emily Hahn continued to write and published many books and articles including her 'partial' autobiography, China to Me, *from which this extract comes. In the mid-1990s she was living in England.*

One of the irritating things about the British point of view which you noticed in the Hong Kong residents was their stubborn refusal to consider the Far East situation. The war meant to them the war in Europe. That they took very seriously. The women learned now to do nursing so that they could stay in the Colony, the young men all joined up and wore uniforms, and there were bazaars and benefit balls one after another, to collect funds for airplanes. The airplanes, however, were all to be sent to Europe and used against Hitler; that was the theme of all the propaganda we were given. Hong Kong, unlike Shanghai, has always been a place where people planned to live permanently. Old people who had spent their twenty-five and thirty-five years in the Colony built houses on the Peak and sat down on their pensions, intending to end their days in a warmer and more comfortable climate than obtained at home. They lived at less expense than would have been possible in Europe, even in the cheaper Riviera towns, and they lived an ideally British sort of life. They had their golf and their races and even their hunts, when they wanted to make the effort. Charles was somewhat contemptuous of the people who went in so knowingly and enthusiastically for horses in Hong Kong when they had never done anything of the sort at home. But they loved it, and it was all harmless enough. There was sailing. There was tennis; that goes without saying.

But nobody among those British ever gave China a thought. You could go through the day, from the eleven o'clock drink in the Grips through lunch at someone's house and tea somewhere else down to dinner, stately· on the Peak with plenty of cut glass and damask linen and heavy silver, and nobody would talk of the war in China except as a far-off exotic manifestation of the natives. In Charles's office, it is true, there was a group of young men who made the natives their special consideration. One officer was good at Cantonese and so they nominated him to be a sort of liaison man with the local Chinese. His job, theoretically, was to be friendly with the people who made up most of the town's population, to keep in touch with their trends and ideas, and to write reports on all of this. The difficulty was that he was too British ever to be particularly friendly with anybody at all. . . .

I found an entirely new (to me) kind of Chinese living in Hong Kong. The Cantonese who make up the bulk of the population have stubbornly resisted change, and in Hong Kong you will find many old customs and traditions flourishing in a lively manner which you can't find anywhere else in China. Perhaps this is because the rest of China has been exposed to the progressive influence of the Chiangs [Chiang Kai-shek and his wife] and their sort; I don't know. The streets of the city were always full of long funeral processions, gay with costumes and discordant with brass bands. There were still brides carried about in sedan chairs, their face hidden. Now and then I even saw a naked baby with a little lock of hair braided into a queue on the top of his head.

We went out a lot with the gayer young British people with French or Dutch residents. (Charles's gift for languages made him an unofficial expert on all 'foreigners'. Most of the other Army people were simply terrified of them.) The general hated entertaining, so he left all that to Charles. This let us in for a lot of big cocktail parties in the Hongkong Hotel. It was much the existence I would have been leading in London, save for the fact that with a few exceptions the people we saw were not as amusing as those I could have dug up elsewhere. I didn't mind it as much as I would have under different circumstances. I enjoyed it. But after a few months I was homesick for China. . . .

My servants were Hong Kong's servants, May Road style,

respectful and distant. Ah King didn't exactly disapprove of me—later he was to like me a good deal—but several things about me were startling him a lot. My Chinese guests, for example. Before me I don't think he had ever entertained Chinese for his masters except at large, stiff, formal receptions when oriental diplomats would not be out of place. Then one afternoon a Sikh policeman from Shanghai dropped by for tea, and both Ah King and Gunga Singh were embarrassed. In the Indian's case it was that damned Hong Kong atmosphere which had such a bad effect. . . .

'I don't know what's the matter with this town,' he said fretfully. 'I'm staying with a cousin down in Happy Valley, and I mentioned that I was coming up to tea with you and I asked him if he knew you. He said, "You're going up to May Road? Why, that's on the Peak. They won't let you go up the Peak. You'll be turned back." What's the idea, Mickey?'

I shrugged it off and we talked about other things. But Ah King, perfect servant though he was, peered fearfully at the turbaned Gunga Singh when he brought in the tea tray.

A Chinese boy who worked in one of the news agencies in Chungking took me one evening to an 'escort bureau', where he had a girl friend. You may not be aware that prostitution doesn't exist in Hong Kong. It has been abolished by order of Parliament or something. Once upon a time there used to be prostitutes there, as there usually are in seaports, and a government doctor examined them every week, and the venereal disease problem was fairly well under control. But along came an idealistic lady writer named Stella Benson, and she was horrified to discover that such things existed in a crown colony. (Actually what she took exception to especially was the slave-girl setup, but she went the wrong way about abolishing it.) A lot of other idealistic English ladies turned to with Stella Benson, terrifying their menfolk into legislation, and prostitution was abolished. So afterwards no government doctor went around inspecting the women, and the venereal disease problem, though it had no official existence, was really very bad.

And instead of prostitutes, Hong Kong had 'escort girls'. They lived in crowded places upstairs in the houses along the harbour front, and these places were known as 'clubs'. The place young Chang took me to was an athletic club. Like other houses of its kind it had a catalogue, a printed leaflet with photographs of the girls who lived there or who dropped in now and then as they made their rounds. If you had just come in from out of town, as many Chinese countrymen did, you telephoned this club and explained that you wanted a guide, or escort, to show you around. You made your choice from the photograph and the girl came to call on you, or if you were an intimate of the place you dropped in and played mah-jongg there, and kidded with the madame. But it wasn't prostitution, no indeed. The police visited the clubs periodically for their tips, but even when the managers paid squeeze regularly the government occasionally made trouble. My athletic club, for example, when Chang first introduced me there, was a dark hovel, long and narrow and built something like an old-fashioned Pullman, with cubicles up and down the hall, and an open space in the back for mah-jongg. Each cubicle had a wooden bed in it and not much else. One of the periodical purity drives came along soon afterward, and when I called in again there were no cubicles; they had been abolished by order of the police. All the partitions had been taken out, and now when anyone wanted privacy they just put movable screens up around the chosen spot.

Chang's girl, Ying Ping, could speak good Mandarin and I needed practice. Not many people in Hong Kong did speak it well enough to be good for my vocabulary. When you are talking with someone who is not a teacher you get along better, for a teacher, whether he wants to or not, usually confines his talk to certain dull subjects and talks down to you, in a stilted fashion beyond which you seldom progress. The people at the athletic club, Madame, and the man who made the dates at the telephone, and the girls, and Ying Ping herself, all thought me slightly mad for calling on them at all, but I didn't care. Ying Ping didn't either. I took up time that she couldn't have used more profitably with male clients because I always came early, in the afternoon, after one unfortunate experience which I'll describe in a minute. I paid her the regular rates for 'entertainment' and we just sat there in the crowded, noisy, cheerful room, talking Mandarin. After a few visits I got to know all the girls by sight, and a few who could speak English would hail me cheerfully when we met in the street.

The unfortunate experience was all my own fault. It happened that one evening after dinner, while I was still living in the hotel, I had nothing to do, and I thought I'd walk down to the escort bureau to see Ying Ping. When I arrived I realized, even before I went upstairs, that I might be making a mistake. Before when I had called, by daylight, it was all dull and quiet. I would go along Queen's Road, past the big market, until I came to an open-front shop that sold toothbrushes and such odds and ends. Next to this shop was a dark, narrow staircase up which I went, past a sinister-looking dentist's office and on to the top floor, which was the club. In the afternoon it was somnolent there. Old amahs shuffled around with buckets, for there wasn't a drop of running water in the building, nor any toilet. That condition was not unusual in Hong Kong. Girls slept soundly on the beds and couches scattered about the long room. They slept as they had fallen in the early morning, dressed in their tinsel finery, their faces smudged with enamel. They slept in crowds, piled on top of each other, anywhere, like kittens. About three or four they would begin to wake, yawning and stretching. I watched with amusement as they dressed over again for the evening, for the wardrobe was communal and they pulled dresses out of drawers any old place, wearing anyone's that pleased them or happened to fit.

That night Queen's Road was jammed, though, with a different sort of crowd, not a shopping crowd but a lot of young men looking for pleasure or mischief. When I had climbed the staircase next to the toothbrush shop and entered the club I knew I had made a mistake in coming. Lights blazed over the room and a lot of men were crowded around the mah-jongg table with some of the girls, playing. Chinese playing mah-jongg make a terrific noise. It's not at all like the quiet ladylike games we used to have in the States. They try to be noisy. They slam the tiles on the bare table and shout their signals, and everyone screams with laughter. A girl was playing the 'pip'a' [Chinese lute] and singing. I was blinded and deafened. Unfortunately my entrance caused a lot of commotion and Ying Ping spotted me and rushed over and made me sit down. . . .

We sat halfway down the corridor from the mah-jongg table near the door, while I tried to think of a graceful way to get out. Suddenly the door blew open and two husky young men staggered in and started down the hall toward the mah-jongg table. One of them glanced at me, paused, went on, and then turned around and came back. He tossed an apple in my lap.

'Hello', he said in a pleased surprise. Then he spoke in

Cantonese, and when I blinked at him uncomprehendingly he turned back to English. He reached out and grabbed my hand and pulled me to my feet, saying, 'Come on and have a drink'.

There was great consternation among the little girls. They fluttered around us like butterflies, explaining to him that I was not part of the club, but a client like himself. He didn't quite understand, naturally, but after a bit he apologized, sat down, and made polite conversation. I got out soon, though, without any more protest from Ying Ping, and hurried home to the Gloucester. I never again went back after dinner to the club. . . .

Christmas was riotous that year [1940]. Charles and I always invited everybody to our parties, and accepted practically all the invitations that came along. Later Charles usually grew more sober about the outside parties, but he never regretted or reneged on his own—or on mine. One time he stampeded my flat with the entire personnel of a large drunken stag cocktail party, at eleven in the evening. For Christmas Eve we blithely made three dates, which we didn't discover until it was time to sort things out and compare notes.

Never mind. We decided to do them all, pausing only to settle on one house for dinner, so that we could notify the other hostesses in time. . . .

The evening ended at a typical bright young colonial party, with discreet flirtations everywhere, sleek, beautiful women and dashing young men in uniform, all being incredibly childish, so it seemed to me, and playing charades. . . . We played out charades, we drank at the funny little bar, we giggled, we saw Christmas in. Half the men I remember that night, horsing around, are dead, and the girls are standing in line at Stanley [internment camp] with cup in hand, waiting for a handout of thin rice stew. Does that sound banal? It isn't. It hits me sometimes like a slap in the face. It has no implications; I'm not moved to philosophy when this happens, but there it is. It dazes me.

It shouldn't amaze me as much as all that. Charles, standing behind his barbed-wire fence in Argyle Camp [Kowloon internment camp], is not being dazed; I'm sure of it.

He kept telling me in his off-guard moments. There was one afternoon when he dropped in after a walk. Sometimes when he had the time after work he would change his clothes and go striding up to the Peak and down again at a pace nobody else could keep up, and he stopped in on the road down for a glass of beer. One evening he said:

'You'd better go away. If you're having a baby you won't be able to run very fast, will you?'

'Run from what?'

'The theory is that it would be the maddened populace, before ever the Japanese got in. Personally I believe that if the Sikhs were first there wouldn't be much left of any of you, even the Chinese. But that's only my own idea.' He added, as he always added, 'But it's entirely up to you of course. . . .'

'I said impatiently, 'Darling, the whole world's going to hell anyway. Suppose I go now; it may catch me wherever I am. Let's take whatever time we have left right here. I like Hong Kong.'. . .

I had better explain before we dive into the war that the whole Colony had already been warned for some months that we would in case of emergency go in for 'billeting'. The authorities were suitably vague as to why they would want a lot of housing space in such a case, but they were definite in saying that they wanted it, and this was the way they proposed getting it: all of us were to move at the first sign of war. Those of us who lived on mid-level, as I did, would be given addresses on the Peak. We were to lock our best things up but leave all our rooms but one free for the billetees, and our bedding and cooking implements were to be left for their use.

People living at sea level would be moved uphill too. People in Kowloon were to be brought over to the island. Nobody said what was going to happen to Kowloon.

Afterward we pieced it out. The 'defence plan' stipulated that the troops were to hold the enemy off as long as possible, probably three weeks. When at last they retreated the civilian population of Kowloon was to have been safely transported to the island, and there we were supposed to hold out against the besiegers for three months. It was all planned down to the last ridiculous detail, and there wasn't anything wrong with it except that it didn't work. We couldn't hold the enemy off at all as it happened.

The cocktail party went on to a buffet supper, but none of us was really merry. Charles' uniform, and the fact that he sat at the radio most of the evening, had a dampening effect on our spirits. People went home about midnight. I stayed. We listened to a broadcast from Tokyo at four in the morning, but there wasn't anything special in that, and at five o'clock I had to go home. Carola [her baby] was to be fed at six. I climbed the hill, holding my long skirt out of the dew and watching the cracked stairs carefully in the dawning light. . . . It was a lovely fresh morning, just turning cool. Hong Kong nights are often stuffy, but the dawns are better. It had been raining.

I was feeding Carola when the phone rang at six.

'Mickey?' said Charles. 'The balloon's gone up. It's come. War.' ▨

49

POEM, 1943

LIEUTENANT A. POTTER

Lieutenant A. Potter found himself incarcerated in Shamshuipo Prisoner of War Camp after the Battle for Hong Kong and the fall of Hong Kong on Christmas Day, 1941. Although with limited poetic expression, his verse speaks of the yearning of the men in the camp. With many other prisoners, he sailed to Japan on the ill-fated Lisbon Maru *in September 1942. The ship was torpedoed with heavy loss of life. This poem, dated May 1942, was found copied by Robert Owens, among the letters in his collection.*

M y prison window opens out
Upon a vista wide
An island studded harbour set
With hills on every side.
And right ahead aye calling me
A passage to the open sea.

My prison house is fenced around
With lines of knotted wire
And weaponed guards keep vigil there
To foil my heart's desire.
'Tis naught for fancy lets me free
Through yonder channel out to sea.

When morning comes along the hills
And floods the bay with light
I rise from my dream-haunted bed
And first direct my sight
Where running tide goes flowing free
Through that blest channel out to sea.

When night enshrouds the silent camp
And slumber holds me fast
'Midst all the dreams of distant ones
That conjure up the past
The constant vision comes to me
Of that near channel out to sea.

Though comfort small this place affords
My constant joy is found
In all the sweep of hill and bay
That rings the camp around
And for supremest luxury
I have my passage out to sea.

In selfsame manner in our life
In narrow limits cast
In action cramped with vision wide
Our mortal days are passed
But freedom for eternity
Waits through that channel out to sea.

And when the sun a flaming ball
Stoops westward to his bed
And Tsing I Lole stands castle-like
Against the flaming red
The sunset streamers beckon me
To sail that passage out to sea. ▩

50

THE YEARS AT STANLEY

JEAN GITTINS

Jean Hotung Gittins was born on Hong Kong's Peak in 1908, one of ten children of the prominent Eurasian community leader, Sir Robert Hotung. They were the first family with Chinese origins given permission to live on the Peak, and they owned three houses there. Jean Gittins attended the University of Hong Kong before the war, leaving to marry Billy Gittins, from another Eurasian family, who later died a prisoner in Japan. During the war she was interned at Stanley with many Westerners. Eurasians could choose whether or not to go into internment; many thought that food and accommodation would be better in the camps than in the rest of Hong Kong. Jean Gittins also hoped that there would be an exchange of prisoners from Stanley, and that she would be able to join her children in Australia. After the war, she moved to Australia, remarried and worked at the University of Melbourne. Her autobiography, Eastern Windows, Western Skies, *from which this chapter is taken, is one of the liveliest portrayals of Eurasians in Hong Kong, and of the continued strength of a particular woman.*

Had the Japanese set out with the intention of looking for a haven in which we would recover from our stresses, they could have found no better place than Stanley. As a haven for a small community it would have been perfect. Stanley peninsula juts into the sea from the south and more beautiful side of Hong Kong island. . . .

Before the war, Stanley had been a quiet resort where one could spend an afternoon away from the bustle of city life to enjoy the gentle breezes that came from the ocean, and to listen to the sound of water lapping against the sand. Rows of bathing sheds lined the beach, and weekend houses dotted the hillside below the green-tiled Carmelite Convent.

On a ridge rising from the peninsula end of the isthmus were the school buildings and bungalow type staff houses of St. Stephen's College. On the southern end of the ridge stood several blocks of residential flats of modern design. They were quarters for the British prison warders and their families. Below the flats was the prison hospital. On the other side of the road were the single warders' quarters and the prison officers' mess; in a sheltered hollow, between these and the sea, were seven blocks of drab looking flats built in the shape of a semicircle around a football field—quarters for Indian warders. Up on the ridge between the modern flats and the college buildings was an old cemetery, quiet and peacefully overlooking the boundless sea to the south and the island-studded bays on the west. Some of the gravestones, erected over one hundred years before, were weather-worn and shaded by scrub and small trees, the soil being too poor to support anything more lush. Here lay the dead of Hong Kong's first garrison. Many had succumbed to malaria. Some, it is said, had died as a result of drinking water which had been poisoned by the villagers who had resented the presence of the British.

During the fighting in December, 1941 there had been a gallant last stand in Stanley. Word of the surrender had not reached the troops in this area. After all else was sad and silent, the guns of Stanley fort could still be heard. Here, too, had been the scene of the most shocking of all atrocities. A band of drunken Japanese soldiers had invaded St. Stephen's Casualty Hospital. Medical Officers endeavouring to stop their progress into the wards had been cold-bloodedly shot and then bayonetted; nursing staff were raped and then raped again; patients were brutally bayoneted in their beds. The carnage was unbelievable.

As soon as the camp site was determined, advance parties had been sent to clear and to clean. They did their best under the circumstances. In a mass grave in the cemetery, they had laid to rest the remains of those who had given their lives but they could do nothing to obliterate the blood stains on the walls, the stairs and the grounds of the College. These remained throughout the war years, bearing mute testimony to their violent story.

But it was not as a haven that Stanley had been selected. It was merely a convenient spot in which to segregate the enemy aliens from the rest of the inhabitants of Hong Kong. Had the entire peninsula been made available, the area would have been utterly inadequate; to thrust some three thousand internees into a camp, the perimeter of which was defined by a barbed wire fence, enclosing a pitiful half a square mile, was an act of sheer barbarity unheard of in modern times. We later found out it took exactly seven minutes of brisk walking to reach the farthest boundary from any given point in the Stanley Civilian Internment Camp. Within this confined space we existed for over three and a half years.

The first batch of internees soon arrived and, to them, after the unspeakable conditions of the hotels in town, the camp was a delightful refuge. Boatload after boatload poured in. The buildings became filled to overflowing: as many as thirty people were packed into a flat and nearly fifty in a bungalow of average size. And still they came. There was no privacy granted to women, no consideration given to the aged. Strangers of both sexes were pushed into the same cubicle. Single men were housed mainly in the College where classrooms became dormitories, while in the gallery, along the passages and under the stairs, one stumbled across people trying to make a home—just anywhere.

Those early days were perhaps the most distressing. Overcrowding was only one of the many problems. Another was a lack of furniture or equipment of any kind. No one expected luxuries but even such necessities as beds and cooking utensils were not supplied. Many slept for months and some even for years on the floor. The rations were even worse than the rooms. Rice, vegetables and either a few buffalo bones, or a little bad fish, comprised the main delivery for the better days. . . .

The privations in camp brought out the worst in some people, as undoubtedly the better side of their nature emerged from others. Early on, members of our police force had found their way into one of the nearby godowns. They organized nocturnal raids on the stores. Instead of making the information available to the starving community, they hid their stolen goods in their own quarters and sold them piecemeal to the highest bidders at preposterous prices. Few had any scruples. Thieving was rife—a blanket was stolen from a sleeping infant when its mother left it alone for a few minutes. One day I saw something glint in the sunlight.

It was a gold Rolex watch. Three weeks slipped by before it was claimed. The owner said he never thought that anyone finding a gold watch would dream of returning it, so he had not even bothered look at the notice boards!

Like many others, Bill Faid [Jean shared quarters with the Faid family] had often thought of growing vegetables to supplement our diet but, because of the thieving, he had decided that it would be a waste of effort. Bill felt hungry all the time, yet he was unable to swallow the rice. It was pathetic.

'Why don't we have a garden on the roof?' I asked him one day.

'You must be quite mad, Jean Gittins. Who ever heard off growing vegetables on malthoid roofing?'

'We could make a garden,' I replied. 'I've been thinking about it for days. Here is my plan:

'You will have to persuade Mr. Pegg to let us have some short lengths of angle iron so that we could make some stairs to the roof. Once there we will build some beds against the alcoves for shelter. There's plenty of soil—good leaf mould—on the hillside. Our vegetables would be safe then as the only approach would be from this flat.'

By promising him a quarter share in the garden produce, we persuaded Mr. Pegg to get us the angle iron supports which were plugged into the wall to form steps leading to the roof. Bricks were collected at night and were piled two-high in front of the alcoves. Bill brought in bucket after bucket of soil and, before very long, we had a thriving garden with dwarf tomatoes, mint (for their vitamin A value), and shallots. Watering and a lack of tools presented problems of a minor nature but Bill, who was a Tynesider and had many friends among the Police, managed to get from them an old watering can and, with the bucket as well, we carried the water up the roof in reasonable comfort. As far as tools were concerned, we improvised as we went along. My experience with the Girl Guides had taught me always to find some way out of a difficulty. Practical application to theory, combined with long interest in gardening, had formulated the idea which Billy Faid put into effect. The vegetables certainly made the rice much more palatable and Bill was able at least to satisfy his hunger to a limited extent. Above all the joy of achievement was worth many times more than the effort expended.

As the warmer weather came on we drifted into a listless routine. The Japanese opened Tweed Bay for swimming. This was a godsend for the children, but it was a long walk to the beach and not many adults made the effort. Besides there were innumerable queues to attend. One day I had just returned from queueing for our midday meal when I found Bill Faid waiting for me with bad news. 'Billy?' I enquired. This was ever uppermost in my mind, especially as it had recently been rumoured that dysentery had reached epidemic proportions in Shamshuipo Camp.

'Oh no! Nothing like that. Just bugs on your bed.'

I knew that many people had them but I couldn't believe that I could be so afflicted. Yet I knew it must be true. Bill would not have said so otherwise. My heart sank.

'Come. I'll show you.' Bill said gently.

My bed was a folding camp stretcher which, knowing of the need for one in camp, I had bought in 'Cat Street' for a dollar. I had scrubbed it with a strong solution of lysol. Bill Faid now took the end support and showed it to me. I shall never forget the absolute horror and revulsion I experienced at the sight. It was not just a bug or two—they were there by the thousand, so full of blood and every human anaemic. I burst into tears. I felt so humiliated. As soon as lunch was over Bill said:

'Come on, Jean. Let's try to get rid of them.'

We poured boiling water over the wooden framework and along the seams of the canvas. Then, standing an old kerosine tin over our hotplate, he boiled the folded camp stretcher, first one end and then the other. This settled our immediate problem but there would always loom the dread of their return—this was the prisoners' curse of curses.

In May, 1943, we had a wonderful surprise. It was suddenly announced that 'as an act of grace' the Japanese authorities had agreed to repatriate the women and children, the sick and the aged. Relief had come at last! The excitement was terrific. We were instructed to advise our own camp office immediately of our preferred travel companions and destination, so that lists could be drawn up. . . .

Knowing that I would be going to Australia, Mr. Pegg asked if I would travel with his wife, Bobby, as she was to go to New Zealand. Naturally I agreed.

'I hope you will accept the advice of an old friend, Mrs. Gittins,'

Mr. Pegg said. He used to live in a house which overlooked ours on the Peak. 'As soon as you reach Australia, you must tell people who you are—that is, who your Father is. I have just returned from a visit over there. I assure you that this would mean a lot to your acceptance in that country.'

'I would prefer people to accept me for myself, Mr. Pegg.'

'Knowing you, I was afraid you would say that. Never mind. If you won't tell them, I'd have to see that Bobby does.'

It was as well that Plans for our repatriation never materialized.

As the days went by our meagre rations dwindled. It was now obvious that Hong Kong was being very effectively blockaded. We had meat but rarely for several months. Stocks of flour were low and could not be replaced. Colliers were not getting through from north China and Japan and, as a consequence, electricity was strictly rationed. Before long, the power supply gave out. We did not mind putting up with more restrictions and shortages because relief seemed so near at hand; but when the Canadians left in September and still there was not the slightest sign of our longed-for repatriation, we sank into a despair too deep for words. . . .

In January 1944 the administration of the Camp was changed from civil to military and the next six months proved some of the hungriest for many of us. We were put on Japanese army rations, which meant an additional four ounces of rice per day instead of flour and, in place of meat, we had an issue of four ounces of peanut oil and a dessert spoonful of sugar every ten days. The ration for an infant equalled that of a grown man. The military regime introduced one improvement. They organized communal gardens and issued extra rations to workers whom they considered in their employ. These included hospital personnel, kitchen workers and gardeners. Other workers drew their awards from the communal rations but no one begrudged them their extras. The garden produce certainly proved a welcome addition to the diet and, indeed, at many a meal we were entirely dependent upon it. ▦

51

LETTERS FROM THE CAMPS

ROBERT OWENS, WILLIAM OWENS, & SYBIL OWENS

Captured in the Battle for Hong Kong, Robert Owens (known as Bertie) became a Prisoner of War in Shamshuipo Camp in Kowloon for the duration of hostilities. Meanwhile, his brother William (Willie) Owens, a mechanical engineer, was interned on Hong Kong Island at Stanley. Also at the Stanley camp were the Owens brothers' sister-in-law Sybil, a trained nurse, and her young son, Bill. Sybil's husband, George Owens, spent the war years in India, while William's wife Jean and daughter Kathleen were in Australia. During the war, the internees sent censored postcards—many limited to twenty-five words—between the Hong Kong camps, and to the Owens brothers' sister Sadie in London. The photograph shows Sybil's wedding to George Owens in June 1939. Robert Owens is on the right.

3rd September, 1943

Dear Sadie,

Your October letter received August, glad getting news of all. Nothing from George for a long time. Please write him. Had card from Bertie July (Shamshuipo, Hong Kong), he was well then. See Willie most days, he is keeping fairly well.

Bill grows quickly, quite a little boy. Talks a lot about his Daddy. I am sure both his grandfathers want to see him. Its such a pity that George has missed so much of his first two years. I am longing for the day when we are all together again.

Our love to all in Derry,

from Bill and (Mrs.) Sybil Owens.

24–12–43

Longing for news of you all. Hope all well. Bill big boy growing rapidly. Wille, Bertie well. Please write George. Hope meeting soon.

SYBIL

William Waugh Owens, Block 8/Room 4
Stanley Civilian Internment Camp
Hong Kong, October 29th 1943

Dear Robert

Sybil, Bill—growing daily—send kind regards. We keep well, trust you are likewise. Time passes quickly, mornings occupied carpentry, repairs. Afternoons—mathematics, mechanics, electrical classes. Evenings—lectures, general subjects. Regards Bertram. Take care of yourself. Keep well. Write soon.

Wishing you every good.

Your loving brother,

Willie

*

Robert Andrew Owens
Hong Kong Prisoners of War Camp 'S'

Dear Father

Am well. Heard from Willie and everyone fine. Hope to hear from home soon. Wishing you all the best.

Your loving son,

Robert

*

From Robert Andrew Owens
Prisoner of War Camp
Hong Kong 1–11–44

Dear Father

Received (censored) card from George. Glad all are well at home. Self and Stanley folk well. Longing for recent home news to see where each member of the family is and what doing. Red Cross parcels received recently. Hope shall all be reunited again.

Your loving son,

Robert

Just after the war, Robert Owens writes to his sister.

Hospital Ship Oxfordshire
At Kowloon Wharf
Kowloon 1 Sept '45

My Dear Sadie,

After such a long absence in writing I hardly know how to begin again. Anyway it is a great relief to us all now that the war is over and we can write without any restrictions.

My temporary address I hope won't give any of you any cause to worry about me. Although I am not as fit as I should be I am not so unwell as to give you the impression that I am an invalid. . . . I only went into hospital about three months ago so it's just a pity the war didn't finish a bit sooner otherwise I might have avoided it. Well it can't be helped now, the wonder is that some of us who were really ill in the winter of 1942 are still to the fore. Those days I will not write about now, the loss of the 'Lisbon Maru' was just one thing you probably know more about it than I do but there were many men that I knew that went on that ship.

Conditions in camp for us were really bad then but it is all over now. Our spirits and determination to see a better day has now come and the same will carry us on till we are fit for work again.

We will probably sail from here in a few days time perhaps for Manilla where I think we will remain for a few weeks until the various nationalities are sorted out and they decide where we are to be sent to recuperate. No doubt I will be anxious to get home to see father and you all, but if we do go to Australia or South Africa possibly it will be better for us who won't get clear of hospital for the best part of a year. My pay as a lowly private in the H.K. V.D.C. [Hong Kong Volunteer Defence Corps] won't be much I suppose 2/6 per day, but the govt. will have to us put right again and perhaps if this illness had to be maybe it is a blessing in disguise. There is one other Hong Kong Electric man with me here. George Everett he was always very good to me. He went ill about a year ago and is running around now. His is the same complaint.

I have seen Willie frequently during the past ten days. He is well considering everything and expects to be going back to the China Light (and Power) any day.

217

He looks thin but that is only to be expected. He hasn't heard from Jean for a long time. I hope all is well with she and Kathleen. Sybil and Bill are quite O.K. I'm glad to say. Conditions ashore are quiet. There will be communal feeding and living arrangements for the essential feeding and living arrangement for the essential service people like Willie etc. and they will be provided for until things become more normal, so I don't think you need worry over anything.

I've just had the first good dinner for a long time. I'll see how my inside reacts after nearly four years of rice and boiled potato tops without meat and scarcely any fats. Tea after dinner instead of hot water and a slice of bread for breakfast is a luxury now. During all this time I received 7 Red Cross parcels. I expect we should have received one per month but that's what the Japs are like. Nothing was received from the *Awa Maru* [supply ship] although she arrived here with supposed Red Cross stores.

I met quite a few Irish chaps in camp attached to all branches. I was introduced one night to a young airman named Gargin from Dromore County Down.

Some of the Electric Staff and China Light Staff are in Japan having gone on various drafts. Those who are fit to go back to work are going but the power stations are in a bad mess. The China Light Station in Kowloon is now supplying Hong Kong and wood is the fuel. I've just seen Steve of the Hong Kong Power Station engineers and he says we hope to get half pay from the Company.

Six of the Hong Kong Electric employees have passed away that I know of. Some from wounds including the manager. Of him I had great regard. Three of us are on this ship. Considering everything, we are all very lucky.

I hope that you all at home are very well, that you have not suffered in health through worry or lack of food. We are all very vitamin conscious now for we realize how essential fats are and eggs, milk and cheese not to mention cigarettes. They have been the currency of Shamshuipo for nearly four years. It has been amazing what has been bought and sold for cigarettes there in the early days of the camp.

I hope you have not been deprived yourselves of the necessities of health. I just hope that times will soon be back to normal and from now on my meals will be my hobby.

I won't waste any more time to write more things that are indefinite. Manilla, Australia, where? Wait and see and eat, eat, eat all you can for never have we survived so long on so little. When I will eventually get home I won't say. Maybe I'll be expected to go back to Hong Kong again. The Hong Kong Electric won't let me down but I'm sure they won't give away any more than they can help. If I could get work in a better place than Hong Kong so much the better, that was my intention before the war, and if ever I could give advice to anyone going abroad I would say *go to a white man's country out of the tropics—lesser wages and health is more profitable.*

Well, I wish Father and you all the best and my usual XXX from your loving brother,

Bertie

*

With the war over, many civilians remained at Stanley Camp until they could be repatriated.

Stanley Camp
Hong Kong
Sept. 3rd, 1945

My Dear Sadie,

Thank God that this dreadful ordeal is over and that there is peace again. It is so nice to be able to write what one wants instead of 25 words. Do hope you are all well, you are always in our thoughts and prayers and Bill constantly talks of when he can help his grandfather dig the garden and pick some flowers, and that how long will it take the big ship to get to London and Londonderry.

That we are eagerly waiting news of George keeps us in a state of nervous tension but I know that as soon as possible, he will cable. His last letter was over a year ago.

Bill has long whispered conversations with him each night before he goes to sleep. Bill is a big boy but now needs a change of climate and food. Thank God, I have been able to keep him fairly fit, but it has been a struggle quite often to know what to give him to eat. Naturally—I am thinner but with better food and a change and reunion and all the joys of civilization and peace. This 'existence' of being a Prisoner of War has ended but it has made us all a bundle of nerves with all its unpleasant conditions and congestion. But we'll be OK soon.

Have just had a delicious surprise. My little Amah has just paid me a visit—complete with 2 bags of fruit, $\frac{1}{2}$ doz. eggs, and the *most* delightful pair of shoes for Bill of whom she was very fond. She has had to walk all the way here about 14 miles but I hope she can get a lift back. She seems just about the same. 'Missie— I can look and see Bill for you', she said straight away. But as we expect to go away at any moment I have given her a letter to the Matron of the Kowloon Hospital, which they hope to open up again quite soon and she would be good for she knows so many of my friends. The Chinese are very devoted servants.

This is a rather disjointed letter I am afraid, only we are living at such a pace these days and it is rather hard to concentrate.

A friend has taken Bill down to the beach. He can just 'swim' (dog paddle) and can write his name and he is left-handed and has hair the same colour as Sandy. Oh! how I am looking forward to being with you all again and to have a home to live in.

The most wonderful moment in our lives was the ceremony of Hoisting the Union Jack. Bill got a great thrill out of it. I just wonder if he is old enough to remember it later.

How is everyone—Bertie, as I expect you heard, went on the first 'Hospital' ship. He has a lung condition but hopes to get better with treatment. Willie, altho' thin, is standing by to go back to his old job.

Love to everyone.

Sybil

Hok-Un Power Station
China Light and Power Co. Ltd.
Kowloon
Tuesday 4th Sept. '45

My Dear Father,

Just a few lines to let you all know at home that I am well and busy at the moment in the Power Station trying to keep light power supplies going. The Japs have left things in a bit of a mess—but we will be able to carry with essential services and gradually get things straightened out.

Sybil is well, also Bill—both still out at Stanley camp and likely to be repatriated as soon as transport is available. Bertie has already left on board Red Cross ship. He is reasonably well—slight touch of chest trouble and generally in run down condition. I reckon that in a few months he will be as well as ever again. Myself had a talk with the Senior Military doctor looking after him—he said there was no need to worry in the slightest. A course of GOOD FEEDING and restful voyage home was all he needed and by the time he got home he was certain to be almost if not quite as fit as ever he was—so don't worry about him.

I long to see you all again—but do not expect to get away from the colony for a few months yet as all the Public Utilities—Essential Services—etc. are all under Govt/Military control and will be for some time until the life of the colony gets back to something near normal routine.

For myself, I am well, a bit thin but now that I am getting food have put on 12 pounds in the last 14 days and feeling so much better now that I am back at work again.

Have had no direct mail or news either from yourselves at home or from Jean in Australia for almost 3 years—but indirectly have learnt from time to time that you are all well.

Must close now, Dear Father, with best love and good wishes to you all from your ever loving son.

Willie

PART IX

AN INTERNATIONAL ENTREPÔT
1950s-1960s

'Life in Hong Kong had a feverish beat to it.'

ANTHONY LAWRENCE, 1958

'To operate illegally was infinitely easier than to obey the law. So it was in many aspects of life in Hong Kong.'

ELSIE TU, 1950s–1960s

52

THE WORLD OF SUZIE WONG

RICHARD MASON

*Throughout Hong Kong, certain elderly ladies still claim to have been
the model for Suzie Wong, and many people fail to realize that she
was a fictional character. Although the book—published in 1957—
now reads as an expatriate period piece, it continues to be one of the
most vibrant Hong Kong novels. The following extract is from the
opening of the novel, and introduces Suzie by her Chinese name,
Mee-ling.*

She came through the turnstile and joined the crowd waiting
for the ferry: the women in cotton pyjama suits, the men
with felt slippers and gold teeth. Her hair was tied behind
her head in a pony-tail, and she wore jeans—green knee-length
denim jeans.

That's odd, I thought. A Chinese girl in jeans. How do you
explain that?

I watched her hold out a coin to a squatting vendor in a battered old felt hat. The vendor twirled a piece of Chinese newspaper into a cone, shovelled in melon seeds, and exchanged it for
the girl's ten cents. She turned away, absently picking the seeds
with red-painted nails, and stopped only a yard from me.

Probably some wealthy taipan's daughter, I thought. Or a student. Or a shopgirl—never could tell with the Chinese.

She cracked a seed edgewise between her teeth, peeled back
the shell, popped the kernel into her mouth. Next to her an old
man in a high-necked Chinese gown leant on an ebony stick,
stroking his white, wispy, foot-long ribbon of beard. A baby peeped
from its sling on a woman's back, blinked its black contented eyes
in perfect infantile security. A youth in horn-rimmed glasses and
threadbare open-necked shirt held a book close to his nose. He

was studying a graph. The book was called *Aerodynamics*.

The girl nipped another seed between her white even teeth. Just then her eyes caught mine. They seemed to linger, so I said, 'I wish I could do that.'

'Hah?'

'Crack melon seeds—I've never been able to learn.'

'No talk.'

She turned her face away haughtily, looking over the barrier behind which swarmed the ten-cent passengers for the lower deck: the coolies in blue tattered trousers and the remnants of shirts, the Cantonese fisherwomen in conical straw hats and shiny black suits. She chewed self-consciously.

I tried not to feel snubbed. Well, I was always hopeless at pick-ups, I thought. I haven't the nerve.

And then she seemed to be . . . yes, she *was* relenting. Giving me a secret glance from the corner of her eye. Wondering if she had misjudged me.

She looked away quickly. Stole another glance. Then said guardedly:

'Are you sailor?'

'Me a sailor? Good Lord, no!'

She relaxed a bit. 'You're sure?'

'Oh, positive.'

'All right, we talk if you want.'

'Well, that's fine,' I laughed. 'But what have you got against sailors?'

'Not me—my father.'

'You mean your father doesn't like sailors?'

'No. He says sailors catch too many girls, make trouble.'

'So he won't let you talk to them?'

'No. He says, "If you talk to sailor, I beat you!"'

'Well, he's probably very wise.'

'Yes—wise.'

The ferryboat came churning alongside and the crowd moved forward. We jostled together up the gangplank—and chose one of the slatted, bench-seats on the covered top deck. The ferries were Chinese owned and run, and very efficient, and we had hardly sat down before the water was churning again, the engines rumbling, the boat palpitating—and we were moving off busily past the Kowloon wharves, past anchored merchant-ships, past great clusters of junks. Ahead, on the island across the channel, was Hong Kong, squeezed into a coastal strip a few hundred yards wide, with the miniature skyscrapers in the centre and on either side the long waterfront, stretching for miles, wedged with sampans and junks and behind rose the steep escarpment of the Peak, shedding the town and the lower social orders as it climbed, until at the higher altitudes there remained only a sprinkling of white bungalows and luxury flats inhabited by the élite.

We rounded the tip of the Kowloon peninsula, heading slant-wise across the channel for Wanchai, the most populous district of Hong Kong's eastern flank. I turned to look at the girl beside me. Her face was round and smooth, her eyes long black ellipses, and her eyebrows so perfectly arched that they looked drawn—but in fact they had only been helped out with pencil at their tips. Her cheekbones were broad, with hints of Mongolia.

'Aren't you a northerner?' I said

'Yes, Shanghai.'

'But now you live in Hong Kong?'

'North Point.'

'That's a good district.' And it accounted for her being on this ferry, since North Point lay beyond Wanchai—the expensive sub-urb beyond the slums—and the Wanchai pier was the nearest ferry-point.

'Yes, only I like Repulse Bay better. Nicer house.'

'You mean you've got two houses?'

'Four.'

'Four.' I knew that Chinese taipans, who made the richest Euro-peans seem like paupers, often owned two or three houses, but four was surely a record. 'You mean all in Hong Kong?'

'Yes, Hong Kong. My father is very rich, you know.' She looked pleased with herself, boasting with the naïvety of a child.

'Well, so I gather. And where are the other two houses?' She counted off the first two on her fingers and went on, 'Number three, Conduit Road. Number four, Peak. Number five—'

'Not *five*!'

'Yes, I forgot—number five, Happy Valley. But that's just small, you know—only ten rooms.'

'Oh, nothing at all,' I laughed. 'And what about cars? How many of those has your father got?' The Chinese collected cars even more assiduously than houses.

'Cars? Let me think.' She puckered her brow, counting on her fingers again, then gave up with a giggle. 'Oh, I forget how many cars.'

'I suppose you've a car of your own?'

'No, I'm too scared to drive. But I don't mind tramcars, you know—I like riding in tramcars.' She proferred the ten cents' worth of melon seeds in their newspaper cone. 'You want one?'

'Yes, but I honestly can't open them,' I said. 'You'll have to teach me.'

'Try first.'

I tried several, but one after another the seeds splintered between my teeth, crushing the kernels inextricably. My ineptitude sent the girl into delighted giggles; she buried her face in her hands, her pony-tail comically whisking and bobbing, then recovered herself, still twinkling with merriment, and gave me a demonstration—nipping a seed edgewise, peeling back the shell, handing it to me with kernel intact.

'Well, that's exactly what I did,' I said. 'Yours must have been an easy one.'

'No, all the same.'

'Then I give up. What's your name?'

'Wong Mee-ling.'

'Mee-ling—that's charming.'

'And you?'

'Robert Lomax—or Lomax Robert, your way.'

'Lobert.'

'No, "R".'

'Robert. Where do you live?'

'Well, actually. . . .'

'Peak?'

'Well . . . yes, mid-level. I live in a boarding-house—Sunset Lodge.' Well, it was nearly true—I had lived at Sunset Lodge until a few days ago, before moving down to Wanchai. And I couldn't very well tell her about the Nam Kok—not, at least, without knowing her better.

'You work Government? Bank?'

'No, neither. I used to be a rubber planter, but I chucked it up a couple of months ago to try and paint.'

'Paint?'

'Pictures.' I started to feel for my sketch book to show her, then remembered that all the sketches were of the Nam Kok and thought better of it.

'I know—artist.'

'Well, I don't call myself that yet.' Then, since we seemed to be getting on so well, I asked her if I could take her out to dinner one night; but she flatly refused.

'Then lunch?' I said.

'No.' She shook her head firmly so that the pony-tail wagged.

'But I'd love to see you again, Mee-ling. Can't we meet sometime?'

'No.'

'But why not?'

'I get married soon.' The marriage, she explained, had been arranged by her parents, according to Chinese custom, and she had not yet met her husband-to-be, though she had seen his photograph and thought him very good-looking. He also had plenty of money. However, even if she had not been getting married she could not have met me, for Chinese girls were not permitted the same liberty as English girls. The latter, she knew, could have boy-friends—could even allow their boy-friends to anticipate the role of husband—without seriously prejudicing their chance of marriage. She had even heard of one English girl, from the upper contours of the Peak, who had taken four boy-friends in as many years, and then been married to a high-ranking government official in the Hong Kong cathedral. But for a Chinese girl such behaviour was unthinkable—for purity was an indispensable condition of marriage, and on the day of marriage the husband's relatives were traditionally entitled to seek proof. And if the girl was found wanting the contract would be annulled; there would be nothing left for her but the streets.

'So you see, I have never had a boy-friend,' Mee-ling declared solemnly. 'I have never made love yet.'

'No?' I said, startled by such frankness.

'No, not once.'

'Well, you've still plenty of time.' I wondered if this kind of conversation, at first meeting, was typically Chinese.

She looked at me innocently. 'What do you call that in English?'

'Call what exactly?'

'I mean, if you have not made love—not with anybody.'

'Well, you call it "being a virgin",' I said.

' "Virgin"? Like that?'

'Yes.'

'Yes, virgin—that's me.'

She said this pointing to herself with a red finger nail. I burst out laughing.

'Mee-ling, you're marvellous!' I said. 'Anyhow, now we've got that point cleared up, won't you have dinner with me? I mean, if I promise not to try and spoil your record?'

She shook her head again stubbornly. 'No.'

'But—I'd love to paint you.'

'No. We say good-bye in a minute.'

The boat shuddered through its frame as the engines went into reverse. It nudged against the Wanchai pier. The gangplank clanged down and I followed Mee-ling off the boat in the crush of passengers. We paused outside on the quay where a group of rickshawmen sat idly between the down-tilted shafts of their rickshaws. Only a hundred yards along the quay was the Nam Kok, and I could see the blue neon sign over the entrance, and my corner balcony on the top floor, and my easel standing out on the balcony with the white square of canvas: the painting of Gwenny that I had started this morning.

Mee-ling followed my glance.

'What's that place?'

'Which . . .?' I said vaguely. Then I quickly reclaimed her attention, saying, 'Where are you going now?'

'Hennessy Road.'

'To catch a tram?'

'No, there is a car to meet me in Hennessy Road.'

'Can I come with you to the car?'

'No, the driver might tell my father.'

'And I suppose your father would beat you?'

'Yes—perhaps.'

'And you won't be a devil and change your mind about dinner?'

'No. I go now.'

She held out her hand for a formal good-bye, gave a sudden little giggle as I took it, as if at the daring of our encounter, then turned and bolted off down the side-street to Hennessy Road, her heels flying, her plume of hair bobbing. She looked back, briefly fluttered a hand at me, then was swallowed up by the foodstalls and rickshaws and pedestrian swarms.

Gone, I thought, gone. *Partir c'est mourir un peu* . . . And I turned away and crossed the quay to the Nam Kok; and as soon as I got up to my balcony I stood the drawing-board on the easel over the canvas of Gwenny, found a piece of charcoal on the cluttered table and made a quick sketch of Mee-ling while the memory was still fresh. I sketched her with that mischievous-innocent look in her eyes, one hand holding the melon seeds, the other pointing to herself; and underneath I wrote, 'Yes, virgin—that's me.'

It was not very good, but it made me smile, and I kept it. I have just looked at it again now. It is very smudged, and has been torn—by Mee-ling herself, who did not like it—and repaired with Scotch tape. But it still amuses me, because it was my first sketch of her. And I have been wondering how many times I have sketched and painted her since. Well, I never could count. But probably more times than there are melon seeds in that cornet—and more times than there are hairs in that pony-tail plume.

53
THE ERRANT COW

AUSTIN COATES

Austin Coates came to Hong Kong in the early 1950s as a Special Magistrate assigned to the New Territories. He relates his experiences in Myself a Mandarin—*from which this extract comes. In it he learns much about Hong Kong—and about himself.*

The Special Magistrate—need I explain?—had no court. The Chief Justice, the Senior Puisne Judge, the Puisne Judge, all the Judges, sat on the high benches in full-bottomed wigs with the Royal Arms behind them, in the splendour of teak-panelled courts, with a clerk to announce their comings and goings. No such trappings were apparently considered necessary to signal the dignity of the Special Magistrate. He, as it were, just sat down and was.

He had not been sitting down for more than five minutes when the door opened.

'Can you hear a case, sir?'

'Yes, certainly.'

The Chinese clerk-interpreter, lined, benevolent, judicious, circumspect, aged fifty-two or so, years of experience behind him, withdrew slightly to usher in five Chinese peasants, three men, two women, all dressed uniformly in black, the women with black cowls over their heads, their thick brown toes splaying out beyond the width of their clogs, their rough fingers spreading beyond the width of their wrists—those firm, inexpressive hands and feet accustomed to earth and animals, those hands on which the lives of every one of us depend. Without looking at me they sat down at the bidding of the clerk-interpreter in a row of black silence facing my desk.

By an ordinance promulgated when the New Territories were

leased from China, it was permissible for litigants to choose whether they would have the magistrate hear their suits according to the common law, or according to Chinese law and custom. The Special Magistrate thus had to be versed in two very different types of law, one English, the other Chinese.

The Special Magistrate knew nothing about the common law, and very little about Chinese law and custom. Faced with an element of choice on the part of litigants, however, he perceived the need to orientate his own views on the matter.

It was difficult to think of anyone in the legal profession, except the Special Magistrate, who would not know a great deal about the common law. A mass of literature existed around it, by means of which fine points could be argued or challenged. On the subject of Chinese law and custom, on the other hand, there was only one known textbook, written by a French Jesuit in the eighteenth century. Only one copy of this book was known to exist, owned by the University of Hongkong. It could not be borrowed, and it was in French.

Having in mind the possibility of appeals—to, say, the Chief Justice—against his decisions, the Special Magistrate saw certain advantages in adhering strictly to Chinese law and custom, about which he must quickly learn as much as possible, building himself into the entrenched position of an expert. Cognate to this was a visit to the University Library, there to find the Jesuit book—though without asking for it—to read as much of it as possible, and then secrete it in a most unlikely place at the top of a twelve-foot ladder, thereafter moving the ladder.

The Special Magistrate, however, as in the space of very few moments he was about to learn, had entirely misjudged what he was up against.

'Chinese law and custom, I presume?' I said to the clerk-interpreter, with a firm overtone of warning against the unwisdom of replying in the negative,

He nodded. He was a wise old bird. For twenty years he had served in the same district. He must, I judged, know it and its people backwards. The essential incongruity of the situation—that it should be I who was hearing the case, and not he, who must know far more than I ever would—made me wish we could change places. I then reflected that he probably knew nothing about my ignorance of law. A bold showing was indicated. I must not let the side down.

'Well, what's all this about?' I asked.

To my dismay, instead of framing the question politely in Chinese, he almost barked at them:

'All right, what have you come for?'

The man in the centre, not actually looking at me, in the strange way Chinese villagers have when face to face with a foreigner they do not know, replied:

'It's about the cow.'

It was an unpromising beginning. Instinctively I glanced from one to the other of the two women, wondering if by any chance the man was referring to one of them. Neither made any sign of being implicated. I collected myself.

'What cow?' I inquired.

'The cow that eats our grass.'

'Your grass?'

'Yes, the grass in our village.'

'Which village is that?'

He named a place I had not heard of. A query of the interpreter elicited the fact that it was a remote hill village in a roadless area in the eastern mainland part of the district.

'So there's a cow eating grass in your village?'

'Yes.'

'Why shouldn't it?'

I began to feel more magisterial. I also began to glimpse an understanding of my interpreter's firm approach to them. They had evidently come before the court with some reason, yet they had a peculiar resistance to explaining what that reason was.

'It won't eat the grass anywhere else,' the man answered. 'It's in our village every day.'

'That's true, Magistrate,' put in the man on the right, clearly identifying himself as a village elder. 'It passes my door every day.'

'You mean it's a cow from another village?' I inquired.

There was slight stir of relief. I had got the point.

'Yes.'

Groping back through textbooks, my memory came to rest on grazing rights. This was a tricky legal point.

'Is the grass it's eating on private or common land?'

I did not know it, but I had already collided with a buffer. In a Chinese village there is no such legal distinction. I did not catch what the interpreter said, but the man did not understand it.

'It's our grass,' he repeated.

This was not good enough. The magistrate was not to be fooled by rustic simplicity.

'Your grass? What do you mean? Is it your own grass, or grass on land owned by the village?'

'It's our village grass.'

It was evidently common land. What, I wondered, was the position regarding grazing rights on common land, whether under the common law or under Chinese law and custom? I had by now been a magistrate for just fifteen minutes, and was already at sea.

'Which village does the cow come from?' I asked.

He named another place I had not heard of. The interpreter explained it was another remote hill village about a mile distant from the first.

'Then someone must bring the cow each day to your village.'

'No.'

'Are you telling me that this cow walks by itself all over the mountains every day to eat grass in your village, and then goes home in the evening all by itself?'

Becoming somewhat irritated, I was relieved to observe that the interpreter's temper was rising in harmony with mine, only rather more so. He had twenty years of it, after all. The five villagers, now I came to think of it, were facing me with the obstructiveness of five armoured tanks.

The procedure of the court gradually became apparent to me. Its function was not to provide a means whereby complainants might express their grievances. At least, not all at once. The procedure was less explicit, more defensive. Faced with five or six unknown people, it was the magistrate's duty to find out why on earth they were there.

'No, the cow doesn't come by itself,' said the man in the centre.

'Then someone must bring it.'

'No.'

'Who milks the cow?' I demanded.

The interpreter repeated my question angrily before recalling himself to common sense. A tremor of embarrassment at such an odd and faintly improper inquiry passed along the five. The interpreter hastily explained to me that cows are not kept for their milk, but as draught animals. It was stupid of me. I knew quite

well that Chinese did not drink cow's milk, but somehow . . . a
cow. . . . We were in a mess.

'If the cow doesn't come by itself,' I asked, 'how does it get
there?'

'Get there?' the man replied in a puzzled tone.

'Yes? How does it come from its own village to your village?'

'It doesn't.'

'But you've just been telling me it does, every day!'

The temperature was rising. The interpreter was near to shouting at the man. For my own part, I could not recall ever having
had my way so completely blocked by a cow.

'It doesn't come every day.'

'But you have just said that it does!'

'No. Not every day.'

'Then it doesn't eat your village grass every day.'

'Yes, it does.'

'For goodness' sake, Mr. Lo,' I expostulated to the interpreter,
'what is this man talking about?—Look. Either this cow comes
from the other village every day and eats your grass, or it doesn't
come from the other village every day. And if it does come from
the village every day, someone must be bringing it.'

'No. No one brings it.'

'Then it doesn't eat your grass every day!'

'Yes, it does.'

Even the villager's temper showed signs of rising by this time.
He seemed to have adopted the attitude that it was I who was
being stupid, not he.

'Then, for heaven's sake, how does it get home to the other
village at night?'

'It doesn't go home to the other village.'

'Well, where does it sleep, then? On the mountain?'

Mr. Lo, I was glad to note, was participating full-blast in this
battle of intellect. The impatient *hauteur* with which he sniffed
'On the mountain?' would have reduced anyone other than a
New Territories villager to shamed silence.

'No,' the villager said calmly. 'It sleeps in our village.'

Mr. Lo sighed and shook his head. I took a deep breath and
started again.

'Now, let's get this straight. A cow from another village eats the
grass in your village every day, but it sleeps in your village.'

'Yes.'

'Well, what does the owner of the cow say to that?'

'Nothing.'

'Well then, what are you complaining about?'

Dead silence.

'Repeat the question, Mr. Lo.'

'What are you complaining about?' the interpreter repeated. He looked very angry. If I had been the villager I would have been terrified. None of the five armoured tanks expressed the slightest reaction.

I leaned back deeply in my chair, and took out a cigar. In moments of stress, nothing is so soothing as a cigar. Mr. Lo was watching me cautiously. I had a slight sense of guilt. There was no Royal Arms behind me. I had no wig or clerk of court. Yet . . .

'Is it considered proper to smoke while hearing cases, Mr. Lo?'

'Most district officers find it a help, sir.'

'Good. Can you ask someone to find me a match?'

The necessary orders were issued. A box of matches appeared. In ancient China, part of a magistrate's duty was to soothe the people. In the modern world, the more cogent factor seemed to be the soothing of the magistrate. A film of blue smoke went up.

'Now then,' I resumed, 'do you use the cow in the fields?'

'A little.'

The expression he had actually used was a Chinese ambiguity which could mean 'Yes,' 'Hardly at all,' or 'No.' Mr. Lo, taking his choice, had settled for a middle course.

'A little!' I exclaimed. 'What do you mean by that? Do you or do you not use the cow?'

'No.'

'Have you ever used it?'

'Yes.'

'Did the owner complain?'

'No.'

'But he's complaining now?'

'Yes.'

'He wants the cow back in his own village.'

'Yes.'

I clenched the desk.

'But when you came in here, you began, if you can remember, by complaining that a cow from another village was eating your grass!'

'Yes. There's no suitable grass in the other village.'

It was incomprehensible.

'Who is the owner of the cow?' I asked.

'Her,' said the man, using a rough, off-hand word, indicating the woman on his right.

Beneath her black cowl, the half-hidden little face stirred.

'Ah!' I said. 'Now we're coming along. You are the owner of the cow?'

'Yes.'

'Yes, *what*!' the interpreter snapped at her.

'Yes, Magistrate,' the woman said demurely.

It was too awful for words. At the very entrance of a woman into the picture, the interpreter's voice had hardened. I did not, of course, know at the time that this was another outcome of my skilled interpreter's experience—that it is hard enough to get sense out of a village man, still worse to get sense out of a village woman, and that a woman litigant or witness, unless dealt with from the outset with the utmost firmness, will set any case in the wildest disorder.

'You are from the other village?' I said.

'Yes, Magistrate.'

'And you want the cow back?'

'Yes.'

'How did this man start using your cow in the first place? Did you allow him to?'

'Yes.'

'And now you've changed your mind?'

'Yes.'

'Did you charge him any money for the use of it?'

'No.'

'But you want the cow now for use on your own fields?'

'I have no fields, Magistrate.'

'Then what do you want it back for?'

'I want it back.'

'What d'you want it back *for*?' the interpreter barked at her.

The little face beneath the cowl hardened.

'I want it back.'

'Is it true,' I asked, 'that there isn't enough suitable grass in your village to feed the cow?'

'There isn't much.'

'There's none,' said the man.

'Then would it not be more sensible,' I said to the woman, 'to continue to allow this man the use of your cow, but charge him for it?'

'I wouldn't pay!' said the man sharply.

There was something in the way he said it. And at this moment, the magistrate, lulled by the cigar, became subject to a brainwave.

'You say you come from the other village?' I asked the woman.

'Yes.'

'Where do you actually live?'

'In *his* village,' she said, nodding at the man, and using the same off-hand expression he had used about her.

'Mr. Lo, there is a relationship of some sort between these two people. Can you find out what it is?'

The interpreter asked a rapid question. There was a scowling silence, then a word from the man. They were husband and wife.

'Ah!' I said, and addressing the wife, 'The position is that you want to go back to your village, and you want to take your cow with you. Is that it?'

'Yes, Magistrate.'

We had arrived. It was a divorce case.

By this time, the magistrate felt he had had about enough. He also felt it was about time the staff started exerting themselves on his behalf.

For this was what lay behind the manner in which the case had been presented to me—neat, as it were. It was a new officer's first day, and the staff were unsure of themselves, waiting to find out what methods the new officer would use, and also—perhaps more salient—how much he knew. It was almost certainly with this latter point in mind that the clerk-interpreter had introduced the case without making any prior inquiries of his own, leaving me to make all my own mistakes.

The district, with its population of some 250,000, and its large and rapidly expanding industrial zones, was a hectically busy place. If the district officer was to deal personally with every case from the start, the work of the office would rapidly come to a standstill.

'Mr. Lo, will you please take these people out to your office, disentangle the facts, and when you are able to explain the thing to me clearly, bring them back, and we'll go into it.'

Thereafter, this became the procedure. It did not eliminate the absurd misunderstandings of which my own ignorance was a main cause; but it did at least minimize them.

About an hour or so later, Mr. Lo returned with the group, and the case came to make sense. The woman on the man's left—the one who so far had said nothing—was a second wife, married about a year previously. The first wife, who had been married to the man for four years, and had brought the cow with her, complained that the husband was cruel to her, neglecting her in favour of the new wife. She wished to divorce her husband, and return to her own village.

The village elder insisted that the case was nonsense, that the husband was not in the least cruel to the first wife, that on the contrary the woman had a shocking temper, and should learn to be more kind to her husband.

By the degree of the elder's intrusion into the affair, however, I hazarded an unspoken guess that he had a stake in it. He spoke gravely of the disgrace of divorce, of the pointlessness of the woman returning to her own village. My private conclusion was that he did not much care whether the woman left her husband or not. The elder's moralizing had an un-Chinese ring about it, specially prepared for foreign ears. What he did not wish to see leave the husband was the cow, which the elder was probably using on his own fields.

As for the husband, it was hard to say whether he was more concerned about his wife or the cow. It looked to me like a bit of both, coupled with the fact that his second wife gave him more comfort than the first.

The relations between the husband and the first wife were clearly very bad indeed. They had not looked at each other once. When one spoke of the other, each turned stiffly the other way. The wife was tense, her pride injured. The husband was sour and aggrieved, possibly knowing somewhere he had done his first wife an injury by marrying the second, but far too obstinate ever to admit it.

In general—but I do not think I was aware of it till that moment—I dislike anything in life involving the severance, in anger and unforgiveness, of attachments through the medium of which sympathy and understanding have once flowed. Whether in marriage, friendship or parental relations, such severances seem to me to dishonour life. Basic in the approach to a case of divorce—and I was surprised by the strength of my own conviction—it seemed to me to be the magistrate's duty to struggle to prevent divorce, to restore harmony. But when they are sitting in front of you, with faces like these, how to set about it?

The question I wished answered was the one which could not be asked: whether or not the wife's motive in seeking divorce was that she had a lover. This inadmissible, there remained the factor which had not so far entered into the case—law. Could it not perhaps be used, albeit in a somewhat unlikely way? As a warning rattle.

'Are you your husband's *kit fat*?' I asked the first wife—a *kit fat* is the first wife a man takes, ranking senior to any other wife he may subsequently take.

'Yes.'

'Mr. Lo, I thought that, in Chinese law and custom, there was no such thing as divorce between a husband and his *kit fat*.'

'That's long ago, sir. Nowadays, divorce is recognized custom.'

My first attempt had failed.

'Have you any children?' I asked the wife.

'Two girls.'

It was old Chinese law and custom that, in divorce, boys go to the husband, girls to the wife.

'You realize you will be solely responsible for the girls' upkeep?'

She was silent for a long time. There was always the possibility that foreign magistrates might not know the old Chinese laws.

'Yes,' she said at last.

'Do you think you can feed them? You have already told me you have no fields.'

'I shall try my best.'

'How will you do it?'

'I don't know.'

The elder had craned forward tensely. The husband was scarcely breathing. It inclined me to think there was not a lover. What seemed to be at issue was the cow.

'Don't you think you'd better think it over carefully for a week, and come and see me again? I don't want to give you a divorce, and then find you here a month later, asking for social welfare for the upkeep of your children. If that happens, the government will blame *me*.'

For the first time in the hearing, the woman raised her eyes and looked straight into mine. It had obviously never occurred to her that a magistrate could be in trouble because of her. Unconsciously, I had touched something. In some peculiar way, I had become personally involved in the affair. She was not, as the elder had insisted, a scolding woman. That was not the truth. There was something else to it. But what? She was a nice little woman.

I looked down the line of faces, stern, withdrawn. How to find out the truth from behind such barriers of reticence? Whom to question? What to ask? How to avoid the easy, but unsatisfactory, decision? How to gain access to the right one?

In a Western court, someone would have to prove cruelty, with witnesses publicizing all kinds of unpleasantness, much of which might be faked. Here, no such thing. There they sat in front of you, awaiting your decision, in an atmosphere of suffering and frayed tempers, waiting for you to help them; and there you were, with no sure facts, no definite evidence, nothing much to go on, but such small corners of truth as they were prepared to show, beyond which lay something else hidden, unidentifiable.

A week later they came again. In the intervening time we had heard quite a number of other cases, and Mr. Lo was beginning to feel more at ease with me. Actually, the staff as a whole had now time to assess me. What their real verdict was, I would never know, of course; but they seemed to have decided that I needed help. Mr. Lo had done some homework on the divorce case; and as he entered the room, something about his appearance suggested that he had arrived at the root of the problem.

'I didn't realize,' he said, 'but that second wife, the one who said nothing—she has a son.'

'A son? The husband's?'

'Yes. Only a few weeks old.'

I leaned back contentedly in my chair.

'Ah! I see! And the first wife only had two daughters.'

'That's it.'

That was indeed it! And to think I had thought of asking everything else except that! I had, as it were, been mesmerized by the cow.

'Ask the first wife to come in, Mr. Lo—and the diagnosis was confirmed. What was closer to the bottom of it than anything else we could find (you never quite got to the bottom of any case) was that she had lost face dreadfully by the birth of the second wife's son. This ascertained, I went all out to reason her back into staying with her husband.

It was then I began to appreciate the wisdom of Mr. Lo's hardness of tone when it was a woman he was questioning. The more understanding of her problem I tried to show, the more impossible she became. Her response to every artifice of reasoning was to put forth yet another demand, which her husband must obey if she was to remain with him. These mounted in number and ferocity till, had we brought wife and husband to written agreement, the result would have read like an armistice between victor and vanquished.

Worse still, I observed that I was alienating Mr. Lo, whose temper, like a balloon of which someone has surreptitiously cut the moorings, was rising independent of the human will it was supposed to serve. Seeing I was on a wrong course, and anxious not to be left behind by the rising balloon, I finally feigned an outburst of temper superior to Mr. Lo's.

'I've had enough of this nonsense!' I said to the wife. 'You're darned well going to stay with your husband; and I'm not so sure I don't believe what the village elder says about your being an impossible woman to live with.'

She quietened down immediately. I felt remorse.

'Don't worry,' I said. 'Maybe you'll be the next one to have a son.'—A rumour of a smile across her lips showed that this was not beyond the bounds of possibility.—'And you must admit it will be nice for your cow to be able to eat the grass it likes.'

At that moment I learned another lesson. The magistrate should never try to be funny. She burst into tears.

The problem now was that we had the facts of the case, but the Special Magistrate was at the end of his resources. How to settle the affair?

'What d'you think we ought to do, Mr. Lo?'

He reflected an instant.

'I should just give them a talking-to, sir.'

'A talking-to?' I said, aghast. 'What d'you mean? A sort of old-fashioned homily?'

'Yes, I think that would do.'

And so, I called them in, and gave them a homily—the first of many, in many different cases. Throughout my years as a magistrate I was never able to reconcile myself to this Chinese method of settling matters. To the end, I always found my own homilies acutely embarrassing, mainly because I could never believe they would settle anything, and they seemed so dreadfully glib.

But when, later on, I came to hear cases assisted by other members of the staff, I found that they too agreed with Mr. Lo on the importance of a homily as a means of bringing peace. As one of the staff explained to me, many of the people who were brought to us by their village elders (as had happened in this divorce case) were brought for the express purpose of being given a homily—being told what to do, and how to behave—after which there would be peace, the magistrate's word being law.

In other countries, of course, a magistrate's word is law; but really, only when he is delivering his findings. In this antique Chinese village world, amid the shadows of departed dynasties, there was the difference that the Magistrate's *every* word was law. One had to be very careful what one said.

In this, my first case, therefore, I began by declining to agree to a divorce. Addressing the husband, I told him he had done a very foolish thing in taking a second wife. He should have been more patient. His first wife might very well bear him a son. He had, however, been impatient, and would have to take the consequences. Instead of having to bear the taunts of one wife, he now had to bear the taunts of two. Instead of having to be fair and patient with one wife, he now had to be fair and patient with two. Let him see that he was. He was the master of his own house. If he were giving a feast in his house, he would not wish to see some guests well provided for, while others did not have enough to eat. It was the same with his wives. As guests are invited to a feast, so had he invited them to his house. As guests must be provided for equally, so must it be with wives. If he remembered this always, there need be no trouble. And let him never forget that he was the master, which meant that while he had his duties to every person under his roof, it must also be he who gave the orders.

To the first wife, I said I realized she had had a distressing and difficult time. This, however, did not mean that she could disobey her husband, and do what she would. She must always obey her husband. It was good that she had brought her case before me, because she was in distress, and did not know what to do. If she was ever in distress again, she must come at once and tell me about it. She had nothing really to complain of. She was the senior wife; and the little boy born to the second wife would have to call her Mother. Nothing could shake her position in the family, unless she herself was foolish enough to shake it—which I felt sure she would not be, particularly now that she knew she could come at any future time, and ask the court to help her. She was a woman of means owning her own cow, and being senior wife to a hard-working and well-thought-of farmer. She should be proud of her position.

To the second wife, I said I was very glad to know she had borne a son. She was a fortunate and happy woman, married to a good and sensible man. Her position in the household was that of second wife, bound to obey the orders of the first wife. I was aware from her behaviour in the court, I said, that she had appreciated this from the first day of entering the house. I trusted she would continue to do so. She should guard against boasting about being the mother of her husband's eldest son, as I was sure she would, since boasting about a son brings ill-luck; and the loss of a son would mean ill-luck to the whole family.

The second wife, who had been expressionless throughout, unexpectedly smiled.

'I see you know what I mean about not boasting,' I said. 'Does your little boy have a girl's name?'

'No, Magistrate,' she said, in hasty confusion.

'What do you call him, then?'

She blushed, and did not know where to look.

'We call him Pig,' she whispered.

'Very wise,' I said. 'Then heaven will not take him away from you; and all of you in this united family will have prosperity. Make sure your little boy, when he is old enough, always obeys his Elder Mother. And may there be many more sons among you!'

I went with them to the door, and, holding Mr. Lo beside me, in a friendly European, but highly improper Chinese, way laid my hand beneath the wrist of the senior wife.

'No more nonsense from you,' I said, when the others were out of earshot. 'But if it's serious, come and see me at once.'

She was terrified and ran away. I felt as if I had made an indecent suggestion.

We never saw them again—not surprising, some might say.

But did it signify success or failure? That, as I was soon to learn, was the most hauntingly worrying of a magistrate's problems—never knowing the full extent of one's own failures. Some of the failures returned quickly enough. But what of these others, of which the only outcome was silence?

In the office they said that, in most cases, silence could be interpreted as success. I was never sure myself. Sometimes—many times, I fear—it was the silence of disappointment at the magistrate's inability to understand. Because, being a European, one never does *quite* understand. . . .

I walked back slowly towards my desk, and a final incongruity struck me. Before me, between two windows looking out on a small, tree-covered hillock, was a portrait of Her Majesty the Queen. What more simple example of the strangeness of Hongkong could there be than the scene this room had just witnessed? There we had been, beneath the beneficent gaze of our Christian sovereign, quietly engaged in promoting harmony among concubines. 🔳

54

FOREIGN CORRESPONDENT

ANTHONY LAWRENCE

Anthony Lawrence's dispatches from Hong Kong cover four decades and have made him one of its most knowledgeable and respected foreign correspondents. This passage covers his early days in the Colony in the late 1950s.

Hong Kong Harbour was bathed in strong sunset light that turned the water to a kind of molten metal and gilded the warships, ocean-going freighters, junks and sampans and the walls of high business buildings on the further shore. Packed with me in the ferry, home-going Chinese office-workers turned tired faces to this western sky; and next to me the old Catholic priest in his dirty, cream-coloured soutane looked up from his Chinese newspaper.

I asked him whether it would take long to know enough characters to understand the news. He said it was a difficult language but not impossible. He pointed out certain characters to show how simple they were. He said: 'You will learn it one day if you really want to.'

What did his newspaper say about the bombardment of Quemoy [Jinmen] and Matsu [Mazu]? Nothing new, he said, only the same agency reports as in the English-language papers. What would happen? Who could tell? His own life was with the boat people of Hong Kong, the Tankas who dwelt on the junks and prayed to Tien Hau [Tin Hau], the goddess of the sea. He did not concern himself much with government.

Two hundred miles to the north the Communist guns blasted away. The mainland armies might launch an invasion of the islands at any time. War between China and Chiang Kai-shek. War between China and the United States, Chiang's ally!

Fear is a factor that counts heavily in assessing news. Troubles of faraway people you know nothing about rarely make the front page. But if world war might result? If the Americans are involved? That's different. It brings in something familiar—and disturbing. People in the West felt varying emotions towards the Americans in the autumn of 1958, ranging from gratitude to loathing; but everyone agreed that a war between the United States and the most populous nation in the world would be a most explosive event. There had been a taste of it in Korea in 1950. Another chapter would be far more serious.

Every evening at seven o'clock I'd be waiting in a studio of Radio Hong Kong by the waterfront and London would call me on the radio link, via Ceylon and Africa, for a despatch on the latest developments. They were always wanting more.

Arrangements grew more complicated. Reporters on Formosa, seat of the Chinese Nationalist Government, had instructions to telephone me during the late afternoon so that their reports could be relayed to London on my radio circuit. But most of all the London office needed assessment of events. That was where Hong Kong was useful—you could listen to diplomats, journalists, businessmen, captains of ships, and come to reasonable conclusions. My reports grew long, but London used every word. For the first time since coming to the Far East I led the radio headlines for days running.

I had a room in the Gloucester Hotel, a solid grey pile near the water-front in the big business and banking district. Life in Hong Kong had a feverish beat to it. Three million Chinese fighting to keep alive and grow rich in a no-holds-barred, *laissez-faire* jungle of energy and tumult. The purposeful crowds in the street, seen from the fifth-floor hotel window, were not like ants or any herds of animals; they were thousands of individuals, fiercely pursuing their private destinies. Passing among those crowds you looked into the face of a human nature as amorally predatory as praying mantises or the sharks waiting off the islands. Here the Cantonese merchant, the well-tailored Shanghai speculator and the British banker looked each other over and approved what they saw. Hong Kong was a place where a shrewd man might make a staggeringly large amount of money—and legally, too.

What made the place so restless, so excited and feverish after Singapore was the need to make your money quickly. The future of Hong Kong was uncertain, so hurry up and do what you have to do, make your fortune and buy shares abroad.

In the early weeks of that visit I was not primarily concerned with Hong Kong. It was simply a listening post for the action further up the China coast. But living there for several months brought me much closer to the Chinese people of the South and I had a taste of what China, the real China, might be like. Compared with these quick-thinking, tireless Cantonese, the people down in Singapore seemed like plodding provincials. The Cantonese in Hong Kong were big-city types and they did not consider themselves as Overseas Chinese at all. Hong Kong was China and they were part of it. Hong Kong a British colony? What did that mean? Barbarians come with guns and trample on you in your time of contempt, and put barbed wire along one of your rivers and call it a frontier. But in the end they will all have to go home.

Of course in the short term three million Chinese found it best, for reasons of politics or money, to come to live in Hong Kong under the barbarian flag. But they never thought of Hong Kong as a country separate from China, a place a man owed allegiance to. The Chinese are used to living with the insecure, the provisional. Now in Hong Kong they followed with their usual absorbed attention the artillery duels around the off-shore islands, the airbattles over the Formosa Straits. What would it mean for them, for their survival?

Foreign journalists from many capitals came to Hong Kong in those days to cover the story, but the men I remember most clearly were correspondents already based in the colony. To me, a newcomer, they appeared as picturesquely larger than life, endowed with great knowledge, shrewdness, and generous feelings. They were helpful to the green and ignorant in circumstances where without their help and without enough background knowledge it would have been only too easy to make serious mistakes and appear a fool on the air.

That kind of good nature within the profession is hard to repay. What you can do is seek to imitate it in later years in dealing with still newer men. But I should have to improve greatly on present performance to count myself in the line of Richard Hughes, Ian McCrane, Gordon Walker, Bill Stevenson, Francis Lara. 🔳

SETTING UP SCHOOL

ELSIE TU

As a political and inspirational force from the 1950s to the 1990s, Elsie Tu (formerly Elsie Elliott) has often been in the news, speaking and acting in the interests of the Chinese in Hong Kong. She arrived in the Colony as a Christian missionary and remained in the Territory after leaving the mission. In her eighties, she was still serving as an active member of Hong Kong's Legislative Council. This extract from her autobiography begins in 1956: she has just left the mission in order to found a school for Chinese children.

Having put behind me the battles of the church and home, I was now able to concentrate on the wider issues of the community. Even before I left the church, my friends and I were fully aware of the political situation in Hong Kong. It was not possible to live amongst the workers, as we did, without seeing how they were exploited by industry and squeezed by corrupt officials. The very house we lived in would not have existed if the owner had not paid to build it illegally. We knew that squatters came under pressure from triad members (*ba wongs*), who took over an area and only allowed people to build if they paid their dues to the triads. When there was no land left in the area on which they could make a squeeze, it was common for the triads to burn the buildings to the ground and start over again. No hawker could operate without paying a bribe and taking an occasional turn at being arrested in order to keep up statistics for hawker arrests. One of our English church members—an employee of the Public Works Department—told us incredible stories of corruption within the government, stories which I now know were entirely true.

But no matter how unjustly people were treated, I was not permitted by the church to do more than mention it among friends. To take up the cudgels with the authorities, or even to write a letter to the press, was absolutely taboo. . . .

We tried especially to take care of our pupils and their families. Fires in the hut areas were frequent, and totally destructive. Fire precautions were scanty or even totally lacking in the squatter areas. Usually the whole area would burn itself out. Some squatters said that the fires were arranged by the triad gangs and the Fire Services Department: once an area was full of huts, the triad gang would attempt to destroy it and start again. I do not doubt that there was some truth in these allegations. A friend in the Fire Services, a European, told me that he once overheard the firemen in charge bargaining a price before putting out a fire. Another friend said that when a fire occurred in the factory next to his, he had to pay a large sum of money to dissuade the firemen from opening the doors and allowing the fire to spread to his premises. Another had to pay to prevent them turning the hoses on his goods after a fire had abated. It was sheer blackmail. One hopes that the firemen today are of a different calibre.

Our pupils all lived in huts, and inevitably some were involved in fires. We would rush to the scene of a fire, usually during the night, to see how we might help. The other children would then take the victims of the fire, if they were students, to buy new books and clothes. The poor understand the sufferings of the poor, and try to help each other. I found this repeatedly in those days. It is unfortunate that as circumstances improve, people often become more selfish. Fortunately, it is not always so. . . .

My work in the school often took me to the Education Department. At that time, the government was interested in educating the children of the rich, but I wanted to expand our school for the underprivileged. Two incidents perhaps indicate the attitude of the Education Department in those days.

On one of my visits, the Assistant Director offered me a job teaching European children, as they had a vacancy. I explained that I could have done a job like that in Britain but had come to Hong Kong to educate the underprivileged local children. The Assistant Director replied, 'We have built housing for the underprivileged. Do you expect us to give them education, too?'

I replied that I did. It took the government a long, long time to discover that either education or prisons must be provided in a place where wealth and poverty are so close in proximity that idleness in youth may lead many to crime. It says much for Chinese family life that so few young people took to crime. Nevertheless, some did, and in 1978 the government acknowledged this by providing free education for children up to the age of fifteen.

The second incident was an encounter with the Director of Education. A child of nine had just left our primary school to go to work because his family needed his earnings. I felt distressed about this, and mentioned it to the director. He replied, 'It will do him good.'

I sat amazed, and finally retaliated, 'Of course, if he were your child, you would not talk like that.' With such people in charge of education, it is small wonder that it was so frustrating to run a school for poor children. No one was interested. . . .

In order to register a private school, one has to satisfy the requirements of the Public Works Department for loading, the Fire Services Department for fire risk, and the Education Department for academic standards. No one could complain about that, because ostensibly it was for the protection of children in schools. But in those early days it was almost inevitable that one had to pay one or all of them a bribe, and my problem was that I offered no bribes. Very few Europeans, I suspect, paid bribes, perhaps because corrupt officials knew that they might report corrupt practices. It was easier to intimidate Chinese people, for it was a case of pay up or no registration. . . .

One of the buildings we rented was on the top floor of a building that had shops on the ground floor. When the Fire Services came to inspect it, they said that the premises were too high: they had no ladders long enough in case of fire. I wondered what the domestic tenants would do if there was a fire. I discussed the matter with the Director of Fire Services, pointing out that rooftop schools in government housing estates were even higher than our building and that they were registered. He sympathized, and it was unusual to get sympathy from a bureaucrat. 'Technically,' he said at last, 'your building is too high. But how can I apply rules to you which I am not required to apply to government schools?'

Finally he agreed to measure the distance only to the floor of the top storey, instead of to the ceiling, which he was supposed to do. 'After all,' he mused, 'we rescue people from the floor of a building, not the ceiling.' I shall forever be grateful to this understanding official.

But another snag arose with that same building. The shop below our school had applied for a licence to sell kerosene. If the licence had been obtained, we could not have registered the school. A different official was involved on this occasion. 'Never mind,' he assured me, 'we'll accept your application because it came first, and reject the application to sell kerosene.' We thanked him.

A few months later, an official rushed into our school. 'You'll have to close your school,' he said. 'The shop below you is selling kerosene and the children are in danger.' I explained the arrangement that had been made, and took him to the school office so that our manager, Mr. Tai, could confirm that this was true. Mr. Tai looked hard at the man. 'Yes,' he said, 'that was the arrangement, and *you* were the one who made it.' He had obviously forgotten his promise.

'All right,' he said, embarrassed, 'forget about it.' And he left. We heard no more of the matter, but I did worry in case the kerosene continued to be sold and the children were endangered. . . .

What surprised me was the number of premises used as schools which did not carry out any of the regulations whatsoever. All they had to do was to operate without registration, and then anything went. For example, seating arrangements were intended to protect the children's eyesight. The regulations stipulated that no child must be too far from the blackboard. If the room was too long or too wide, the number of pupils permitted in a classroom would be considerably reduced. One room in our school was large enough to accommodate over forty children, but when other regulations came into play, the number was reduced to twenty-six. That made it impossible to pay the rent and the teacher. But the illegal school next door to us divided a room of the same size into two parts and taught sixty children in each part. When I asked why they were allowed so many children in the classrooms, I was told that the school had not applied for registration and so the rules did not apply. Theoretically, an illegal school was subject to prosecution, but the law was seldom enforced. To operate illegally was infinitely easier than to obey the law. So it was in many aspects of life in Hong Kong. ▩

PART X

A COLONIAL FINALE
1960s-1990s

*'Hong Kong's likely to be a good bargain for China
for some time yet.'*

CHRISTOPHER NEW, 1960s

*'With a good eye and a bit of luck, you can buy priceless treas-
ures for next to nothing at the most unlikely places in Antiques
Alley.'*

NI KUANG, 1987

*'The city has become
adjunct to its airport'*

LOUISE HO, 1990s

56

LUNCH AT THE HONG KONG CLUB

CHRISTOPHER NEW

Christopher New—British academic in the Philosophy Department at the University of Hong Kong—has lived in the Colony for almost thirty years. He was in Hong Kong during the 1960s, the era of China's Cultural Revolution which spilled over into Hong Kong, suddenly unsettling the lives of everyone as terrorism became a threat to normal daily life.

In this extract from Christopher New's novel, The Chinese Box, *Dimitri, a university lecturer in Hong Kong, reports British police brutality—but some feel he is letting the side down at a difficult time. As Dimitri is probed about his wife, Helen, and his mistress, Mila, the sometimes gossipy, claustrophobic nature of life in Hong Kong emerges.*

Peter Frankam: H.K. Club 1 p.m. Lunch.

Dimitri got out of the taxi at Statue Square. The tall fountains rose still and glistening in the breathless sunlight, unnoticed by the swift-stepping crowds crossing and recrossing the square in dedicated pursuit of the fast buck. Neatly dressed typists, clerks or businessmen, all were hurrying to hatch deals or place bets over lunch or coffee, a thousand dollars or twenty-five, each bargaining relentlessly to the last profitable cent. Yesterday, several bombs had been planted here. One man was shot and thirty-seven people injured by shrapnel. Today, there were still a few dark, ignored stains on the sun-glaring white paving stones. Tomorrow even they would be gone, scuffed out by a million scurrying feet.

Overlooking all this restless activity stood the ugly concrete masses of the Hongkong and Shanghai Bank, the Chartered Bank and Prince's Shopping Arcade. Somehow, through their bare, characterless windows, they seemed to emanate a bleak air of proprietary approval at the manifest triumph of capitalism before their doors. Directly opposite were the Supreme Court and the Hong Kong Club, revealing, in their nineteenth-century architecture, a certain restraint the twentieth century lacked. A little to the east, the Bank of China rose, narrower, but even higher than the others, its top spiky with iron bars to prevent police helicopters from landing. The Bank of China was the unofficial Chinese embassy and, although it had directed many of the riots and demonstrations, neither the police nor the army had ever entered it, tacitly admitting its diplomatic immunity. Its windows were smaller and more forbidding than the other banks' and, whatever expression they wore, Dimitri smiled wrily, if certainly wasn't approving.

He walked slowly across the square, letting the crowd scurry ant-like round him. He could just hear the hissing spray of the fountains above the noise of the traffic and it occurred to him that none of the people dodging past him were talking. Each one was a separate parcel of energy and aims, without any interest in the others, except as possible rivals.

The club was the oldest building still standing in the city centre, colonnaded and shuttered on three storeys. Dimitri was not a member and the doorman eyed him unsurely until he asked for Mr. Frankam.

Peter was giving the lunch in an upstairs room. Waiting for the lift, Dimitri glanced round the lobby. The walls were painted a fading lime green. A number of rubber plants stood along them, their leaves shiny as if they had been polished. The notice board beside him caught his eye.

In accordance with article 329 (Payment of Monies) the undernoted member's name is hereby noted in the main hall for non-payment of dues: Mr. J. E. Johns

The lift doors slid open and he stepped in. The faint mustiness, the green of the walls and the tone of the notice recalled smudged memories of his school in England. It was as though this place too were damp, cold and gloomy, despite the summer's heat—a rheumatism of the heart. He walked down the long, worn, red carpet of the hall, silent and empty as a cathedral, and paused at the doorway. He felt as vaguely apprehensive as he used to feel when called to the headmaster's study at school. Glasses were chinking with ice, voices were chatting smoothly and suddenly he wanted to run away before Peter saw him. There slipped into his mind a memory of the school photograph his mother used to keep on her bedroom wall. He could see his face in the second row left, head down, with drawn eyes shyly, almost sullenly, peering up at the camera, arms stiffly folded across his chest, the cuffs of his grey school jacket much too short.

'Dimitri, how are you?' Peter came to meet him. He was as sleek as ever, fair hair too beautifully in place and tie, a delicate purple, too carefully chosen for effect against the pale blue shirt and trim grey suit. 'Glad you could come. We haven't met for months, it seems. How is Helen?'

Three equally well-dressed, but more imposing-looking men were standing together in the room, drinks in their hands. They turned to Dimitri, glowing corporately, it seemed, with the warmth of self-satisfaction.

'I expect you know everyone?' Peter began, with only the faintest trace of doubt in his slightly unctuous voice.

'The exact contrary, I'm afraid.'

'Oh.' A little discomposed by his abruptness, Peter introduced him quickly to a judge with a deep suntan and slightly pendulous jowl, a Chinese manufacturing taipan who bowed and smiled with

256

reserved politeness and a colonel in the Gurkha Brigade wearing a Christ Church tie, who had just arrived in Hong Kong. Dimitri remembered their names from the gossip columns of the press, where every official who opened a fair, or came or left, was solemnly commemorated.

He felt the three pairs of eyes estimating him while Peter ordered a drink from the white-jacketed waiter. 'I have the advantage of you all,' he began with an awkward dryness, 'I know all about you from the newspapers, whereas you can't possibly know anything about me, since I'm never in them.'

'Oh, Peter's been telling us what a brilliant chap you are and all that,' drawled the colonel in unmistakably Christ Church tones. 'And I dare say he's more reliable than your average newspaper. . . . ' There was a suggestion of irony in his voice, strengthened by the narrowing of his rather close-set brown eyes, which hinted that his Wodehousian manner was merely a carefully preserved facade behind which some fairly deft mental operations were being conducted.

'His information is more accurate, I'm sure, but his editorial comments may be equally. . . .'

'Perverse?' suggested Peter, smiling faultlessly at himself as he handed Dimitri his glass. I was just telling them about this trial you're involved in.'

'Fortunately, I won't be trying it,' interrupted the judge. His pendulous jowls gave him a mournful look which his phlegmy, sepulchral voice did nothing to alleviate. 'Otherwise one of us would have to leave.'

'When are you stepping into the box?' the colonel asked.

'Couple of weeks now.' He turned to Peter, who was fingering his tie. 'Have there been any murmurs of dissatisfaction about it? About prosecuting two policemen, I mean, at a time when they're all getting picked off by the opposition?'

'No doubt there was some heart-searching before the decision to prosecute was taken.' Peter pursed his lips consideringly. 'The morale of the force was very important just then—still is, of course. They're still the main target for bombs and knives and so on. . . . I would imagine the average bobby here feels rather aggrieved that his colleagues should be tried for getting their own back in what is a time-honoured way, after all. . . .'

'Yes, we had the same problem in Cyprus.' The colonel stretched and threw back his shoulder—Terrorism always provokes some kind of counter-terrorism. And that's how revolutions get their martyrs, I suppose. You never get a decent revolution without a bunch of martyrs, after all. Absolute *sine qua non*. Absolute.'

'Well, I hope these aggrieved coppers won't try to tamper with the witnesses. . . .' Dimitri was wondering how far he could probe.

'Have you been tampered with?' asked the taipan.

'I'm probably not so vulnerable as . . . others might be.'

'Oh, I think that sort of thing always comes to light, you know,' the judge wheezed a little. 'After all, we do have a rule of law here. '

Dimitri shrugged, thinking of Mila's warning. The others resumed the conversation his entrance had interrupted, profitable investments in the Hong Kong stock market. Dimitri sipped his drink, half-listening. The taipan spoke in thick fluent English about the speculative nature of the market and the possibility of making vast profits just then because the communist disturbances had pushed share prices down to an unreal level.

'But if the disturbances grow worse?' asked the judge.

'Yes, yes. It is all speculative,' the taipan opened his hands and laughed. 'If your horse dies before the finishing post, you lose your money. It happened in Shanghai.'

The colonel began to reveal the alertness Dimitri had suspected, comparing quotations on the Hong Kong and London exchanges with the taipan. Peter tried to bring the judge and Dimitri into this discussion, but neither responded. The judge turned to Dimitri behind the taipan's back, eyeing him thoughtfully.

'You don't sail a boat by any chance, do you? At the yacht club?'

'No, I'm afraid not.'

'Ah. Thought I might have seen you there.' He looked down at his glass resignedly. 'Well, I always was bad on faces—'

The soup was placed on a table beside the lace-curtained window. Dimitri sat between the colonel and the taipan, who had to adjourn their financial discussion. The colonel had no difficulty in changing topics, though.

'And what are all the brilliant minds thinking at the university these days?'

'Many of them are as keenly interested in the stock market as you are,' Dimitri returned the irony, 'although that doesn't always indicate a brilliant mind, of course.'

'Dimitri is too modest to mention that he's writing a book.' Peter bent towards him from the head of the table.

'No doubt it will be brilliant,' murmured the colonel.

'How is it going, Dimitri?'

'Backwards at present.'

'Oh, I'm sure that's more false modesty—I've told everyone already that you're the only person in Hong Kong who's equally at home in Russian and Chinese literature.'

He couldn't let me be a mediocrity. Dimitri crumbled some bread on the tablecloth. *It would never do to admit he knew anyone undistinguished.*

'And what do you think of Confucius, Mr. Johnston?' the taipan asked, dabbing at some soup on his hairless chin. 'Can he be translated?'

'Only by a schizophrenic.' *I suppose that's why each of us has been invited, to impress the rest and glorify his nibs.*

He talked stiltedly with the taipan, who was careful to let him know he had his suits made in Savile Row, about Shanghai before the communist take-over. It was better than Hong Kong, the taipan said, because the profits were even higher.

'The workers knew it was work or starve. So they worked.' And his shrewd eyes sparkled as he laughed.

On Dimitri's other side, the colonel was maintaining the Gurkhas were such good fighters because they had no imagination and so no fear.

'Still, don't you think they'd fight in vain if they had to defend Hong Kong against the PLA?' Peter asked.

'Oh, I suppose we would fight a holding action until the necessary notables had been evacuated. . . .' He scratched his bristly grey moustache. 'Not that I think it's a probability any more, you know. . . . There were some tricky months, of course, but I can't see Peking doing anything now, since it didn't move when things were more critical. After all,' he raised his eyes quizzically towards the taipan, 'wouldn't you say John Chinaman knows a good bargain when he sees one? Whether he's a Maoist or a mandarin? And Hong Kong's likely to be a good bargain for China for some time yet, with all the foreign exchange and information she gets through here. Barring unforeseen accidents, I should say the worst is over. . . .'

The next course came and Dimitri withdrew more and more

from the conversation, unable either to follow or break the conventions of brittle sophisticated chatter in which the others, except the melancholic judge, excelled. He gazed out of the window at the heat-hazed hills of Kowloon, beyond which the colonel's unimaginative Gurkhas were preparing patiently for the battle he thought would never come. And remote beyond them was Mila, *gone now for three weeks and no idea when she's coming back. Or if. She may even miss the trial.* His eyes, following his thoughts, started searching amongst the crowded buildings of Kowloon city for the block where her now empty flat was. Though unsuccessful—the Ocean Terminal building was in the way—his search composed an image of her in his mind, built up of fluctuating memories of her gestures and expressions. *If she does come back and tells her story at the trial, she might go to England anyway. And now that I've missed that job, I'll just stay here and rot. Yes, I shall rot here.*

The colonel's voice recalled him to the public world. 'You've been here a long time—born here, so Peter tells me. What's the view like from the seat of learning in your ivory tower? How d'you find the place?'

'It's a good place to rot in.'

'Oh come, that's a bit severe.' He laughed. 'I don't mean to rot here.'

'Nobody *means* to.'

'Can't say I share your rather depressing *Weltanschauung,* all the same.' He laughed again, glancing round at the others for support.

'I wouldn't say that writing a book was rotting exactly.' Peter bridged the gap of silence. 'I mean composition is hardly a form of decomposition, would you say?'

'P'raps he means his book is rotten, what?' the colonel asked genially, with a full display of his Wodehousian manner. 'Most books are, after all . . . No doubt in his case it's false modesty, though.'

Dimitri shrugged, smiling helplessly down at his glass, as much ashamed of his absurd rhetoric as annoyed by their imperturbable complacence.

The taipan saved him from further baiting by asking Peter whether it was true that he was going to become head of his department in the government.

Peter glanced down with a modesty that must have been studied.

'As a matter of fact you've hit the nail on the head.'

'Ah.'

'It's not official yet, of course, so don't breathe a word, will you?'

'Good show,' muttered the colonel, while the judge murmured some indistinct sounds of congratulation.

The taipan raised his glass gaily. 'To our next Director-General.'

The others drank with slightly forced enthusiasm, while Peter smiled and shrugged deprecatingly. Watching him over his up-lifted glass, Dimitri thought that this was why the lunch had been arranged, so that Peter could let his promotion be known and admired. Ever since he had first met Dimitri at Cambridge, Peter had been trying to impress him. Failing to get a first-class degree had only intensified his determination to extract at last the tribute that Dimitri had always a little contemptuously withheld. Peter's glance, meeting his and then dropping again, seemed to confirm his intuition. Now that he was to be head of his department he could clearly be seen, in his own eyes, to have got ahead of Dimitri. But Peter wanted him to see it too. Dimitri finished his wine musingly. *Which of us is worse off—he with his pathetic craving for praise or me with my inability to do anything that deserves it?*

He left as soon as the coffee had been served. Peter walked with him to the door, lighting a cigar as he talked. His face was flushed with well-being and wine, but his eyes flickered inquiringly at Dimitri, still seeking the acknowledgement of his due. As Dimitri stolidly withheld it, though, Peter prompted him.

'You won't take it any further, Dimitri, will you? My elevation to the demigods, I mean. It won't be official for a month. . . .'

'No, of course not.' He still held back maliciously from con-gratulating him. 'I won't even tell Helen.'

'Ah,' he recovered quickly, 'and how is she, by the way? When is she coming back?'

'According to her last letter, as late as possible.'

'She doesn't want to?'

'Not particularly. She's never really liked the place. And then. . . .' He felt he was giving away too much, but he let it go now, 'and then there is the *ennui* of matrimony too. . . .'

'Mm.' Peter glanced at him sideways. 'And perhaps some of your . . . extramural activities have come to her notice as well?'

'Extramural?'

261

'A certain dancer?' He smiled and winked. 'A lady sometimes seen on television.'

Dimitri felt his face flushing.

'Mum's the word, eh?' He was leering roguishly now. 'I'll keep quiet about you and you'll keep quiet about me, eh?' He drew on his cigar and let the blue smoke waft up between them, smiling at Dimitri all the time with slightly bloodshot eyes.

'It's most considerate of you to show such tender regard for other people's wives.' He realised that Peter must be very drunk. 'I'm sure you'll make an excellent Director-General, with so much information at your disposal. Provided you always hold your liquor like a gentleman, of course.'

He walked slowly away down the long, red-carpeted hall. Someone was waiting by the lift, so he went down by the stairway. He let his hand brush the stone balustrade, thinking of Peter's goatish face. If Peter knew about Mila, other people must know too. Sooner or later it would get to Helen, but he felt his will was paralysed, unable to choose either sooner or later. Perhaps it would all be over by then, anyway. Peter's gloating assumption that Mila could be only a *fille de joie*, a stealthy pleasure taken while Helen's back was turned, almost amused him, but there was another thought that nagged. *Does he know more than he said? Does he have any idea she's been got at about the trial? If so, the getting at her must be an official plan. In which case, the whole thing's been cooked beforehand.*

He walked out past the silent rubber trees into the bustling square. It was late October, but the sun was still fierce. A beggar was squatting in the shade of the courts of justice, holding out a red plastic beaker for alms. *Surely an official conspiracy would have prevented a prosecution altogether?* Nobody gave the beggar any money, but he held his beaker up all the same. *Well, perhaps we'll know in a couple of weeks, one way or the other. I'll hold up my bit of evidence like he holds up his mug.* 🔲

57

HONG KONG 1976
(AN UNFINISHED SYMPHONY FOR
5 MILLION INSTRUMENTS)

WALTER SULKE

Of German-Jewish birth, Walter Sulke lived in Hong Kong for forty-six years, becoming Chairman of the Zang Fu Company, known for its Mercedes dealership. He was made a Justice of the Peace in 1976 and received an OBE (Order of the British Empire) in 1979. In his collection, Myself and Words, *Walter Sulke tries to capture and reflect the impressions and pace of the city in poetic images.*

ALLEGRO

*h*iGH riSe BuilDINgs squeezing the breath out of the city
humid heat cloud pressing down
NOISE reverberating reverberating reverberating
piledrivercementmixerdieselbuspneumaticdrillshipshornstraffictraffic
and time shoving escalating deadlines through
telephonelinessatelliteearthstationstvsetsradiostelexmachines
clattering cacophony culminating in sixtysecond pulses
of screaming jet takeoffs and landings. ▨

58

A GE-WARE BURNER WITH 'FLYING' HANDLES AND SIX LEGS IN CRACKLED *FENQING* GLAZE

NI KUANG

Ni Kuang has been called Hong Kong's most popular writer. Although he is best known for his science fiction and martial arts writing, this story comes from Antiques Alley, *his 1987 collection of seven short stories. 'Ge-Ware' is a valuable, highly imitated ceramic from the Song Dynasty.*

'With a good eye and a bit of luck, you can buy priceless treasures for next to nothing at the most unlikely places in Antiques Alley.'

Myths of this nature are fairly common, and there are also a lot of true stories to back them up.

Though there are several hundred stands and shops in Antiques Alley, they're not organized in any way, and so there's no reason to suspect that all the proprietors spread such tantalizing rumours. None the less, such rumours have enticed numerous people to test their eye and try their luck in Antiques Alley. Doubtless the idea of acquiring a valuable antique for a song has an almost irresistible appeal.

In the Alley there's one rather unique stand that specializes in small ceramics. Instead of laying its wares out on the ground like the other stands, here they are displayed in a glass cabinet, which is something of an antique in its own right, since its framework is made entirely of wood. Ever since aluminum cabinets came into vogue, wooden cabinets like that have become extinct!

The proprietor of this stand is something of a character. He sits on a wooden bench behind his cabinet in exactly the same

posture all day long, hardly moving at all, and is exceedingly fond
of picking the wax from his ears.
As he sits there keeping watch
over his inventory, he works at
his ears non-stop, using for the
purpose a bamboo ear spoon
which is stained a dark maroon
from years of handling. First he
cleans his left ear, then his right, after which he goes back to his
left ear, and so on.

Because of this habit, he never holds his head straight up, and
when he tilts it to one side and half-closes his eyes, it's hard to tell
if his joy is derived from ear-picking, or from the novelty of watching the world go by at such an odd angle.

Most of the stands on Antiques Alley operate on a self-service
basis; customers are free to pick up and examine whatever objects
strike their fancy. But because this particular stand is equipped
with a glass cabinet, it's impossible to get to the items on display
from the front of the cabinet, so if customers wish to see anything
they have to ask the proprietor sitting on his wooden bench to
take it out for them. But because the proprietor always seems to
be preoccupied with his ears, most customers—unless they're especially eager to buy something—resign themselves to examining
the objects through the glass. The proprietor himself never does
much in the way of trying to stir up business.

That afternoon, the three of them came once again. I say 'again'
since the three of them have been coming to this stand three days
running; this was their fourth visit. The proprietor could recall
what had taken place the first day. The middle-aged man, who
bore all the marks of a connoisseur, had come alone that time. As
he passed by the glass cabinet, he stopped dead in his tracks, a
strange glimmer in his eyes. Pointing with two fleshy fingers at an
item in the case he said, 'I'd like to look at that incense burner
with the "flying" handles'. 'Flying handles' is the term used to
describe tall vertical handles on ceramic incense burners. There
wasn't a wide selection of items in the cabinet, so the proprietor
reached in with one hand and took out the incense burner, which
was about the size of his fist, and handed it to the middle-aged
man, who began to examine it with great care.

265

While the proprietor gave his ears a workout, the middle-aged man remarked somewhat ironically: 'This is a very strange incense-burner. It has six feet.'

The proprietor responded with a 'humph', and went back to his picking. The middle-aged man said: 'What do you call it?'

The proprietor switched his ear spoon from one ear to the other and said: 'It's a Ge-ware incense burner with six feet in crackled *fenqing* glaze.'

The middle-aged man laughed out loud, which instantly drew a small crowd of curiosity seekers around them. Still laughing, the middle-aged man said, 'Ge-ware? Ha ha! There isn't a dealer on this street who wouldn't make the same claim!'

People who run antiques stands in Antiques Alley generally have a bit more patience than the average person, so the proprietor good-naturedly laughed alone with the man. But he never for a moment ceased picking his ears, and it was that his smile and laughter were merely skin deep. Let them take their time, the proprietor thought, I've got enough wax in my ears for a lifetime of picking.

Though the middle-aged man had made fun of the proprietor, he continued to examine the incense burner quite intensely. 'How much do you want for this?' he asked.

For a moment, it seemed, the proprietor actually held his head erect. 'Three thousand dollars. No bargaining.'

The middle-aged man laughed again, put the incense burner down and left.

The next day, the middle-aged man returned, this time with another man, and together they spent a long time examining the incense burner. Though the middle-aged man had asked this person along to give him advice, everything he said was pure rubbish!

'If it's authentic Ge-ware in *fenqing*, then three thousand is too cheap. Three hundred thousand'd be more like it. If it's a fake, though, three thousand's an absurd price; I wouldn't give you three bucks for it.'

On the third day, the middle-aged man brought a third person along, whose judgments were somewhat more reasonable. His comment: 'It's only three thousand dollars, so if it's a fake, so what? You might as well buy it.'

The middle-aged man was hesitant. 'I'm not worried about the three thousand dollars,' he said, 'It's just, you know, if it's a fake, it can be a bit embarrassing. How will I ever live it down?'

The middle-aged man was evidently a noted authority on antiques, otherwise why would he worry so much about damaging his reputation by making a bad purchase?

As usual, the proprietor remained a passive spectator, allowing his customers to make up their minds for themselves. The price had been set at three thousand dollars, no more, no less, regardless of whether it was real or fake; everything hinged on the price.

And then today they came for a fourth visit. When the proprietor noticed them approaching, he removed the ceramic incense burner from the cabinet and placed it on the counter.

The middle-aged man picked it up and began to examine it as usual. The three of them used a lot of technical jargon, like 'spur marks' and 'dripped glaze'; they sounded like real experts.

But when it comes down to distinguishing the genuine from the fake, the greatest expert is in the same boat as the rank amateur.

Ten minutes passed, and the middle-aged man said: 'Please be frank with me, is this real or is it fake?'

The Proprietor replied with a laugh: 'You expect a little hole in the wall like this to give you a certificate of authenticity? My friend, you ought to know by now, what counts in buying second-hand goods is a good eye. Look, if you're not sure about it, don't buy it, 'cause if you don't, somebody else will.'

These words had the effect of setting the middle-aged man's pants on fire, and he reached into his pocket and took out the three thousands dollars that had been burning a hole there for the last three days. 'If you say three thousand, then three thousand it is. I'll take it.'

In an unprecedented gesture, the proprietor put down his ear spoon and started to count the three piles of bills the man had handed him. Before he had finished, however, the middle-aged man interrupted him. 'There's a dirty part here I don't seem to be able to rub off....'

Very casually, the proprietor said: 'Don't worry about it, I'll get you another one.'

For a split second they all froze, like a freeze shot in a movie.

59

AN OLD COLONIAL BUILDING

LEUNG PING-KWAN

As a member of the Department of Comparative Literature at the University of Hong Kong, the office of poet and novelist Leung Ping-kwan is in the stately Main Building, complete with fish-ponds, columns, and flowering plants in glazed Chinese pots. Hong Kong's colonial buildings are a fast-vanishing reminder of its heritage.

–1–

Through sunlight and shadow dust swirls,
　　through the scaffolding raised-up around
　　the colonial edifice, over the wooden planks
men live on to raise it brick by brick, the imperial
image of it persisting right down, sometimes,
to the bitter soil in the foundation, sometimes finding, too,
the noble height of a rotunda, the wide, hollow corridors
leading sometimes to blocked places, which, sometimes,
knocked open, are stairs down to ordinary streets.

–2–

Down familiar alcoves sometimes brimming
with blooms sometimes barren I go to xerox
glancing at the images caught in the circular pond,
now showing the round window in the cupola as duckweed
　　drifting,
day and night caught in the surface, no longer textbook
clean, but murky, the naive goldfish searching
mindlessly around in it, shaking the pliant lotus stems
and the roots feeling for earth, swirling orange and white,
gills opening and leeching, in and out of the high window bars.

Might all the pieces of ruins put together present
yet another architecture? Ridiculous the great heads on money,
laughable the straight faces running things. We pass in this
   corridor
in the changing surface of the pond by chance
our reflections rippling a little. We'd rather not bend;
neither of us in love with flags or fireworks.
So what's left are these fragmentary, unrepresentative words,
not uttered amidst the building of chrome and glass, but beside
a circular pond riddled with patterns of moving signs. ▣

60

HONG KONG AT THE CROSSROADS

LOUISE HO

As one of Hong Kong's premier poets and prose-writers, Louise Ho Shew-wan depicts the problems and frustrations of Hong Kong with whimsy and perception. She taught at the Chinese University of Hong Kong, the 'New University' in New Territories, before moving to Australia. Her short story, written in 1990, touches on many modern Hong Kong topics.

HONG KONG AT THE CROSSROADS

The city has become
adjunct to its airport.
The airport has become
a mere coach station
for families strung out
across oceans and continents.
'The family at home'
used to refer to one place at a time.
It will now be redefined.

HOME TO HONG KONG

A Chinese
Invited an Irishman
To a Japanese meal
By the Spanish Steps
In the middle of Rome
Having come from Boston
On the way home.

CITY

No fingers claw at the bronze gauze
Of a Hong Kong December dusk,
Only a maze of criss-crossing feet
That enmeshes the city
In a merciless grid.
Between many lanes
Of traffic, the street-sleeper
Carves out his island home.
Or under the thundering fly-over,
Another makes his own peace of mind.

Under the staircase,
By the public lavatory,
A man entirely unto himself
Lifts his hand
And opens his palm.
His digits
Do not rend the air,
They merely touch
As pain does, effortlessly.

*

THREE MEN IN A LIFT,
NOT TO MENTION THE WOMAN WHO DIDN'T GET IN

It was a University function held at the Arts Centre on the Island. The Arts Centre is a fifteen-minute walk away from the city centre, what the locals call prime-land. This was for some years the most costly piece of land in the world, it is now the third most costly, after Tokyo and London. The city, represented by the Urban Council, had been hankering after such a centre for decades, neither private nor public sector paid any attention, the arts being hardly a lucrative activity. It was finally built because some clever bureaucrat detected an angle of space in between two high-rise buildings which could be made in a triangle. At least it would be a variation on going round and round in circles. It is aesthetically interesting too. It's like fitting a neat compact triangular Pompidou Centre of a box in between the legs of a sleeping giant. And so the New University had seen fit to mix and mingle with the suave urbanites in their environment instead of holding the reception out in the wilds of the countryside campus.

Guests and university personnel alike were arriving in hordes, jamming the triangular lobby, waiting to take the lifts that would take them to higher triangles. Men in dark suits, women dripping in jewels and finery jostled about elbowing their way everywhere. This was twenty-first century civilization where a dissociation of finery from fine manners had firmly set in.

Bringing up the rear, about a lift-load away, was a group of four trying to make conversation and visibly straining. I was later to learn that the three men were high-ranking administrators in a university run by administrators and the woman only an academic, and a junior one to boot. The unspoken rationale was that any academic who rose high enough in the ranks would become an administrator. Indeed, the administration was the university. Academics were incidental additions as somehow courses had to be offered and students somehow had to be taught. The young-looking man on the left was Petronius Ong, recently Harvard PhD'd and positively glowing, now dean of students in one of the colleges. The one on the right was Aloysius Jing, son of a pre-communist Chinese mandarin, American educated, just returned from Cambridge, UK, full of praise for 'the civilised manners of the English'. The man in the middle was T. S. Tan, president of one of the colleges, who refers to Lord Todd by his first name, etc., etc.

The lift arrived. People got out. People got in. As the four neared the lift entrance, it became clear there was only room for three. As if caught in mid-sentence, for a split second facial muscles tensed up and the four shared a blank look. No one actually made a mad dash, they just straightened their backs and looked vague.

Then everything happened very quickly. The three men moved toward the lift and just as they did so, the woman took one big deliberate step backwards. It was at this point that she caught my eye and we burst out laughing together.

She came up to me as I leant against the counter and explained that that was perhaps the refugee spirit which was so infectious in the colony. Three presumably civilised men couldn't resist getting into a lift as if it was the last lift available, the last meal, the last boat, the last chance. You're a journalist, she called to me as she was about to board an empty lift, write about it, make someone laugh!

There was a last gesture that struck me as interesting. I wonder if she noticed, perhaps women don't. The tableau of the lift doors about to close, the three men were standing in a straight line, all three of them held their hands together in front of their trousers, as if protecting themselves. I know, a lot of nonsense has been made of Hitler and his hands-over-his-crotch pose. However, can there really be some truth in man's fear of castration being the basis for all other fears, including the fear of missing out on a lift? I'll be damned if I'm going to find out! ▓

BIBLIOGRAPHY

Ai Wu, 'One Night in Hong Kong', translated by Zhu Zhiyu, first published in *Renditions*, Hong Kong: The Chinese University Press, 1988.

Andrew, Kenneth A., *Chop Suey*, Ilfracombe, Devon, England: Arthur H. Stockwell Ltd., 1958.

Auden, W. H., 'Hongkong' in *Journey to a War*, with Christopher Isherwood, London: Faber & Faber, 1939.

Ba Jin, 'Hong Kong Nights', translated by Zhu Zhiyu with Don J. Cohen, *Renditions*, Hong Kong: The Chinese University Press, 1988, pp. 54–5.

Ball, B. L., *Rambles in Eastern Asia, including China and Manilla, During Several Years Residence*, Boston: James French & Co., 1856.

Belcher, Edmund, *Voyage Round the World Performed in Her Majesty's Ship H.M.S. Sulphur*, San Francisco: Book Club of California, 1969.

Benson, Stella, *Documents and Letters*, Cambridge: Cambridge University Library, Add: 8367 350–396.

'Betty,' *Intercepted Letters*, Hong Kong: Kelly and Walsh, Ltd., 1905.

Bille, Steen Anderson, 'Early Days in the Colony', reprinted in *The South China Morning Post*, 3 October 1930.

Black, Gavin, *The Eyes Around Me*, London: Fontana Books, 1966.

Blake, Amanda, *The Colony Club*, London: Sidgwick & Jackson, 1988.

Blunden, Edmund, *A Hong Kong House*, London: Collins, 1962.

Brassey, Lady Anne, *Around the World in the Yacht 'Sunbeam'*, New York: Henry Holt & Company, 1879.

Bullen, Fiona, *A Limited Season*, London: Warner Books, 1993.

Carré, John le, *The Honourable Schoolboy*, London: Hodder and Stoughton, 1977.

Chailley-Bert, J., *The Colonisation of Indo-China*, translated by Arthur Baring Brabant, London: Archibald Constable & Co., 1894.

Chase, James Hadley, *A Coffin From Hong Kong*, London: Granada

Publishing, 1964.

Chekhov, Anton, *Letters of Anton Chekhov*, translated by Michael Henry Heim with Simon Karlinsky, London: The Bodley Head, 1973.

Clavell, James, *Noble House*, London: Hodder and Stoughton, 1981.

Clavell, James, *Taipan*, London: Michael Joseph, 1966.

Clementi, Sir Cecil, *Poems*, London: privately printed, 1925, reprinted, 1978.

Coates, Austin, *Myself a Mandarin*, New York: Frederick Muller Ltd., 1968.

Coates, Austin, *The Road*, New York: Harper & Brothers, 1959.

Danziger, Nick, *Danziger's Travels: Beyond Forbidden Frontiers*, London: Grafton Books, 1987.

Darrell, Elizabeth, *Concerto*, New York: St. Martin's Press, 1994.

Davis, John Gordon, *The Year of the Hungry Tiger*, London: Michael Joseph, 1974.

Des Voeux, Sir G. William, *My Colonial Service in British Guiana, St. Lucia, Trinidad, Fiji, Australia, New Foundland, and Hong Kong with Interludes*, London: John Murray, 1903.

Dilke, Charles Wentworth, *Greater Britain: A Record of Travel in English Speaking Countries*, London: Macmillan and Co., 1894.

The Directory and Chronicles for China, Japan and the Philippines for the Year 1872, Hong Kong: The Daily Press, 1872.

The Directory and Chronicles for China, Japan and the Philippines for the Year 1925, Hong Kong: The Hong Kong Daily Press, 1925.

'Dolly', *Tales of Hongkong in Verse and Story*, Hong Kong: Kelly & Walsh, Ltd., 1902.

Edwards, Henry J. Anderson, 'Letter to Jardine, Matheson & Co., September 23, 1886', Cambridge: Cambridge University Library, Unpublished papers of Jardine Matheson & Co., Local Letter Book, B/20/2.

Elegant, Robert, *Dynasty*, New York: Fontana, 1977.

Elegant, Simon, *A Christmas Wedding*, London: Piatkus, 1994.

Forster, L., *Echoes of Hong Kong and Beyond*, Hong Kong: Ye Olde Printerie, Ltd., 1933.

Franck, Harry A., *Roving Through Southern China*, New York & London: The Century Co., 1925.

Freeman-Mitford, A. B., *The Attaché at Peking*, London: Macmillan and Co., 1900.

275

Gardam, Jane, 'The Pig Boy' from *The Pangs of Love*, London: Abacus Books, 1991.

Gillman, Dorothy, *Mrs. Pollifax and the Hong Kong Buddha*, New York: Ballantine Books/Fawcett Crest, 1985.

Gittins, Jean, *Eastern Windows–Western Skies*, Hong Kong: South China Morning Post, Ltd., 1969.

Gordon-Cumming, Constance, *Wanderings in China*, Edinburgh: William Blackwood and Sons, 1888.

Hahn, Emily, *China to Me: A Partial Autobiography*, Philadelphia: The Blakiston Company, 1944.

Halcombe, Charles J. H., *The Mystic Flowery Land: A Personal Narrative*, London: Luzac & Co., 1896.

Hardy, The Revd. E. J., *John Chinaman at Home*, London: T. Fisher Unwin, 1905.

Haslewood, Mrs. H. L. and Lt. Comdr., *Child Slavery in Hong Kong*, London: The Sheldon Press, 1930.

Ho, Louise Shew-wan, 'Three Men in a Lift, Not to Mention the Woman Who Didn't Get In', from *Local Habitation*, Hong Kong: Twilight Books Company in association with the Department of Comparative Literature, University of Hong Kong, 1994.

Hoe, Susanna, *The Private Life of Old Hong Kong*, Hong Kong: Oxford University Press, 1991.

James, H. E. R., 'Correspondence of H. E. R. James' (1894), Hong Kong: Unpublished manuscript in University of Hong Kong Library. Acquired 1973.

Jardine, Matheson & Co. 'Letter to Sir Jamsetjee Jejeebhoy, 7 December, 1846', Cambridge: Cambridge University Library, Archive C 9/1, 148/160, Unpublished papers of Jardine Matheson & Co.

Johnston, A. R., 'Note on the Island of Hong Kong', London: *The London Geographical Journal*, Vol. XIV, 1843.

Kipling, Rudyard, *The Writings in Prose and Verse of Rudyard Kipling*, Vol. 15: *From Sea To Sea*, New York: Doubleday and McClure, 1899.

Leung, Ping-kwan, *City at the End of Time*, Hong Kong: Twilight Books Company in association with the Department of Comparative Literature, University of Hong Kong Cultural Series Nr. 3, 1992.

Lawrence, Anthony, *Foreign Correspondent*, London: George Allen and Unwin Ltd., 1972.

Legge, James, 'The Colony of Hong Kong', London: *The China Review*, Vol. I, 1872–3, pp. 183–76.

Malraux, André, *The Conquerors*, London: Jonathan Cape, 1929.

Mason, Richard, *The World of Suzie Wong*, London: Collins, 1957.

Maugham, W. Somerset, *The Painted Veil*, London: Heinemann, 1925.

Meigh, William, *Reminiscences of a Colonial Judge*, London: Privately printed at The Kingsgate Press, 1907.

Mo, Timothy, *The Monkey King*, London: André Deutsch, 1978.

Morris, Jan, *Pleasures of a Tangled Life*, London: Barrie and Jenkins, 1989.

New, Christopher, *A Change of Flag*, London: Bantam Press, 1990.

New, Christopher, *The Chinese Box*, London: W. H. Allen, 1975.

Ng, Peter Y. L., *New Peace County: A Chinese Gazetteer of the Hong Kong Region*, Hong Kong: Hong Kong University Press, 1983.

Ni Kuang, 'A Ge-Ware Burner with "Flying" Handles and Six Legs in Crackled *Fenqing* Glaze', translated by Don J. Cohen, published in *Renditions*, Hong Kong: The Chinese University Press, 1988.

Owens, Robert, William and Sybil, Letters and cards, 1943–5, unpublished.

Peplow, S. H. and Barker, M., *Hongkong, Around and About*, Hong Kong: Ye Olde Printerie, Ltd., 1931.

Potter, Lieut. A., 'Poem', 1943, unpublished.

Poynter, Mary A., *Around the Shores of Asia*, London: George Allen & Unwin Ltd., 1921.

'A Resident', 'Letter from Hong-Kong, Descriptive of that Colony, by a Resident', London: Smith, Elder & Co., 1845.

Scott, Justin, *The Nine Dragons: A Novel of Hong Kong, 1997*, London: Grafton Books, 1991.

Smith, Albert, *To China and Back: Being a Diary Kept, Out and Home*, London: Egyptian Hall, 1859; republished, Hong Kong: Hong Kong University Press, 1974 with an introduction by Henry James Lethbridge.

Smith, Joyce Stevens (ed.), *Matilda: Her Life and Legacy*, Hong Kong: Matilda and War Memorial Hospital, 1988.

Sulke, Walter M. 'Hong Kong 1976' in *Myself and Words*, Hong Kong: Libra Press Ltd., 1982.

Thielicke, Helmut, *Voyage to the Far East*, translated by John W. Doberstein, Philadelphia: Muhlenberg Press, 1962.

Thomson, John, 'Hong-Kong Photographers', London: *The British Journal of Photography*, Vol. XIX, No. 656, p. 569, 29 November 1872, and No. 658, pp. 591–2, December 13, 1872.

Tiffany, Jr., Osmond, *The Canton Chinese, or An American's Sojourn in The Celestial Empire*, Boston and Cambridge: James Monroe and Company, 1849.

Tu, Elsie, *Elsie Tu: An Autobiography*, Hong Kong: The Longman Group, 1983.

Unsworth, Mrs., 'A Lady's Impression of Hong-Kong', in *The Journal of the Manchester Geographical Society*, 1900, pp. 218–22.

Verne, Jules, *Around the World in Eighty Days*, Boston: James R. Osgood & Company, 1873.

Queen Victoria, *The Letters of Queen Victoria: A Selection from her Majesty's Correspondence Between the Years 1837 and 1861*, Vol. I (1837–1843), London: John Murray, 1907.

Wang Tao, 'My Sojourn in Hong Kong', translated by Yang Qinghua, published in *Renditions*, Hong Kong: The Chinese University of Hong Kong, 1988.

Woolf, Bella Sidney, *Under the Mosquito Curtain*, Hong Kong: Kelly & Walsh, Ltd., 1935.

Wood, William Maxwell, *Fankwei; or, The San Jacinto in the Seas of India, China and Japan*, New York: Harper & Brothers, 1859.